Praise for *Pondering th*

D0789785

"*Pondering the Passion* maps the landscape of issue ~~~~~~~~~~~~~~~ on the accounts of the death of Jesus in the Gospels and Christian theological tradition as well as the controversies raised by Mel Gibson's move, *The Passion of the Christ*. Christians and Jews will be challenged by the essays in this book. These essays push both Christians and Jews beyond the debates of 'history' versus 'faith' or 'liberal' versus 'conservative.' They seek to establish the boundaries of what constitutes a proper discussion about fundamental religious reflection for both communities in the twenty-first century." —**Michael A. Signer**, Abrams Professor of Jewish Thought and Culture, University of Notre Dame

"The essays in this collection ask vitally important questions about one of the most outrageous American media events of the young 21st century. The authors make it plain that every viewer of *The Passion of the Christ* must address the questions. Most importantly, the authors offer sober, thoughtful, well-informed perspectives from which to seek answers. Representing a remarkable range of scholarly expertise, they bring resources from the many disciplines that bear on any portrayal of Jesus' Passion—history, scripture, theology, drama and film, music, religious education, and even psychology. The contents of this book offer many of the tools we need to handle this explosive film without doing collateral damage to our Jewish neighbors. Whether we are successful depends on our answer to the books' implicit central question: will the riches of this scholarship continue to be squandered? We do so at our own risk." —**Peter A. Pettit**, Director of the Institute for Jewish–Christian Understanding and Assistant Professor of Religion, Muhlenberg College, PA

"Even if Mel Gibson's *The Passion of the Christ* has peaked as a box office golden egg, the debate it sparked about the murder of Jesus and the relations between Jews and Christians remains as heated and muddled as ever. We are deeply grateful to the contributors to *Pondering the Passion* for helping us think more clearly and critically about the biblical, historical, theological, and artistic issues surrounding the passion of Christ. Scholarly yet accessible, passionate yet well-reasoned, open to dialogue yet deeply rooted in the Christian faith, these essay must be required reading after every showing of *The Passion of the Christ*." —**Dr. Peter C. Phan**, Ignacio Ellacuría Professor of Catholic Social Thought at Georgetown University, author of *Many Faces, Once Church*.

Pondering the Passion

What's at Stake for Christians and Jews?

Edited By
Philip A. Cunningham

A SHEED & WARD BOOK

ROWMAN & LITTLEFIELD PUBLISHERS, INC.
Lanham • Oxford

A SHEED & WARD BOOK

ROWMAN & LITTLEFIELD PUBLISHERS, INC.

Published in the United States of America
by Rowman & Littlefield Publishers, Inc.
A wholly owned subsidiary of The Rowman & Littlefield Publishing Group, Inc.
4501 Forbes Boulevard, Suite 200, Lanham, Maryland 20706
www.rowmanlittlefield.com

PO Box 317
Oxford
OX2 9RU, UK

British Library Cataloguing in Publication Information Available

Library of Congress Cataloging-in-Publication Data

Pondering the Passion : what's at stake for Christians and Jews? / edited by
Philip A. Cunningham.
    p. cm.
  "A Sheed & Ward book."
  Includes bibliographical references and index.
  ISBN 0-7425-3217-8 (hardcover : alk. paper) — ISBN 0-7425-3218-6 (pbk. : alk.
paper)
  1. Jesus Christ—Passion—History of doctrines. 2.
Judaism—Relations—Christianity—History. 3. Christianity and other
religions—Judaism—History. I. Cunningham, Philip A.
  BT431.3.P66 2004
  232.96—dc22
                                                          2004019981

Printed in the United States of America

♾™ The paper used in this publication meets the minimum requirements of
American National Standard for Information Sciences—Permanence of Paper for
Printed Library Materials, ANSI/NISO Z39.48-1992.

Dedicated to the Memories of John M. Corcoran and Samuel J. Gerson
A Catholic and a Jew
United in Their Enthusiasm and Support for the Mission of
The Center for Christian-Jewish Learning at Boston College

~

Contents

~

Introduction: The Passion—What's at Stake for Christians and Jews?

Philip A. Cunningham

Seldom do the covers of national news magazines feature such lead articles as "Who Killed Jesus?;"[1] "The Real Jesus;"[2] and "Why Did Jesus Have to Die?"[3] The release of the controversial Mel Gibson film *The Passion of the Christ* generated these and other media explorations of questions at the heart of Christian self-understanding, not to mention the conflicted history of relations between the Christian and Jewish communities.

In January and February of 2004, the Center for Christian-Jewish Learning sponsored a multi-week speakers' series at Boston College upon which this collection builds and expands. Since the Center for Christian-Jewish Learning is devoted to the development and implementation of new relationships of mutual enrichment between Christians and Jews, it was only natural that my Boston College colleagues and I would be interested in the public pondering of the Passion[4] and its impact on Christian-Jewish relations. We are delighted to be joined by friends from other universities in this volume's consideration of the meaning of the Passion for Jews and Christians. The recent widespread discussion has brought to light several important realities. What's at stake for Christians and Jews when the Passion is discussed?

Contrasting Perceptions

Recent media exchanges illustrate the fact that Christians and Jews construct their respective communal memories very differently. They find it difficult to enter into each other's frame of reference. A brief discussion of the respective Jewish and Christian contexts will help make this clear.

Feelings of anxiety and alarm arise in the Jewish community when the crucifixion of Jesus becomes a highly visible subject in the public arena. Even if many Jews do not know all the details, they share a widespread consciousness that over the centuries Christian retellings of the story of the crucifixion of Jesus regularly produced suffering for Jews. In addition, Jews for the most part are deeply aware, as one Vatican document has put it, "that the Shoah took place in Europe, that is, in countries of long-standing Christian civilization."[5] Consequently, many at least subconsciously connect that abominable genocide with the primary symbol of Christianity, the cross. Many Jews have also personally experienced being called "Christ-killer."

Such Jewish concerns are not much alleviated by Christian reassurances that, "We don't hold the Jews responsible; Christ died because of the sins of every human being," a concept articulated in the 1566 Catechism of the Council of Trent. While Jews are unfamiliar with Christian theological niceties, it is obvious to them that this particular idea did little to curb antisemitism in recent centuries. Neither was the teaching of universal guilt for the crucifixion accompanied by the abandonment of the Christian claim that Jews lay under a divine curse. That notion was, in fact, not repudiated until after the Shoah. As late as 1938, for example, Catholic theologians advised Pope Pius XI that a proposed document condemning racism include the statement that "the authentic basis of the social separation of the Jews from the rest of humanity . . . is directly religious in character. . . . This unhappy people . . . whose misguided leaders had called down upon their own heads a Divine malediction, [became] doomed, as it were, to perpetually wander over the face of the earth. . . ."[6]

Moreover, some Jews are puzzled why Christians should focus on the sufferings of one first-century Jewish individual when the Roman military crucified thousands and thousands of Jews. Understandably having little acquaintance with Christian ideas about salvation, the intense emotional response of some Christian viewers to questions about *The Passion of the Christ* only makes these matters even more mystifying to Jewish moviegoers.

Christians, on the other hand, are generally ignorant of the antisemitic ways in which their ancestors customarily told the story of the Passion of Jesus. Most Christians today are honestly unfamiliar with the centuries-old Christian presumption that "the Jews" were under God's curse for crucifying Jesus. Some Christians are actually bewildered when they hear it; since the Shoah, virtually all churches have ceased to teach the notion of a divine curse on Jews. Most Christians simply don't know that this charge was conveyed for centuries in Christian art and music, preaching, and theatre, often in connection with Passion-related observances. Therefore, many Christians are baffled when other Christians or Jews express alarm about the antisemitic possibilities of a current retelling of the Passion. Combine this with the prevailing secularization of American society today, and it is little wonder that those Christians who view the world as divided between belief and unbelief might ask, "Why can't we just depict and proclaim our faith without being attacked or criticized? Is religion so odious in our culture?"

These contrasting perceptions of the Jewish and Christian communities can be bridged only by experiences of trust-building and open interreligious dialogue among people who have become friends. A process for local Christian and Jewish congregations, *Walking God's Paths: Christians and Jews in Candid Conversation*, has recently been produced by the Center for Christian-Jewish Learning on behalf of the U.S. Bishops' Committee on Ecumenical and Interreligious Affairs and the National Council of Synagogues. This is one tool that can help Jews and Christians enter into each other's traditions and frames of reference.[7] This dialogue can also build on available educational materials that illuminate the history of Christian anti-Jewish teachings and artistic expressions. Several of the essays in this collection contribute to increasing the level of this awareness.

Thus, the contemporary relationship between Jews and Christians is at stake when Christians retell the story of the Passion. Whether that relationship is enhanced or diminished depends on how the story is retold.

An Impoverishment of the Christian Tradition

Recent public conversation has also revealed a widespread lack of appreciation for the richness and diversity of Christian thinking about the Passion. Many commentators seem to feel that there is a single, universal understanding of the redemptive meaning of the cross. However, over the centuries, Christians have produced a rich variety of understandings of why the life, death, and resurrection of Jesus are universally saving. This wealth of insight is apparent even with a cursory glance at the distinctive ideas of some New Testament writers about the significance of Jesus' death.

For Paul, Jesus' death is important because one who shared equality with God emptied himself and experienced human mortality—even death on a cross. Therefore God exalted him to Lordship (Phil 2:5–11) and made him the forerunner of all who will be resurrected to new life (1 Cor 15). For Mark, writing with resurrection faith, only the experience of the cross reveals that Jesus is God's Son. The climax of the Gospel of Mark occurs when the centurion at the foot of Jesus' cross declares upon seeing Jesus' death "truly this man was God's Son!" (Mk 15:39). This is the first human character in that Gospel to perceive correctly, by Marcan standards, the true identity of Jesus. Matthew's Gospel adds the perspective that Jesus' death and resurrection represent the human rejection and divine exoneration of God's Wisdom. The resurrected Jesus, to whom all authority in heaven and earth has been given, commands his followers to teach all the nations what Jesus has instructed (Mt 28:16–20), the decisive instance of "Wisdom [being] vindicated by her deeds" (Mt 11:19). In Luke's Gospel, the crucifixion is seen as the martyrdom of God's ultimate and most righteous prophet. That is why "it is impossible for a prophet to be killed outside of Jerusalem" (Lk 13:33) and why the Lucan centurion at the foot of the cross exclaims, "Surely this man was innocent!" (Lk 24:47). For the Gospel of John, the cross is the hour of Jesus' glorification (Jn 17:1), when all people are drawn to him (Jn 12:32) and can share in the eternal life of the world above (Jn 3:14–15; 14:18–26). The author of the Letter to the Hebrews draws upon the imagery of Temple sacrificial rituals—through which relationship with God was restored or intensified—to portray Jesus as the ultimate High Priest, who offers for all time the supreme sacrifice (Heb 9:24–28).

This rich diversity indicates that no single conception of the significance of the death and resurrection of Jesus fully captures its profound meaning for Christian faith. Yet much public conversation has proceeded as if there was only one authentic Christian perspective on the meaning of Jesus' death. Moreover, that one approach is the highly problematic idea of "substitutionary atonement," whereby Jesus endures unimaginable pain by taking upon himself the just punishment deserved by all humanity, thereby appeasing God. As some essays in this volume will show, the diversity of understanding characteristic of the New Testament itself continued to unfold in the theological reflections of later centuries when a variety of "soteriologies," or ways of understanding the universal saving character of the "Christ event," arose.

Thus, Christian understandings of salvation are also at stake when Christians retell the story of the Passion. Whether that understanding is richly multi-faceted or an impoverished flatness depends on how the story is retold.

Interpreting the Bible

The controversy over the Gibson movie has shone a bright spotlight on the differences between those Christians who feel that little interpretation or study is needed to discern the "plain sense" meaning of the Bible and those Christians who believe that the Bible must be read in some sort of literary or historical context. This is not only a denominational difference; it points also to the degree to which members of churches that officially accept contextual interpretations have internalized their implications.

Distressing to me as a Roman Catholic is the realization that many members of my own church community seem untouched by the renaissance in Catholic biblical scholarship that has flowered since 1943. In that year Pope Pius XII instructed Catholic interpreters to use "the aids offered by the art of [historical and literary] criticism" to discover "the genuine meaning of the Sacred Books."[8] This basic orientation was reiterated by the Second Vatican Council in its Dogmatic Constitution on Divine Revelation.[9]

Of particular significance in regard to the Passion is the Council's teaching that the Gospel writers "selected certain of the many elements which had been handed on, either orally or in written form; others they synthesized or explained with an eye to the situation of the churches."[10] The Council here drew upon an instruction issued the previous year by the cardinals of the Pontifical Biblical Commission that had described the formation of the Gospels in three stages: (1) the ministry of Jesus; (2) the post-resurrection preaching of the apostles; and (3) the time of the writing of the Gospels.[11]

This means that the Gospel passion accounts are not simple historical transcripts, but are, more importantly, theologically-driven narratives written to convey inspired spiritual insights into the meaning of Jesus Christ. It also means that they sometimes incorporate into the narratives of the time of his death later religious arguments about Jesus' identity that did not arise until after the Resurrection. Consequently, "Certain [Gospel] controversies reflect Christian-Jewish relations long after the time of Jesus."[12]

The authoritative Catholic mandate to interpret the scriptures within their historical and literary contexts means that a failure to do so would "create an illusion and display lack of respect for the inspired Scripture."[13] This failure is only compounded by any reading "of certain texts of the New Testament which could provoke or reinforce unfavorable attitudes toward the Jewish people."[14] As Pope John Paul II has declared, "erroneous and unjust interpretations of the New Testament regarding the Jewish people and their alleged culpability [for the crucifixion] have circulated for too long, engendering feelings of hostility towards this people."[15] Regrettably, little knowledge of this Catholic biblical teaching was evident in public comments made by most Catholic proponents of Gibson's movie.[16]

While I have focused here on biblical issues in the Catholic community, similar comments could be made about those churches that also encourage the historical or literary contextualization of the Bible. Therefore, Christian appreciation of the Bible is also at stake when Christians retell the story of the Passion. Whether the Bible is understood in a fundamentalist way that "seeks to escape any closeness of the divine and the human" or incarnationally as "the inspired word of God [that] has been expressed in human language" depends on how that story is retold.[17]

Pondering the Passion

This volume seeks to address some of these matters. The essays by Claudia Setzer, Michael Cook, and John Clabeaux provide important background information about the first-century world and the consequences for the crucifixion of Jesus. The situation of Jews under Roman domination, including the legal authority permitted to Jewish governing institutions, provides a necessary context for understanding Jesus' execution historically.

Two biblical essays by Walter Harrelson and George Smiga consider the Gospel Passion accounts from a range of Protestant and Catholic perspectives. They make apparent the diversity of Christian approaches and the multilayered and religious character of the Gospel texts.

Four essays by Pamela Berger, Raymond Helmick, James Rudin, and John Michalczyk explore examples of the theme of the Passion in Christian visual arts, sacred music, theatrical dramas, and modern movies. As they indicate, in each medium the artist must make choices about how to interpret and utilize the four Gospels. As part of this, the artist must also decide how to deal with elements that have historically promoted antipathy for Jews.

Clark Williamson and Louis Roy discuss the theological significance of the death of Jesus, the former from a Protestant biblical perspective and the latter through Catholic systematic theological thought. In the process, they make clear the dynamic and polyvalent natures of such terms as "salvation," "sacrifice," and "atonement." In addition, both essays manifest the richness of Christian thought on so profound a topic.

The collection concludes with reflections on Mel Gibson's movie itself. This section is introduced by my own analysis of the film in terms of Roman Catholic teaching on biblical interpretation. John Pawlikowski considers Christian ethical responsibilities in a post-Shoah world when retelling the story of the death of Jesus. Maddy Cunningham examines the potential psychological effects of viewing the graphic torture of a central religious figure on film. Mary Boys offers insights on the educational challenges that the controversy over the film has brought to light.

Collectively, the essays in this volume are, among other things, part of the post-Shoah rapprochement between Christians and Jews. The Gibson film has created one of those benchmark moments when each community, each with its own internal diversity, pauses to reassess the relationship.

The situation brings to my mind the prescient words of Cardinal Edward Idris Cassidy in one of his last formal addresses before retiring as the president of the Pontifical Commission for Religious Relations with the Jews. Although delivered in the context of an international Catholic-Jewish dialogue, I believe his remarks can be applied to the Christian world in general:

> Let us then turn to consider the future. Our first aim must of course be to press forward. To stand still is to risk going backwards—and I feel absolutely confident in stating that there will be no going back on the part of the Catholic Church. At the same time, there can be a lessening of enthusiasm, a growing indifference or even a renewed spirit of suspicion and mistrust among members of the Catholic community should our efforts to keep up the momentum slacken. Hence, I would suggest that we need above all to continue to build mutual trust between our communities. Mutual trust is a basic element of all true dialogue. It is this in particular that we have been seeking to achieve over the past thirty-five years. It means first of all deepening our knowledge of the other as the other really is and seeking to understand the other more fully. This is achieved especially when we are ready to take up seriously those problems that are troubling one or other of the parties and attempt together to find a solution. The commitment to achieve such understanding and mutual respect is a process that begins with a change in heart, in our own individual hearts, and spreads through our community out into the world in which we live.[18]

Notes

1. Jon Meacham in *Newsweek*, February 16, 2004.
2. Jay Tolson and Linda Kulman in *U.S. News and World Report*, March 8, 2004.
3. David Van Biema in *Time*, April 12, 2004.
4. Throughout this book, "Passion" will be capitalized to refer to the events surrounding Jesus' crucifixion and also to later Christian theological reflection upon it. When the Gibson movie is being discussed, the full title, *The Passion of the Christ*, will be employed.
5. Pontifical Commission for Religious Relations with the Jews, *We Remember: A Reflection on the Shoah* (1998), II.
6. Georges Passelecq and Bernard Suchecky, *The Hidden Encyclical of Pius XI* (Harcourt, Brace, and Co., 1997), 247, 249.
7. www.bc.edu/research/cjl/meta-elements/texts/education/Walking_Gods_Paths.htm
8. Pius XII, *Divino Afflante Spiritu* (Sept. 30, 1943), §23.
9. See *Dei Verbum* (1965), §12.
10. Second Vatican Council, *Dei Verbum* (1965), §19.

11. Pontifical Biblical Commission, *Sancta Mater Ecclesiae* (1964), §6–10.

12. Pontifical Commission for Religious Relations with the Jews, *Notes on the Correct Way to Present Jews and Judaism in Preaching and Teaching in the Roman Catholic Church* (1985), §21A.

13. Pontifical Biblical Commission, *The Interpretation of the Bible in the Church* (1993), Conclusion.

14. Ibid., § IV, A, 3.

15. John Paul II, *Address to the Vatican Symposium on the Roots of Anti-Judaism in the Christian Milieu*, October 31, 1997.

16. See my analysis of the movie in the last section of this volume.

17. Pontifical Biblical Commission, *The Interpretation of the Bible in the Church* (1993), I, F.

18. Edward Idris Cardinal Cassidy, "Jewish-Catholic Relations: 1990 to 2001," address delivered at the seventeenth meeting of the International Catholic-Jewish Liaison Committee, New York, May 1, 2001, §10.

PART ONE

FIRST-CENTURY HISTORY

CHAPTER ONE

~

The Jews under Roman Rule

Claudia Setzer

Roman Incorporation of Judea

Jesus and his followers were Jews living under Roman occupation. The God of Israel, who in his covenant with Abraham had promised his descendants a certain land, the God who had once rescued them from Pharaoh, had so far failed to rescue them from Rome. Roman control of Judea began in 63 BCE when the Roman general Pompey marched into Jerusalem and captured the Temple. He came as both a conqueror and an invited guest. The Hasmonean dynasty, which had ruled for approximately 100 years since the time of the Maccabean rout of the Seleucids in 164 BCE, began to devolve into fraternal warfare. When the Hasmonean queen Salome Alexandra (reigned 76–67 BCE) died, her two sons, John Hyrcanus II and Aristobulus II, each with his own constituents and foreign allies, wrestled for control of the kingdom. A third group of aristocrats, who favored neither, soon appealed to the superpower Rome to rid them of the Hasmoneans altogether.

The civil strife worked to the advantage of the Romans, the growing power in the region. Pompey invaded Asia Minor, defeated Tigranes of Armenia, and turned Syria into a Roman province by 65. Unable to ignore the powerful general in Damascus, both Hasmonean brothers lobbied for his support. After some delay, Pompey backed Hyrcanus, who promoted his entry into Jerusalem. Pompey captured the Temple where Aristobulus and his party held out, naming Hyrcanus High Priest.

Roman rule only fanned the flames of civil war, and different Jewish groups and individuals appealed to different factions of the Roman Senate.

3

Hyrcanus owed his power to his friendship with Antipater, an Idumean who had ties with neighboring non-Jewish warlords as well as with factions in the Roman Senate. Antipater's ambitions were rewarded when Hyrcanus appointed his two sons to government positions. Phasael became commander in Jerusalem and Judea, while Herod was awarded the Galilee.

Herod the Great

Fortunes were reversed when the Parthians invaded Syria and Palestine in 40 BCE, for they named as king Antigonus, the son of Aristobulus II, Hyrcanus' rival. Hyrcanus himself was captured and had his ear cut off, thus maiming him and making him permanently ineligible to serve as High Priest. Phasael committed suicide, while Herod escaped to Rome. In Rome the Senate named Herod king of Judea and *amicus Romani populi*, friend of the Roman people, a title often given to a client-king, and supported him to reconquer the land from the Parthians for Rome. As Herod produced more successes in Galilee, Samaria, Judea, and his own Idumea, more aid flowed from Rome and Roman Syria. In 37 he finally conquered Jericho and, with Roman troops and his own Jewish troops, besieged Jerusalem in a great slaughter. Antigonus surrendered and was later executed.

Herod lacked Jewish pedigree. As an Idumean he was the descendant of a people that had been forcibly converted by the Hasmoneans, and some called him a half-Jew. Since he was not of priestly descent he could not himself serve as High Priest, but conferred and withdrew the title of High Priest on others at will. Previously an inherited position in the Hasmonean family and held for life, it now became an appointment at the king's pleasure. Seven High Priests were appointed during Herod's reign of thirty-three years, five of whom were non-Judeans, perhaps to prevent a concentration of local aristocrats in the Temple becoming a competing locus of power.

Herod's tenure was distinguished by the incorporation of territories and coastal cities, the Golan Heights, and parts of Syria, as well as by extensive building and restoration projects. He expanded and rebuilt the Temple from a small sixth-century BCE building to a large and magnificent structure with a massive courtyard, financed by Temple funds and taxes. Himself a Roman citizen, he copied aspects of Greek culture and political structure, and promoted his kingdom as a vassal-state to Rome. Court intrigue was thick around him, and he executed family members, including a wife and several sons, whom he suspected of plotting against him.

Nearing death in 5 BCE, Herod appointed the youngest of his surviving sons, Herod Antipas (son of a Samaritan woman, Malthace) as his sole heir. In his last days he relented somewhat, and divided the kingdom into thirds among his sons, making Antipas tetrarch of Galilee and Peraea; Archelaus he made king of Judea, Idumea, and Samaria; and Philip became tetrarch of Gaulanitis, Trachonitis, Batanea, and Paneas. Herod was unable to control matters from the grave, however. Soon after Herod's death in 4 BCE, Archelaus' rule was undone by the Jerusalem aristocracy and popular insurrections. Philip and Herod Antipas were left to rule in peace, the latter presiding over Galilee, the place of most of Jesus' preaching. According to the gospel of Luke (23:6–12), Jesus was even sent to Antipas for judgment, but was returned to Pilate without a ruling.

Judea, however, proved too unruly to be left to a client-king. By 6 CE, Rome had transformed Judea into an imperial province, to be ruled directly from Rome by a series of prefects (called procurators after 44) who would represent the emperor. Their job was to collect taxes and keep the peace. Rome awarded them broad powers to fulfill these tasks, including *ius gladii*, the right to condemn to death.

Imperial and Local Control

While the Romans relied to some degree on the native aristocracy and local institutions of self-government, ultimate power resided with the Roman administrator. A judicious and sensitive prefect needed to balance a respect for native sensibilities and religious traditions with his role as representative of the empire and his assignment to maintain order. Few exhibited such delicacy and skill.

As they did in other provinces, the Romans in Judea left many already-existing institutions in place and relied on local functionaries to carry out their rule. The Jerusalem Sanhedrin, an assembly under the High Priest's leadership that decided matters of religious law, stayed in place, but served at Roman behest. The term is ambiguous, and seems to refer to more than one type of body. The New Testament, Josephus, and the rabbinic sources differ on the composition and scope of the Sanhedrin's authority, as well as the question of whether it was a fixed or ad hoc group, but they agree that it enjoyed some autonomy in religious matters. The High Priest was appointed by the Roman governor and the group could only meet with the governor's permission. The vestments of the High Priest were kept by the Romans in the fortress called the Antonia and parceled out on special holy days, showing both symbolic and literal control of the cult by the empire. A parallel but unequal jurisdiction prevailed, with the political trumping the religious.

On the question of the death penalty at the time of Jesus' death, many scholars accept that the Sanhedrin could pronounce on it for religious crimes. We can hardly be certain, since most evidence about the council is from later Pharisaic/rabbinic tradition, whereas the Sanhedrin and Temple was probably largely Sadducean in the year 30. The gospels and early Passion accounts do not show the Pharisees active in Jerusalem or the Sanhedrin, but refer to chief priests, scribes, and elders. The gospel of John cites Jewish authorities claiming, "We are not authorized to put anyone to death (18:31)," but that might not obviate the possibility of their trying a capital case even if others might carry it out. In the later, fourth- to fifth-century source, the Palestinian Talmud, a tradition states, "For forty years until the Temple was destroyed, the privilege of trying capital cases was withdrawn" (Sanhedrin 1:18a), placing the beginning of the ban at approximately the time of Jesus' death.

The execution of James, the brother of Jesus, provides an example of the ambiguity around the question of who may impose the death penalty. The High Priest Ananus, taking advantage of a temporary absence of a procurator, convened the Sanhedrin hurriedly and condemned James, the brother of Jesus and others to death and had them stoned (Ant. 20.9.1 § 200–1). Certain prominent Jews complained to the emperor about Ananus' high-handedness and met the new procurator on his way to Jerusalem. The High Priest had exceeded his authority and carried out the death penalty without Roman permission, so was summarily removed by the procurator. This case shows that a hotheaded High Priest might successfully maneuver to get rid of a troublemaker. Yet it also shows that trying and executing other Jews independent of Rome was illegal. The complex relationship of the Sanhedrin and the High Priest to the Roman representative, as well as the likelihood that the aristocratic Sadducees dominated the Sanhedrin, suggest that it would have lost moral prestige with the people. The negative gospel portrayals of the Sanhedrin, High Priest, and authorities are likely meant to implicate a particular social class, not Jews as a whole.

Pilate and Caiaphas

If the ideal Roman procurator needed to balance his role as Roman administrator with an appreciation of local religious and ethnic sensitivities, Pontius Pilate was a remarkably poor choice. Although the gospels depict him as a passive, indecisive sort, caving into pressure from the Jewish authorities and the crowd, Josephus cites numerous examples of his deliberate brutality and insensitivity to Jewish sensibilities (War 2.9.2 § 169–78; Ant. 18.3.1 § 55–62; Ant. 18.4.1 § 85–89). He ordered soldiers to bring in Roman standards displaying icons of the emperor's head during the night, certain to rile the Jews who reject graven images, then after six days of Jewish protests, threatened to kill the Jews unless they retreated. Only when the protestors refused did he back down. He also stole from the Temple treasury to build an aqueduct. When Jews arrived at his tribunal to protest, he sent soldiers to beat and kill them. After he prevented some Samaritans from following a prophet in 36 CE, a riot ensued and many were killed. After that he was recalled to Rome to explain himself and never returned. His performance was apparently unsatisfactory to his superiors.

Caiaphas, the High Priest, held his office throughout Pilate's prefecture and was removed the same year Pilate was recalled, suggesting his position was secure only so long as he was in the good graces of this particular Roman official. Appointed by Rome, the High Priest needed to please the Roman prefect by keeping things quiet, not the reverse.

Religious and Class Conflicts

The Roman occupation of Judea was a daily reminder to religious Jews that something had gone dreadfully wrong. God's covenant with Abraham had promised them the land. The empire once presided over by Israel's anointed ones (literally "messiahs"), the kings David and Solomon, had now passed into the hands of Gentiles, practitioners of foreign, polytheistic cults. The situation provoked a variety of responses from different groups, ranging from accommodation to outright rebellion. From at least the time of Herod the Great, bandits or brigands (lēstēs) threatened the social order. Banditry was a loose phenomenon that included armed political revolt, greedy plunder of neighbors' goods and land, and even collusion with shady rulers. It arose from a situation of corrupt rule, unjust distribution of goods, and the desperation of peasants. In this agrarian and pastoral economy, small landholders were eclipsed by larger property owners, especially the royal household. In times of economic stress, large landholders absorbed smaller holdings, and many formerly independent farmers were forced to become tenant farmers, or worse, day laborers. The gulf between rich and poor and the resentment of the wealthy explains the poverty ideal in the gospels, evidenced by parables about wealthy landowners and day-laborers, as well as sayings such as "Blessed are you poor, for yours is the kingdom of God" (Luke 6:20) or "If you would be perfect, go sell what you possess and give to the poor, and you will have treasure in heaven" (Matt 19:21). In the cities, upper classes were associated with large property owners, while the more oppressed peasant class was more prevalent in rural areas. It is no surprise then that cities do not figure in Jesus' preaching (except the special case of Jerusalem). A reader of the gospels would never guess that he preached not far from the active cities of Sepphoris or Tiberias, sites of considerable archaeological discoveries in recent decades.

Jerusalem was unique as the site of the Temple and its wealth and trea-sures, the destination of foreign visitors and pilgrims, which required the sup-port of a population of religious specialists, merchants, and craftspeople. Cut off from the sea and nestled in the hills, it was vulnerable to food shortages and military isolation. At holiday times, when it swelled with extra popula-tion, it would be especially prone to social and political unrest.

Passover was an especially worrisome time for the Romans since its obser-vance constituted a "silent protest" against Roman rule.[1] It commemorated God's rescue of Israel from an earlier oppressor and asserted his power over any foreign ruler. Between the symbolic power of the holiday and the influx of pilgrims with time on their hands, it called for preventative action on the part of the rulers. No wonder that the Romans brought in extra troops at Passover, stationing some in the Temple itself to keep order. The Syrian legate C. Sestius Gallus came to Jerusalem at Passover to stem the revolt gaining steam under the procurator Gessius Florus (64–66). During the Passover of 70, the rebel John of Gischala invaded the Temple and Roman troops began their final assault on the city that ended with the Temple's destruction.

Jewish Sects and Groups

As early as 6 CE, a group rose up to oppose Roman rule openly. In response to a Roman census, Judas the Galilean and a Pharisee named Zadok founded a group whose slogan was "No king but God" (*War* 2.8.1 §118; *Ant.* 18.1.1 § 3–10; *Ant.* 18.1.6 § 23–25). Josephus calls this group "the Fourth Philosophy," in addition to the other three schools (*hairēsēs*) of Pharisees, Sadducees, and Essenes, though he denies them the same legitimacy as the other three. Al-though the Romans crushed this uprising (Judas' sons were executed by the procurator), by the 40s numerous examples of revolutionary movements had arisen. The *Sicarii*, (daggers) were probably the heirs of the Fourth Philosophy. Later, in 67, the Zealots appear associated with the great revolt. While each of these revolutionary groups may have had its own history and character, as current scholarship argues, the appearance of these groups shows that the po-tent mix of religious nationalism and guerilla tactics persisted.

The three other "legitimate" groups mentioned by Josephus (and sup-ported by the New Testament, the Dead Sea Scrolls, and Philo), Pharisees, Sadducees, and Essenes, can be partially categorized by the attitudes they struck toward Rome (*Ant.* 18.1.2 § 11–18.1.5 § 22). As Shaye Cohen notes, one's political, cultural, and social attitudes would vary: "A Jew might be ac-commodating in the political sphere, wholeheartedly supporting the ruling power, but quite unyielding in the cultural or social sphere."[2]

We have no sources from the Sadducees themselves, and what we have are from their detractors, but our sources agree on some general similarities. They were aristocrats, many of them priests, denied resurrection of the dead, claimed to follow only the written Torah and not extra-biblical interpretations, and did not enjoy popular support. As functionaries of the Temple and members of the upper classes, they would be most motivated to accommodate the Roman occupation, although some priestly groups did support the revolt of 66–70. They were probably in the majority of those who controlled the Temple at the time of Jesus' arrest. None of them would have reason to sympathize with a Galilean charismatic who had caused a disturbance outside the Temple and who drew support from the peasant classes.

The Pharisees, on the other hand, were reportedly a larger group who enjoyed popular support, at least in the cities. They were committed to observance of the Torah, especially according to their own set of extra-biblical interpretations, which Mark's gospel cites as "the tradition of the elders" (7:3), probably a forerunner to the later rabbis' "oral law." Like Jesus and his followers, they believed in the resurrection of the dead. Josephus says, and Acts implies, that they are the most legitimate and respectable group, not to be flouted. The Hasmonean king Alexander Janneus, on his deathbed, had recommended to his queen Alexandra Salome that she befriend them; thus they wielded great power during her reign (*Ant.* 13.5.5 § 401). They had also supported Herod the Great. Some also appeared in 66 to argue with some rabble-rousers not to mount a revolt. They did not as a group oppose Roman rule, yet a Pharisee is named by Josephus as a founder of the Fourth Philosophy, and the Pharisee Simeon ben Gamaliel was part of a revolutionary council in Jerusalem in 66. They appear to have been a lay religious elite. Anthony Saldarini characterizes them as Roman "retainers," a literate intellectual class that negotiated between the people and their Roman overlords.[3] Their influence on the people in religious matters is borne out by the fact that they were the only group, besides the followers of Jesus, to survive as a group the disaster of the destruction of the Temple in 70.

The third group, the Essenes, who counted many priests and Sadducees among them, reacted to Roman power by withdrawal, real and symbolic, and aligning themselves with God. Some seem to have remained within society, while others withdrew to the shores of the Dead Sea at Qumran. There they lived a rigorous communal lifestyle, practicing celibacy, sharing goods in common, and maintaining strict standards of ritual purity. The biblical and other texts they copied or composed form the great archaeological find of the last century, the Dead Sea Scrolls. Strongly apocalyptic, they awaited the coming clash between the Sons of Light and the Sons of Darkness, in which

God would raise them up as the righteous army to rout the oppressive Romans. It was not to be; the Romans destroyed them in 68 CE. Although Josephus claims that there were only these four groups, no doubt there were many others. Many Jews probably identified with no particular group, but were just trying to eke out a living and avoid trouble.

Apocalypticism

The Essenes were not alone in their apocalypticism, a perspective that holds the world to have been so overrun by evil that only divine intervention could defeat it. As a natural reaction to the wrong people being in power, apocalyptic thought flourished before and during the period of Roman occupation.

An outgrowth of prophecy, it explains the apparent triumph of evil, the suffering of the righteous, and the eclipse of God. Angels, intermediaries, and visions reveal God's cosmic plan, visible only to the insiders. The end of the world as they knew it was imminent. God was about to break into history and create a new, just society with God at its head, where the righteous would be rewarded and the evil punished. War, the suffering of the righteous, and the seeming triumph of evil were only birth pangs that accompanied God's bringing forth a new world. Early examples of this worldview appear in Daniel, various apocalypses such as 4 Ezra and 1 Enoch, and the Dead Sea Scrolls. It informs the preaching of John the Baptist, who calls people to a baptism of repentance. Jesus' preaching, as presented in Mark's gospel, is apocalyptic: "The time is fulfilled; the kingdom of God is upon you. Repent and believe in the gospel" (1:15). Paul too believed he was living in the end-time, and so discouraged making major changes in lifestyle, "for the form of this world is passing away" (1 Cor 7:31). Heightened expectation of the end must have contributed to the charged atmosphere in Jerusalem at the time of Jesus' death.

Jesus from the Roman Perspective

In the tense atmosphere of Jerusalem at Passover, Roman authorities and their Jewish subordinates would be understandably worried about Jesus, a charismatic preacher promoting a new kingdom of God, causing a ruckus with the Temple money changers, and teaching suspicion of the wealthy and powerful. Could this, they might wonder, be an opponent of Caesar, planning to overthrow the government? The choice of twelve men as his inner circle could be a symbolic statement of the expected restoration of David's kingdom, the unified twelve tribes of Israel. The affirmation of the crowd at Jesus' entrance to Jerusalem, waving palm branches and shouting "Save us"

(*Hosanna*), recalled images of the Davidic messiah. Coming from rural Galilee, a trouble-spot for insurrectionist movements, Jesus was also associated with John the Baptist, another charismatic preacher, who already had been executed by Herod Antipas. The charge over the cross reported in the four gospels, "king of the Jews," attests to the political character of his execution, as does Pilate's question in Mark 15:2, "Are you the king of the Jews?"

Crucifixion

Most of our historical testimony about Roman crucifixion comes from some decades after Jesus. The mid-forties show an increase in banditry, a parade of High Priests, and a succession of brutal procurators. Open revolt erupted in 65–66, when daily sacrifices for the emperor in the Temple were suspended and rebels took the Roman fortress at Masada. But discontent had been brewing since the end of the Hasmonean rule in 63 BCE, and was given a boost with the founding of the Fourth Philosophy in 6 CE. As rebellion mounted, so did public executions.

Crucifixion was practiced by several peoples. Some speculate that the Romans learned it from the Carthaginians during the Punic Wars. The Romans did not employ it for any random crime. It was considered a slave's punishment, also appropriate for foreigners, and those guilty of crimes against the state like sedition. The Romans too, considered it a brutal and disgusting penalty.

Prisoners were often flogged first, and were sometimes forced to carry the crossbeam. The upright piece was set up at all times, both because wood was scarce and as a permanent reminder to would-be revolutionaries of the fate of those who opposed the Roman state (not unlike a gallows in the town square). Prisoners were crucified in different positions, their bodies nailed or tied to the cross. In 1968, archaeologists discovered the skeleton of a man who had been crucified in first-century Jerusalem; a spike is still lodged in his heel bone. His wrists and hands show no clear signs of being nailed, suggesting the upper part of his body was tied to the cross.

The Romans crucified thousands. Josephus reports that the governor of Syria crucified 2,000 Jews in disturbances after Herod's death (*Ant.* 17.10.10). In the revolt of 66–70, the Roman general Titus made a wall of crosses around the city of Jerusalem, and the soldiers made sport of the Jews by putting them in different positions: "Roman soldiers, out of the wrath and hatred they bore the Jews, nailed those they caught, one after one way, and another after another, to the crosses by way of jest; when their multitude was so great there was not enough room for the crosses, and not enough crosses for the bodies" (*War* 5.46). Historical context requires that we recognize that Jesus was crucified *as* a Jew (not *by* the Jews), along with thousands of fellow-Jews under Roman occupation, proclaiming the sovereignty of the God of Israel. He shared the fate of his oppressed and subjugated people.[4]

Notes

1. Bart Ehrman, *Jesus, Apocalyptic Prophet of the New Millenium* (New York: Oxford University Press, 1999), 115–16.

2. Shaye J. D. Cohen, *From the Maccabees to the Mishnah* (Philadelphia: Westminster, 1987), 59.

3. Anthony Saldarini, *Pharisees, Scribes, and Sadducees in Palestinian Society* (Wilmington: Michael Glazier, 1988; repr. Grand Rapids: Eerdmans, 2001).

4. Readers interested in further study of these matters might consult the following works in addition to those already cited in the notes: Raymond E. Brown, *The Death of the Messiah*. 2 vols. (Anchor Bible Reference Library; New York: Doubleday, 1994); Emilio Gabba, "The Social, Economic and Political History of Palestine, 63 BCE–CE 70," vol. 3, *The Cambridge History of Judaism*, (Cambridge: Cambridge University, 1999), 94–167; Martin Hengel, *Crucifixion* (Philadelphia: Fortress, 1977); Seth Schwartz, *Imperialism and Jewish Society 200 BCE–640 CE* (Princeton: Princeton University, 2001); and E. Mary Smallwood, *Jews under Roman Rule from Pompey to Diocletian* (Leiden: Brill, 1981).

~

CHAPTER TWO

The Problem of Jewish Jurisprudence and the Trial of Jesus

Michael J. Cook

"Now the chief priests and the whole council [Sanhedrin][1] sought testimony against Jesus to put him to death" (Mark 14:55). Thus begins the rendering of Jesus' Sanhedrin trial by our earliest—also most basic—source, the Gospel of Mark. The proceeding climaxes shortly after the high priest asks Jesus, "Are you the Christ, the Son of the Blessed?" When Jesus affirms that he *is* and also that his accusers will witness "the Son of man seated at the right hand of Power, and coming with the clouds of heaven" (14:62), the high priest decries this as "blasphemy." On this basis, the entire tribunal promptly condemns Jesus as deserving death.

Clearly, this Sanhedrin episode advances the impression that the Jews were instrumental in bringing about Jesus' execution. Captured and delivered for trial by Jewish conspirators, Jesus is tried by the foremost Jewish court, and condemned for "blasphemy," a Jewish (hardly Roman) concern. Thereafter, when the Roman prefect, Pontius Pilate, offers to free any prisoner whom the Jews desire, the latter opt not for the innocent Jesus but the infamous Barabbas. Pilate himself, reluctantly, will consign Jesus to the cross, but only to satisfy the clamoring by the specifically Jewish throng.

On matters of historicity within the Passion, Mark commands most attention because his is the earliest narrative, and also determinative for others.[2] How credible is Mark's recounting of Jewish jurisprudence in Jesus' day? Is his rendering the original form of the story, or already an embellishment of some earlier nucleus? Are any aspects fanciful, even contrived? What are the most promising ways of determining the proper answers to these questions?

The Sanhedrin in Rabbinic Literature

The fullest descriptions of the Sanhedrin appear in writings by the ancient rabbis. First is the (Hebrew) Mishnah, the oldest extant compendium of rabbinic law and lore, completed in early third-century Palestine. Finished several centuries later is the Talmud, which incorporates the Mishnah and adds lengthy (Aramaic) commentary to each of its paragraphs. Both works feature an entire tractate entitled *Sanhedrin*, detailing the court's structure, composition, and leadership, and its procedures, cases, and tenor of decisions.

These rabbinic expositions seem to offer an ideal backdrop for interpreting the Gospel Sanhedrin accounts. But formidable problems intervene. Rabbinic traditions were not codified until well after Jesus' time. While their antecedents may well have circulated orally generations earlier, we are unsure how much earlier or in exactly what form. Also, although the Mishnah defines how the Sanhedrin managed capital cases, it makes no mention of Jesus at all, let alone of his trial.

Discrepancies between Rabbinic and Gospel Testimony

Such factors might seem less troubling if only the rabbinic depictions of the Sanhedrin more closely approximated, let alone matched, their Gospel counterpart. But the two configurations sharply diverge.[3]

Composition and Leadership

The Sanhedrin's ranks, in the Mishnah and Talmud, seem wholly rabbinic, that is, with no priestly component. The council is headed by the *Nasi* (Prince) followed by the *Av Beth Din* (Father of the Court). Yet the Gospel Sanhedrin was headed by the high priest, with the broader membership designated "chief priests, elders, and scribes" (the *first* dominant).

Capital Procedures Followed

Rabbinic literature forbids scheduling capital trials at night or on a holiday or the day preceding. Yet Jesus' hearing is said to ensue directly after his evening arrest (Mark, Matthew), with his interrogation on the first day of the Feast of Unleavened Bread (Mark, Matthew, Luke) or the day preceding it (John). As for the death penalty, the Mishnah contains the view that any Sanhedrin "that effects an execution once in seven years is branded a destructive tribunal." To this, one authority adds "[or even] once in seventy years," while two others insist that, "were we members of a Sanhedrin, no person would ever be put to death." Underscoring such leniency are so many safeguards for the defendant that convictions become well-nigh impossible. Cases must begin with arguments for the defense so as to predispose judges toward the accused's innocence. Nothing defendants say may be used against them. Acquittal is permitted the same day as the trial, but conviction requires a day's delay—so that judges negatively inclined will have opportunity to reconsider. At least two witnesses to the offense are needed to convict, and the defendant had to be warned in advance not to commit the contemplated crime!

Where, in Mark's rendition (and the other Gospels as well), was any of these protections brought to bear on Jesus' behalf? Here no defense was mounted for Jesus at any time during his trial, let alone its beginning. What he said was indeed used against him. His conviction was virtually immediate, with no statutory delay until the next day.

Condemnation for Blasphemy

As for Jesus' conviction for "blasphemy," the rabbinic litmus test is whether the accused utters God's Ineffable Name (YHWH) in conjunction with the alleged trespass. Certainly, we are never told that Jesus did. Claiming to be the Messiah (if Jesus did so) is not blasphemy under rabbinic law. Further, execution for blasphemy calls for *stoning* at Jewish hands (not crucifixion, as by Rome), so, theoretically, a Sanhedrin death verdict for blasphemy would not have necessitated Jesus' delivery to Pilate![4]

Six Basic Options

Why does the rabbinic Sanhedrin contrast so glaringly with its Gospel counterpart? While the problem may defy resolution, at least six basic possibilities suggest themselves:

Option I: In descriptions of Jesus' trial, so many mandates of rabbinic law were violated that Gospel testimony must stand utterly discredited.

Option II: Jesus was deemed so dangerous that standard rabbinic safeguards were suspended in his case alone. If so, the basic Gospel account appears plausible.

Option III: With the Temple's destruction (70 C.E.), the Sanhedrin was *transformed*. The priests lost dominance. Rome now shifted the reins of authority to the rabbis. However, the Gospels do accurately portray the Sanhedrin in its *pre*-70 configuration, so the basic Gospel depiction of Jesus' trial (around 30) could well be accurate. Rabbinic literature, in turn, is also accurate, but only concerning the Sanhedrin *post*-70.[5] Accordingly, discrepancies between the Gospels and rabbinic literature become of no consequence since each source, respectively, addresses the Sanhedrin as it functioned during a different *time frame*.

Option IV: There were two parallel Sanhedrin systems before 70: one addressing capital offenses *religious* in nature (e.g., murder, idolatry), the other *political* in nature (e.g., sedition). Rabbinic literature describes only the religious-type system, the Gospels only the political type (the latter ceased when the Temple's destruction, in 70, ended the post of high priest). Accordingly, discrepancies between the Gospels and rabbinic literature are of no consequence since each source, respectively, addresses a different type of *court system*. Since the Gospel Sanhedrin matches that of the political system, the basic account of Jesus' trial could be accurate.[6]

Option V: The rabbinic Sanhedrin, as described, was only an imagined idealization, since no society could function when it was virtually impossible to convict capital offenders. Discrepancies between Gospel and rabbinic procedures thus prove moot since the latter were simply never in force.

Option VI: The account of *Jesus'* Sanhedrin trial came into being belatedly as an outgrowth of concerns by the developing church. The discrepancies prove moot because the historical Jesus never underwent the kind of trial described.

Clarifications from Josephus

The first-century Jewish historian, Josephus, effectively reduces these six options by half. To begin with, he outlines a three-tiered scheme of authority operative within the Roman province of Judea around Jesus' time. Uppermost was the Roman Emperor (even if never physically present); second, the local Roman procurator (governor)[7]; third, the high priest. Figures on the two lower tiers were accountable to whoever ranked directly above them. The procurator therefore controlled the high priest or, in Jesus' day, *Pilate dominated Caiaphas*. That Caiaphas remained high priest throughout Pilate's long tenure (26–36) is remarkable given that most other high priests, before or after Pilate, failed to last a year or so without dismissal.[8] No doubt, then, Caiaphas assiduously followed Pilate's instructions.

Second, Josephus tells us that Pilate was a vicious ruler who, far from fearing the Jewish masses, enjoyed inflaming them.[9] Third, Josephus speaks of Sanhedrins during the Roman period as ad hoc privy councils often presided over by the high priest. Frequently, these were specially convened to deal with political crimes, particularly sedition, and to rubber stamp wishes of the second-tier ruler. Fourth, the death penalty was commonly meted out, and procurators could consign suspected seditionists to crucifixion.[10]

Fifth, Jesus' brother, James, was convicted, in 62 C.E., by a Sanhedrin Josephus terms *unlawful*. Here, the high priest Ananus capitalized on a power vacuum when second tier Festus died, and the next procurator, Albinus, had yet to arrive. What Josephus said was *unlawful* is that Ananus assembled this Sanhedrin *without a procurator's consent*.[11]

Options I, II, and V fare poorly under Josephus:

- Compromised altogether is Option I—that the rabbis described the Sanhedrin correctly, and the Gospels, accordingly, stand discredited. Josephus tells of Sanhedrins headed by high priests and trying suspected political offenders. This profile validates the Gospels' depiction while bearing no semblance to that in rabbinic testimony. Based on Josephus, then, we may not pronounce the Gospel account untrue simply *because* later rabbinic literature outlines a Sanhedrin with different contours and procedures.
- Once Josephus has authenticated Sanhedrins generally matching the Gospel configuration, Option V is sidelined. If it is true that the rabbis' notion of the Sanhedrin is merely an *idealization*, it warrants no further attention.
- Disabled also is Option II. Gospel trial scenarios cannot be correct if they contravene Josephus' three-tiered scheme of authority in Roman Judea. That (third-tier) Caiaphas acted independently of, and at cross purposes with, (second-tier) Pilate is simply untenable. Moreover, consider Josephus' report concerning the Sanhedrin condemning James (62 C.E.). If the rule he cites was genuinely in force not only then but also in Jesus' day, then just as the Sanhedrin that Ananus convened was *unlawful* because he did not secure procuratorial consent, the presumably *lawful* Sanhedrin trying Jesus must have been convened *in consonance with* Pilate's own dictates! Such a reality the Gospels never reveal and may even deliberately *conceal*.

Faring better, in light of Josephus, are Options III and IV, for either scenario allows *both* sets of sources (Gospel *and* rabbinic) to emerge as possibly correct. According to III (that the Sanhedrin was *transformed* after 70 C.E), the Gospel and rabbinic traditions accurately refer, respectively, to the Sanhedrin during two different *time frames* (before 70, and after 70). According to IV (that, before 70, there coexisted two distinct Sanhedrin systems), the Gospels accurately refer to one system and the rabbis to the other.

Nonetheless—and this is key—Option VI must occupy us *first*. For if traditions of Jesus' formal trial arose expressly to satisfy church needs during the decades after his death, then there may be no compelling basis for believing that Jesus ever faced any Sanhedrin trial at all. We basically enter here the uncomfortable realm of conjecture, where a judgment call has to be made: is the case for the historicity of Jesus' trial sufficiently compelling or overly problematic? Should Option VI prove even *reasonably* persuasive, the impetus for recourse to Options III or IV would dissipate—although not because either is unimportant or unimpressive on the Sanhedrin problem *in general*.[12] Rather, it would simply be a matter that, if Jesus *likely* had no formal trial, then how can Options III or IV contribute to our discussion?

Is Mark's Sanhedrin Trial Sufficiently Compelling or Overly Problematic?

Our earliest and most basic version of the Sanhedrin trial, Mark 14:55–65, does not appear to have originated as a cohesive unit. Instead, it gives the impression of a composite, a mosaic of sorts, perhaps accumulating over time through the accretion of layers of tradition, possibly added to fill lacunae or correct problems perceived in previous formulations. Separating this paragraph into segments may prove instructive (italics and bracketed material are added to note key terms):[13]

SEGMENT A: 55 Now the chief priests and the whole council [Sanhedrin] sought testimony against Jesus to put him to death; but they found none. 56 For many *bore false witness against him*, and *their witness did not agree.*

SEGMENT B: 57 And some stood up and *bore false witness against him*, saying, 58 "We heard him say, 'I will destroy this temple that is made with hands, and in three days I will build another, not made with hands.'" 59 Yet *not even so did their testimony agree.*

SEGMENTS C–D: 60 And the high priest stood up in the midst, and asked Jesus, "Have you no answer to make? What is it that these men testify against you?" 61 But he was *silent* and made no answer.

Again the high priest asked him, "Are you the Christ, the Son of the Blessed?" 62 And Jesus said, "I am; and you will see the *Son of man* seated at the right hand of Power, and coming with the clouds of heaven."

SEGMENT E: 63 And the high priest tore his garments, and said, "Why do we still need witnesses? 64 You have heard his *blasphemy*. What is your decision?" And they all condemned him as deserving death.

SEGMENT F: 65 And some began to spit on him, and to cover his face, and to strike him, saying to him, "Prophesy!" And the guards received him with blows.

Segments A through D: an Expanding Composite?

Segment A (verse 55) mentions "false witness" but does not reveal of what this consisted. This could explain why the two clauses from Segment A ("[1] bore false witness against him, and [2] their witness did not agree") oddly *reappear* in Segment B, except now the content of the false testimony is supplied *between* the two clauses:

- Segment B repeats (from verse 55) that some "bore false witness against him."
- Likewise it repeats (from verse 55) that "not even so did their testimony agree."
- Between these is now the *content* of the false witness: "we heard him say, 'I will destroy this temple that is made with hands, and in three days I will build another, not made with hands.'"

Despite this improvement, Segment B (verses 57–59) proves unsatisfying in its own right. It begs the new question: what did even more important persons, the high priest and Jesus, say and do?[14] This new information is now, in turn, supplied by Segments C (14:60–61a) and D (14:61b–62): two questions by the high priest and Jesus' response to each.

Yet Segments C and D do not ring true, for several reasons. First, Jesus' demeanor seems incongruous: he is overly *silent* and then immediately overly *strident*. While not impossible in itself, the inconsistency is more likely traceable to the developing church's fondness for two *contrasting* Jewish Biblical motifs:

- Jesus' *silence* reflects Christianity's casting of Jesus as Isaiah's Suffering Servant, who "opened not his mouth; like a . . . sheep that before its shearers is dumb" (Isaiah 53:7; cf. Psalm 38:13–16); and
- Jesus' *stridency* conforms to the warning in Daniel 7:13 (along with Psalm 110:1) concerning "the Son of man seated at the right hand of Power, . . . coming with the clouds of heaven."

Has Mark harnessed two sharply contrasting motifs, and then conformed Jesus' behavior to mirror each? If so, then this could also mean that Mark gears the high priest's questions so as to elicit from Jesus precisely the responses

Mark wants. The impression of artificiality is intensified since Mark may have chosen to *derive* the high priest's two questions, in turn, from the pair that Pilate himself asks Jesus when it becomes *his* turn to do the interrogating![15]

We run the risk here that Mark conveys not a stenographic transcript of actual courtroom proceedings as much as a blend of theological traditions that first became vital for Christians years after Jesus died. Such custom-gathering of "information" about Jesus' presumed trial (if real evidence was absent) is here accomplished by recourse to the Jewish Bible for clues presumed predictive and descriptive of the true messiah.

Thus far, Segments A through D give the appearance of a construction developed in stages. While unsatisfying, it is yet understandable. For to introduce the idea of a formal trial but then to confess to knowing few if any of its particulars would seem artless in a milieu where recording "history" was more art than science! Whether the notion of a Sanhedrin trial began as fact or fancy, much scurrying was required to supply fuller content and correctives where necessary.

Segment E and Jesus' Healing of the Paralytic

Segment E will be decisive in gauging the historicity of Jesus' trial. Here "blasphemy" is identified as the basis for Jesus' condemnation. Mark used "blasphemy" elsewhere only once, many chapters earlier, when Jesus heals a paralytic (2:1–12). Glaringly, however, Mark there *added* blasphemy to the original narrative. Brevity and simplicity were required for traditions to be easily memorized and then conveyed orally to others. But the paralytic episode is overly long and oddly complex because a unit of text was inserted. Fortunately, the underlying narrative remains readily discernible:[16]

> Mk 2:1 And when he returned to Capernaum after some days, it was reported that he was at home. 2 And many were gathered together, so that there was no longer room for them, not even about the door; and he was preaching the word to them. 3 And they came, bringing to him a paralytic, carried by four men. 4 And when they could not get near him because of the crowd, they removed the roof above him; and when they had made an opening, they let down the pallet on which the paralytic lay. 5 And when Jesus saw their faith, he said to the paralytic, 11 "I say to you, rise, take up your pallet and go home." 12 And he rose, and immediately took up the pallet and went out before them all; so that they were all amazed and glorified God, saying, "We never saw anything like this!"

Into this brief and structurally simple story, verses 5b–10 have been rudely inserted (italics added to note key terms):

Mk 2:3 . . . They came, bringing to him a paralytic. . . . 5 And when Jesus saw their faith, *he said to the paralytic,*

"My son, your sins are forgiven." 6 Now some of the scribes . . . questioned in their hearts, 7 "Why does this man speak thus? It is *blasphemy*! Who can forgive sins but God alone?" 8 And immediately Jesus . . . said to them, . . . 9 "Which is easier, to say to the paralytic, 'Your sins are forgiven,' or to say, 'Rise, take up your pallet and walk'? 10 But that you may know that the Son of man has authority on earth to forgive sins"—*he said to the paralytic*—

11 "I say to you, rise, take up your pallet and go home." 12 And he . . . immediately took up the pallet and went out before them all; so that they . . . all . . . glorified God, saying, "We never saw anything like this!"

As scholars have long observed,[17] the double appearance of "he said to the paralytic" (verses 5 and 10) signals that extraneous material has been spliced in between. (Note also the awkward need this creates, in verse 10, to introduce close-quotation marks!) But not commonly recognized is Mark's *motive* for the insertion: he wants to get "blasphemy" on the record as early as chapter 2 in conjunction with the very *first* appearance of Jewish leaders ("some of the scribes"), so as to set the stage for the Sanhedrin's verdict of "blasphemy" in chapter 14!

Why was Mark so preoccupied with "blasphemy"? He was writing around 70 C.E., in the wake of an unremitting Roman persecution of Christians that had commenced under the Emperor Nero, in 64, inflicting "grievous torments"[18] and kindling a litany of anxieties: Christians were informed upon or betrayed; unable to bear up under oppression; uncertain what to say to authorities, or how to face suffering; pressured to express loyalty to Caesar, etc. (12:13ff.; 13:9–13).

Moreover, Judea's uprising against Rome, in 66, raised the ominous specter not only of Roman vengeance against the rebels but of intensified danger for Christians (whom Rome still commonly confused with Jews). Since Jesus had been crucified, the standard *Roman* punishment for sedition, Mark vitally needed to substitute some other accusation, less disturbing to Rome, as the supposed catalyst for Jesus' execution. Mark's insertion of blasphemy into the paralytic's healing (to set up the Sanhedrin verdict) suggests that the crucifixion for *sedition* was the original actual charge, with "blasphemy" only a later attempted corrective!

Reinforcing this observation is Mark's practice, elsewhere as well, of intruding new units of text into earlier materials. This is precisely how he manages to change the Last Supper from an ordinary meal into a Passover observance.[19] Also in this fashion is the Barabbas episode introduced (though possibly earlier than Mark).[20]

Because of Segment E, the Sanhedrin paragraph, already quite problematic, now inspires even less confidence. To be sure, it is the contents of the trial that have lost credibility, not the possibility of a trial itself. Yet to the extent that Segments A through E constitute a mosaic of materials echoing later church interests, this raises the question of whether the *entire* Sanhedrin paragraph is itself a unit inserted, now, where it was originally absent?

The Sanhedrin Paragraph as a Unit

The possibility must be granted that, were the Sanhedrin paragraph never present, Mark 14:53 could seamlessly continue in 15:1 (italics added):[21]

> 14:53 And they led Jesus to the high priest; and all the chief priests and the elders and the scribes were assembled.
>   Omit SANHEDRIN PARAGRAPH (Mark 14:55–65)
> 15:1 And as soon as it was morning the chief priests, with the elders and scribes . . .[22] held a *consultation*; and they bound Jesus and led him away and delivered him to Pilate.

Moreover, these two verses (which now *frame* the Sanhedrin paragraph) could well have constituted the *totality* of the original Christian report of Jesus' arrest. The word "consultation" (in 15:1) could be another telltale clue that originally there was no trial reported here. At least the question is worth pondering: if there had truly intervened here a nighttime trial (culminating in Jesus' conviction), what necessarily remained about which to "consult" in the morning? More to the point: if the "consultation" was the *totality* of what was done vis-à-vis Jesus, would not early Christians have deemed this anomalous? To do adequate justice to Jesus' stature, could anything short of the grandiosity of a Sanhedrin trial be imaginable? Was the term "consultation" perhaps the catalyst that first generated the literary necessity of presenting Jesus as tried before the foremost Jewish court?

What, then, is our judgment call: is the case for the historicity of Jesus' trial sufficiently compelling or overly problematic? The answer need not be conclusively proven. What *may* be set forth with confidence is that the Sanhedrin account in Mark is fraught with irregularities *internally*, and even the historicity of a Sanhedrin trial in itself emerges as improbable.

Concluding Reflections

A pathbreaking document, *Criteria for the Evaluation of Dramatizations of the Passion*, has wisely counseled: "the historical and biblical questions surrounding the notion that there was a formal Sanhedrin trial argue for extreme caution and, perhaps, even abandoning the device."[23] On many points, our most basic Sanhedrin account, that of Mark, appears to be an imagined construction primarily addressing Christian concerns arising only well *after* Jesus' own day. Accordingly, resolving the problem of Jewish jurisprudence and the trial of Jesus requires the admission *that Jewish jurisprudence may be able to shed no light whatsoever on a trial that most likely never occurred!*

Probably, the early Christians knew very little about what had happened to Jesus beyond a rudimentary progression of events: his capture; an interrogation (if even that); a *consultation* about delivering him to Roman officialdom; and the crucifixion. Convinced of Jesus' grandiose stature, however, they naturally assumed that his opponents had recognized the same. Surely, then, he had warranted no mere "consultation" or even interrogation, but rather a formal trial before the foremost Jewish court of all, followed by a personal examination by no less than the Roman procurator himself!

Neither recalling nor, perhaps, exactly comprehending *why* Jesus had been arrested, they naturally retrojected as Jesus' experience problems they themselves were later experiencing from *contemporary* Jewish critics. No doubt, they heard themselves labeled "blasphemers" for identifying the crucified Jesus as a divine figure, so they likely assumed Jesus himself had been similarly misconstrued. This conclusion was not merely logical but expedient for, unlike sedition, "blasphemy" posed no concern to Rome. Instead, it helped diminish the possibility that Jesus' crucifixion as "King of the Jews" would stigmatize post-70 Christians as *subversives*. In the wake of Nero's persecution and the Judean revolt, both in the mid-60s, it was advisable, even imperative, that Christian communities cast themselves as allies of Rome, and cast the "rebellious" Jews as the common enemies of *both*. The belated tradition of a "Sanhedrin trial" contributed to this goal in a fundamental way, transforming a Jew put to death by Rome into a Christian put to death by Jews.

Notes

1. "Council" translates the Greek *synedrion* (rendered *sanhedrin*, in Hebrew).

2. Matthew closely relies upon Mark, Luke somewhat less so. It is uncertain if John knew Mark's Passion account.

3. For what follows: Mishnah *Sanhedrin* 4:1, 5; 5:5; 7:5; *Makkoth* 1:10; Babylonian Talmud *Sanhedrin* 8b–9a; 35a. (*Sanhedrin* 43a is unaddressed; the rabbis there *base* themselves on Gospel tradition rather than contribute anything substantive independent of it.)

4. Those objecting that Jews lacked capital jurisdiction still must reckon with Acts' account (6:11–7:1, 58–60) that Stephen, condemned for blasphemy by the Sanhedrin, is executed by stoning—with no Roman governor or crucifixion involved. John 18:31 ("it is not lawful for us to put any man to death") may only be a device to explain away Jesus' death at Roman (not Jewish) hands.

5. Albeit that sometimes the rabbis, anachronistically, retroject post-70 institutions, etc., to the pre-70 period.

6. Assuming that Christian tradition substituted "blasphemy" (a *religious* crime) to camouflage "sedition" (the *political* crime for which Jesus died).

7. Fourteen ruled Judea from 6 until 66 C.E. (excepting 41–44); Pilate was the fifth. Mentioned below: Tiberius Alexander (#9), Porcius Festus (#12), and Albinus (#13).

8. Josephus, *Antiquities of the Jews*, XVIII. ii. 1–2.

9. Josephus, *Jewish War*, II. ix. 2–4; *Antiquities*, XVIII. iii. 1–2; cf. XVIII. iv. 1–2.

10. E.g., "the sons of [seditionist] Judas of Galilee . . . were James and Simon, whom [Tiberius] Alexander committed to be crucified" (*Antiquities* XX. v. 2).

11. *Antiquities* XX. ix. 1.

12. Defending Option IV is more challenging, given sparse evidence that a pre-70 rabbinic-type Sanhedrin functioned.

13. Factoring out Peter's denial of Jesus (14:54, 66–72), lest it obscure our focus on Jesus' trial. Mark loosely interweaves the two episodes to suggest their simultaneity.

14. Segment F adds information concerning still others present.

15. Pilate's "Are you the King of the Jews?" (15:2) becomes the priest's "Are you the Christ, the Son of the Blessed?" (14:61). The priest's "Have you no answer to make? What is it that these men testify against you?" (14:60) is taken from Pilate's "Have you no answer to make? See how many charges they bring against you?" (15:4). The priest's questions derive from Pilate's (not vice versa) since Mark intends the Sanhedrin passage entailing *blasphemy* ("Son of the Blessed") to displace the Pilate passage, entailing *sedition* ("King of the Jews").

16. Original manuscripts did not number verses, so "11" could directly continue "5."

17. See Michael J. Cook, *Mark's Treatment of the Jewish Leaders* (Leiden: Brill, 1978), 45, 64–65.

18. Suetonius, *Life of Nero* 16; cf. Tacitus, *Annals* xv. 44.

19. The authorities plan to arrest Jesus before Passover (14:2); nothing goes awry. How, then, does the Last Supper become a Passover meal? Mark inserted verses 12–16 between 11 and 17 (Michael J. Cook, "Early Christian Appropriation of Passover," in *Occasional Papers in Jewish History and Thought* #5, ed. Robert Seltzer [New York: Hunter College, 1998], 49–64; "Righting What's Wrong with Church 'Seders,'" *Central Conference of American Rabbis Journal* [Spring 2000], 1–13).

20. The original tradition was likely 15:5, 15b: "But Jesus made no answer, so that Pilate wondered, and having scourged Jesus, he delivered him to be crucified." Into this was intruded the unlikely Barabbas episode: verses 6–15a.

21. Peter's denial of Jesus (14:54, 66–72) must here be ignored: it is a separate entity, placed here only because Mark links it with the Sanhedrin story (cf. earlier

note). Further, as part of a general polemic by Mark himself, it is far removed from early Christian tradition (Michael J. Cook, "Destabilizing the Tale of Judas Iscariot," *A Festschrift in Honor of . . . Walter Jacob* (Pittsburgh, 2001), 109–49, passim.

22. Omit "and the whole council." Mark has committed an editorial error. "Chief priests, elders, and scribes" *are* the entire council (there is no membership *beyond* them). Because Mark used "the whole council" in fashioning 14:55, he uses it here again so his Sanhedrin insertion seems a better fit with the originally sparse narrative.

23. The Bishops' Committee for Ecumenical and Interreligious Affairs (National Conference of Catholic Bishops, 1988), Section C.1.c.

~

CHAPTER THREE

Why Was Jesus Executed?
History and Faith

John Clabeaux

Many Christians would answer the question "Why was Jesus executed?" with the words of Paul: "Christ died for our sins in accordance with the scriptures." (1 Cor 15:3) This comes from the heart of Christian faith. It ascribes responsibility to no particular group. When controversies rage over presentations of the Passion of Jesus, many think this answer eliminates the controversy. "No one is blaming the Jews; we are *all* responsible," they say. But for Christians this theological answer is not enough by itself. It needs to be accompanied by another answer, a historical answer. Consider this reply from Frank Matera: "Historically, Jesus stood trial only once, before Pilate. Persuaded by the chief priests that Jesus was a political threat, Pilate sentenced him to death for insurgency."[1] This is a necessary supplement to the first answer, not a contradiction. But it is not evident from a reading of the Gospels and Acts.

In the four Gospels the Jews seem to dominate the inexorable movement toward Jesus' execution. In *Acts* there are five explicit statements that the Jews had Jesus killed: Acts 2:22–23; 3:13–18; 4:10; 5:30; and 7:52. But one does not read the Bible *well*, if one ignores what else has been written. The Bible is only understood when placed alongside many other writings, which help us determine how the forms of writing employed in the Bible are to be understood. Not all Christians think this is necessary. I write this article with a Catholic understanding of the relationship between *faith* and *reason*. The Catholic position, spelled out in the encyclical *Fides et Ratio*, is to assert vigorously the need for both faith and reason in arriving at the truth. Reason without faith is rejected as *rationalism*. But faith without reason is rejected with equal force as *fideism*. The forceful assertion of both is a difficult position to hold. It is criticized by many as excessively idealistic about the possibility of reconciling faith and reason. In the history of the Church the competing claims of faith and reason have often clashed. New developments in thinking and reasoning led to controversies, and sometimes even violence. But in the end, the Church asserts the reconcilability of faith and reason and rejects a view that silences either one. This view is not peculiar to the Roman Catholic Church. It is held officially or unofficially by many Christian denominations.[2] To many others it seems an unnecessarily subtle approach to reading.

The conviction that *history* is important for good *theology* springs from the Bible itself in that it reveals a God who acts in history. It is also supported by the Christian conviction of the *Incarnation*. Jesus lived and moved in time and space. The world in which He lived is the world in which we live, but Jesus lived in it two thousand years ago. We know his ancient world not only from the Gospels, but also by examining the writings and studies of those who have labored to understand the past.

The Christian Church, which believes in his saving death and resurrection from the dead, also lives and moves in history. And how it lives in the world is due in large measure to how it thinks and talks about the object of its faith. Beliefs strongly held affect behavior and events. The Christian who cares about the world, cares about the history of Christian dealings with Jews for two thousand years—a history which has been tragic.[3] Those who know it are sensitive to the slightest suggestion of Anti-Judaism, since history reveals that this vile inclination has been like gasoline near a flame. Jews comprise less than one-half of 1 percent of the world's population. Adding to their vulnerability is the fact that, as a group that has striven to maintain its distinctive ethnic and religious identity, they are regularly seen as *other*. The world is a dangerous place for people whom most of the world sees as *other*. The Jews are especially prominent in the consciousness of the Christian world, since they are so frequently in the Gospel readings of Christian assemblies. Both they and we have reason to be concerned about what images of the events that took place in the year 30 dominate the minds of Christians.

The Gospels and History

The Gospels contain history, but they are not *histories*. They are the chief witnesses to the events of Jesus' death, but since they were written using the literary customs of long ago, modern readers have to do some hard work if they seek the kind of historical information that was not the prime concern of the authors.[4] On many matters of detail they disagree with each other. Those who engage in historical analysis of the Gospels must go through a process that can be likened to sifting. The Gospels and all relevant literature are the sand or soil that you sift. As you shake the screen, much of the sand slides through, but certain large particles stay on the screen. These are the facts on which all the witnesses agree, like: Jesus died on a cross, or, Pilate was the prefect who sentenced Jesus. The large particles are not merely isolated. They must be examined in relation to all other large particles (strongly established facts) and arranged as a coherent whole. If they create a world in conflict with what is known from careful study of the time period, the construction is not good history. Many medium-sized particles nearly pass through the screen. One must sift gently and watchfully. If these medium-sized particles (plausible or partly established facts) cohere with what is emerging as solid, they can be integrated into the picture. So can quite small elements, providing they do not disrupt the coherence of the whole.

The careful historian must make judgments about the tendencies of particular witnesses. Also, lines of development must be traced, since they may contribute to arguments about what events are confirmed. For instance, if we note a tendency in Christian literature to place less and less blame on Pilate, we should have to conclude that the earliest versions are more historically reliable than the later on the question of his role.

The study of ancient histories reveals an important fact about speeches and dialogues. It is crucial for reading the Passion narratives, since most of their scenes (65 percent of the Passion in John) involve such speeches or dialogue. The ancient world showed much greater latitude for reporting speeches and dialogues than is acceptable today. An Athenian named Thucydides, who was the gold standard for writing history in the Greek speaking world when the New Testament was being written, said that in writing speeches his aim was, "while keeping as closely as possible to the general sense of the words that were actually used, to make the speakers say what, in my opinion, was called for by each situation."[5] Thus, in dealing with speeches and dialogues in the Passion accounts, it is unwise to take these as though they were verbatim transcripts of what was said.

To insist that the Gospel writers broke completely from the standards of communication of their time for narrating past events, and wrote history as twenty-first-century historians should, we would have to adjust our view every time new standards of what constitutes *good history writing* emerged. The position of the Catholic Church and many other groups of Christians is that the ancient authors wrote "as true authors" (*Dei Verbum* 11). Inspiration does not mean that their procedures and proclivities were taken over by God. They wrote using forms and methods they knew.

The Context of the Passion Events

Historically, the execution of Jesus must be placed within the political and social context of first-century Judea. These are matters of which we know relatively little from the Gospels, but a great deal from the writings of the first and second centuries C.E.

The Roman Empire and the Power to Execute

In the first-century Mediterranean world, the Romans jealously guarded the power to kill. As with all historical matters the record is complicated. There are reports of killings by Jews of other Jews for which the Romans punished those who killed without Roman approval.[6] In general it seems that the words attributed to "the Jews" who brought Jesus before Pilate in John 18:31 were accurate: "It is not permitted for us to kill anyone."

The Temple and Internal Jewish Conflicts

A crucial feature of the historical context of the Passion is the situation of the temple as the focal point of Jewish identity and of the conflicts among Jews at this time. Since the rebuilding of the temple in 515 B.C.E., after the return from exile, the temple took on an importance for identifying the Jews as a worshipping people that exceeded its significance in the days of the kings of Israel and Judah. After the exile the monarchy was gone. Israel was a province in a foreign empire. Even the "independence" asserted by the Maccabees in the second century B.C.E. was short lived and limited. In 63 B.C.E. the Romans established control, which they soon delegated to a puppet king—Herod. But the temple and the worship ceremonial that enacted the presence of God in their midst remained. If anything, foreign domination intensified the importance of the great processions to and around the temple altar. The processions embodied "a march that protested against idolatry."[7] However much the people despised Herod or those who ruled after him, they loved the temple. The Romans were usually savvy enough to leave the temple alone. But they possessed subtle forms of control. The Roman prefect had custody of the high priestly garments and could give them or withhold them as he chose. The strongest Roman fortress in Jerusalem was strategically placed overlooking the temple courtyard.

The people's love for the temple did not extend to the high priests. Jewish texts from 165 B.C.E. to 100 C.E. reveal that Judaism was divided into many groups sharply opposed to the other groups, but most especially to the temple authorities.[8] There were not just three groups (Pharisees, Sadducees, and Essenes) but dozens of different factions, with certain traits in common, such as love of the Torah and love of the temple. One thing nearly all groups shared was opposition to the temple authorities. The high priests were appointed by the Romans from Judea's wealthy elite, and they served or were removed at the pleasure of the Romans.[9] The temple establishment represented what sociologists would call the "parent group."[10] They were the group against whom nearly all the other groups defined themselves. Each group accused the others, and especially the parent group, of lawlessness. Most claimed their own legitimate teacher as true interpreter of the law. The rhetoric was highly charged but rarely lethal. The *Sicarii* (dagger-men) and *Zealots* of a later period (post-66 C.E.) are exceptions.

These facts are crucial for understanding the conflict between Jesus and other Jews. It is no accident that his chief opponents in the Passion Narratives are the high priests and not the Pharisees, who only appear in John's passion in a minor role (John 18:3) and in Matthew's version are not mentioned until after Jesus' death. Jesus' conflict with the high priests, and earlier in the Gospels, with the Pharisees, was not a conflict between "Christianity" and "Judaism," but a regular feature of Jewish religious life in this time period. As heated as the debate became, it rarely involved the Romans. But public critique of the temple, at particular times of year, could be seen by the Romans as serious enough to warrant punitive action. And historically, the high priests were in a mutually beneficial relationship with the Romans. It was usual in the Roman system for local officials like the high priests "to maintain and advance the interests of the [Roman] ruling elite."[11] There is little doubt then, that the high priest and his supporters colluded with the Romans in getting rid of Jesus. But the Romans needed little convincing.

It is important to note that Jesus would not have been killed for his teachings or behavior relative to the law.[12] He had engaged in disputes with Pharisees, but they were in no position to bring about his death. Most historians see Jesus' rather violent activity in the temple (in Mark 11:15–19 and parallels) as sufficient to raise the ire of both the Romans and the temple authorities. To this we now move.

The Passion Events Relevant to Jesus' Execution

The Temple Incident
Matthew, Mark, and Luke present the Temple Incident at the beginning of Jesus' final visit to Jerusalem to celebrate the Passover.[13] The commercial

business connected to the sacrificial system was a regular and essential feature of it. Scholars are split on Jesus' intentions in carrying out this act, but one thing is certain: the disruption of the temple system was a disruption of the public order—as important to the Romans as to the temple authorities. The wonder is that he was not arrested immediately. We must assume he escaped due to the confusion common to a pilgrimage season. But people responsible for the public order would have been deeply concerned.

The Arrest

Matthew, Mark, and Luke are vague in their descriptions of the force that came and arrested Jesus. They call it a "crowd from the high priests, scribes and elders" without reference to ethnicity. Such a group sent by the religious leaders could have included Romans. John (18:3) is more specific. He mentions a mixed force, Roman and Jewish, which he describes as "the cohort and attendants from the high priests and from the Pharisees." His mention of the Pharisees is hard to reconcile with the fact that the Pharisees do not appear here in the other gospels, nor do they play any further role in John. But his mention of the "cohort" as a distinct group is supported by a reference in John 18:12 to "the cohort and its tribune." Cohorts at full strength numbered 600—far too many for such an operation. But the mention of a specific Roman officer (*chiliarchos* is equivalent to an American colonel) suggests high-level Roman involvement in the arrest. One wonders why so many presentations of the Passion, which usually follow John in his special details (such as the presence of the mother of Jesus at the cross), leave the Romans out of the arrest. Given the political context, it is more probable that the Romans were involved in the action from the start. There seems to be no reason why John would add them, had they not been there. Mark, however, has a reason for not mentioning them. Robert Beck discerns that Mark's Passion narrative has a tight dramatic structure in which Judas, one of the Twelve, hands Jesus over to the Council, the Council hands him over to Pilate, Pilate hands him over to the soldiers who beat him and kill him.[14] The progression moves toward the most lethal setting (the soldiers). Then the pattern proceeds in exact reverse. A soldier, in fact their leader, declares him "son of God." Pilate then has custody of the body. He is approached by Joseph of Arimathea, a member of the Council, who then hands the body over to the women. The women are told in Mark 16:7 that Jesus will appear to the other disciples in Galilee. There is a clear pattern here of disciples-Council-Pilate-soldiers and then the reverse, with a startling contrast between Judas (one of the Twelve) and Joseph (a member of the Council). It is memorable. You walk out of the drama by the same steps on which you entered it. If Mark had mentioned the

Roman soldiers and their officer as part of the arresting party the tight literary structure would be ruined. But John's mention of the Romans is more probably correct historically.

Interrogation by the High Priest

Here the Gospel record is conflicted. This should not surprise us, since no one from the community of disciples was with Jesus inside the house of the high priest. The *beloved disciple* and Peter get no further than the courtyard (John 18:15–18). We are not told that any official discussions happened in the courtyard. Matthew and Mark describe a meeting of the Sanhedrin. We know precious little about the size and functioning of the Sanhedrin at this time. Mark presents a night meeting. But Luke (22:54–71) says only that they went to the high priest's house, and then he describes Peter's denial which takes place outside. He does not take us inside the house. John does (18:13–24), but it is the house of "the high priest's father-in-law" (Annas not Caiaphas), and there is no trial—only an interrogation. The historian should conclude that we do not know exactly what happened that night, beyond that Jesus was taken to a house of a current or former high priest, and that Peter denied him. John's scenario of an interrogation seems the most plausible, but Matthew's and Mark's are more effective as drama. But, we must stress, they are drama, not courtroom transcripts. The subjects discussed in the trial Mark describes are Jesus' identity, something he said about the temple, and a statement about the coming of the Son of Man, all of which are matters that occur in the sayings of Jesus tradition. They represent what according to the author should have been said given the circumstances. They are not verbatim reports of eyewitnesses to the events. The discussions of Jesus identity in the trials portrayed in Mark and Matthew seem to reflect insights about Jesus from a later stage of Christian reflection. John's representation of an interrogation by the high priest that involved only questions about "his disciples and his teaching" (John 18:19) seems more accurate historically.

And yet, what happened on that night is quite important in answering the question "Why was Jesus executed?" If there were a formal trial by the Sanhedrin, we would have to place more emphasis on the violation of Jewish (rather than Roman) law. If it were only an interrogation by one of the power-brokers of the Jews who cooperated with the Romans, then more weight is placed on Roman interest in public order.

Judgment by Pilate

This was not a *trial* by current standards. Pilate himself was judge and jury. Even in John, which is the longest account, Pilate only asked a few questions, in

Matthew and Mark, only two. Only Jesus, Pilate, and possibly some guards would have been present. Ancient writers were free to construct a dialogue of what is likely to have been said. What is clear in all accounts is the importance of the question of kingship. This was most reasonably the heart of the matter, since it is what appeared on the placard above Jesus' head when he was crucified, and this placard was viewable by the public. The questions about kingship seem an accurate representation of Pilate's chief interest in the matter.

The Release of Barabbas

This episode is almost more important than the Judgment by Pilate in determining the picture one paints of how the decision to execute Jesus was made. In this episode Mark is probably closest to the events as they occurred. Pilate judged Jesus, a crowd approached asking for Barabbas, and, when this was settled, Jesus was led to scourging and death. Luke and John have Pilate making repeated efforts to set Jesus free—exactly three. The power shifts more and more to "the crowd." The term "crowd" is imprecise. We have no idea how large the crowd was, or who was in it.[15] What is clear is that the later the Gospel was written, the more power is given to the crowd, and the less the blame placed on Pilate. In Mark, the crowd has come specifically to demand the release of one prisoner. That would make it a self-selected "pro-Barabbas" crowd. In Luke (23:13) Pilate summoned "the high priests, the leaders, and the people." This implies an entirely different form of "crowd" than Mark's. Luke's version has the ring of a formal summons—the equivalent of "the Senate and People of Rome." Mark knows nothing of this formal summons by Pilate; neither does Matthew, who is rather close to Mark here. But Matthew has "the high priests and leaders persuade the crowds" so that in Matt 27:25 "the *entire people* said, 'His blood be on us and on our children.'" By this Matthew connects the destruction of Jerusalem in 70 C.E. to the rejection of Jesus in Jerusalem a generation earlier. Historicized by Christians over the centuries it has meant horrendous suffering for Jews. Many famous Christians—Justin, Hippolytus, Origen, John Chrysostom, and Augustine among them—have gone on record saying that it explains the wandering and sufferings of the Jews. Such an interpretation was firmly rejected in the Vatican II document *Nostra Aetate*: ". . . the Jews should not be spoken of as rejected or accursed as if this followed from sacred Scripture"(#4).[16]

The historian has to be careful in assessing the importance of the crowd. The role of the crowd in each Gospel narrative has a dramatic function. The selection of Barabbas is loaded with irony and dramatic possibilities. It may have happened, but it may not have happened just at that moment. In any case, the historian cannot dismiss the fact that Christian tradition reflects a steady trend toward diminishing the blame placed on Pilate and increasing the blame placed on the crowd, or "the Jews." Mark does little to deflect the blame from Pilate himself. Matthew and Luke increase the role of the crowd.[17] John intensifies this. In *Acts of the Apostles*, Peter asserts that the Romans tried to release him, but "The Jews" insisted he be killed (see Acts 2:22–23; 3:13–18; 4:10; 5:30; 7:52). By the second century the apocryphal *Gospel of Peter* says that Herod had Jesus killed. Later Christians either excused Pilate (like Tertullian ca. 190) or styled him "a prophet of the kingdom of God" (as Augustine).[18] The trend was continued by fourth- and fifth-century literature like *The Acts of Pilate, The Tradition of Pilate*, and *The Letter of Pilate to Herod* that have Pilate (or, in one case the Emperor Tiberius) become a believer in Jesus. All three place the blame for the crucifixion on "the Jews."[19]

Three historical arguments mitigate against an explanation of the execution of Jesus that assigns a decisive role to the crowd. First, the power to execute rested squarely in the hands of the Romans. Second, Jesus' teaching about *the kingdom of God* and his temple disturbance were enough to alarm the Romans about him. Finally, the little information we have about Pilate indicates that he was ready and willing to use violence against his Jewish subjects. Literary analysis of the Gospel of John suggests that the way in which Pilate is presented in the trial has more to do with "a dramatic character type . . . having to decide between truth and falsehood" than a carefully drawn historical description of the Roman prefect of Judea.[20] John's trial scene was mapped by Raymond Brown as "a series of seven scenes outside and inside the praetorium, . . . Outside the praetorium there is frenzy and emotion as Pilate struggles with the Jews over the fate of Jesus. Within the praetorium there is a mood of awe and fear as Pilate speaks to Jesus."[21] It is powerful drama that takes us into the meaning of the event. But it is not a transcript of what was said.

The custom of a yearly release of prisoners is a problem for many historians.[22] Would the Romans favor such a policy? There is no evidence in Roman writings for such a general policy. Would an individual governor have some such special practice? That we cannot rule out. Given power, individuals often use it in irrational ways. Practically speaking, Pilate may have used such a practice to diffuse popular animosity against the Romans. It is unlikely that he would put himself entirely at the disposal of his subjects. It is hardly conceivable that *any prisoner* would qualify for potential release. If Pilate had such a custom, it was meant to serve his own ends.[23]

Jesus' Death on a Cross

This incontrovertible fact weighs most heavily in answering historians' questions about why Jesus was executed. All four Gospels indicate Jesus was crucified, between two other condemned men described as *brigands* or *insurrectionists*, with a placard containing the words "King of the Jews." Crucifixion was public terror used by the Romans to maintain control of subject populations. Flogging was a normal part of it. The flogging prepared the victim for a bloody death in full view of the public. They reserved this barbaric treatment for "deserters, rebels, and those guilty of high treason."[24] The fact that Jesus was sent by the Romans to such a death, along with two other violent men, with a charge of kingship attached to his cross, all suggest that, to the Romans, the three men crucified were in the same category. Christian attention is focused on Jesus in the middle. But there is no evidence that the other two were treated differently from Jesus. An important detail from the Barabbas incident is that Barabbas was one of those "who [the plural form of the pronoun] had committed [the plural form of the verb] murder during the rebellion" (Mark 15:6). If the Barabbas episode rests on an historical memory from the day or near the day of the death of Jesus, it means that there had been a rebellion and men had killed people. This would cohere with the gospel presentation of two men crucified with Jesus. The Romans were concerned with public order. To them, Jesus and the rebels had disturbed it. We have no way of knowing whether Pilate made much of a distinction between Jesus and the other two. We have no report from him. We have only the memory of three men killed by a means reserved for "deserters, rebels, and those guilty of high treason." Neither Jesus nor the others were soldiers or high-ranking officials, so to the Romans they were some kind of rebels.

The Limits of History and the Need for History

The historical reconstruction of the crucifixion is unsatisfying to most Christians. It should be. It is not a complete description. Christian faith sees more than three men on crosses. There are questions of Jesus' identity, his mission, his conflict with the religious powers of his time. The Gospels seem to highlight the religious conflict and downplay the political motivations of the Romans, because the evangelists were not writing political history. Jewish religious authorities *were* involved. Their conflict with Jesus did include religious differences.[25] And, as Raymond Brown pointed out, to eliminate those religious conflicts from the picture would diminish the message of Christianity.[26] It is good that the evangelists addressed the intra-Jewish conflict, and the fact that many religious people opposed Jesus. This gives Christianity a basis for challenging the motives of (Christian) religious leaders who for reasons of selfishness or ignorance oppose Jesus as he appears in the

Church and the world today. But historically, that emphasis on the death of Jesus as being chiefly due to jealousy or ignorance by Jews (both are mentioned in the Gospels and Acts) does not address important historical realities about the Romans and their forms of control in the Mediterranean world, which, although they may not have been the primary concern to the Christian writers, must be of concern to us. From a twenty-first-century vantage point, we must take the Romans more seriously. Their form of control is repugnant to us. We must place blame where blame is due as we see it. We must learn from the Gospels about the harm involved in religious opposition to Jesus, but we must also deal with the terrible political forces that perpetrate murder in the name of public order. A Christianity which is separated from the hard realities of politics is ripe for manipulation by secular powers— and this has happened in the twentieth century when for the most part organized Christianity stood on the sidelines as Jews were worked to death, tortured, or killed by the Nazis and their many assistants from other countries.[27] And so we must deal responsibly with history. This includes the history of the effect that particular views of the execution of Jesus have had on the Jewish people.

The *view from history* does not replace faith, but people of faith dare not ignore it. A Christianity that is contemptuous of history is a Christianity turned in on itself, that has retreated to a mythical world of individual salvation. Such a Christianity will never fulfill its mission to the world. As Christ lived in the real world, so must the Church.

Notes

1. Frank J. Matera, "The Trial of Jesus: Problems and Proposals." *Interpretation* 45 (1991), 5–16.

2. Some Catholics do not hold to this time-honored view of the relationship between faith and reason, or they understand it in quite a different way. For a detailed discussion of the Catholic stand on this crucial issue see the article by George Smiga, "Separating the True from the Historical: A Catholic Approach to the Passion Narratives" elsewhere in this volume.

3. See Edward Flannery, *The Anguish of the Jews: Twenty-Three Centuries of Antisemitism*, (New York: Paulist, 1985) and Mary Boys, "Jews and Christians in Historical Perspective," in *Has God Only One Blessing?: Judaism as a Source for Christian Self-Understanding* (New York: Paulist 2000), 39–74.

4. Again I refer the reader to the more thorough discussion of this matter in George Smiga's essay.

5. Thucydides, *Peloponnesian War*, trans. R. Warner (Baltimore: Penguin, 1954), 24. That Thucydides was the *gold standard* for history writing is seen from Lucian of

Samosota's essay from about the year 170 C.E., *How to Write History*, in which he refers frequently to Thucydides, and the fact that the opening lines of Josephus' *Jewish Wars* are modeled on the opening lines of Thucydides' *Peloponnesian War*.

6. See Raymond Brown, *The Death of the Messiah* (New York: Doubleday, 1994), 366–84. One important incident is the killing of James as told in Josephus' *Antiquities of the Jews* (20.9.1 #200–03). The high priest convoked the Sanhedrin and they took a decision to kill him after the Roman governor Festus had left and before the new governor (Albinus) had arrived. When Albinus arrived and found out that the high priest had done this, he removed him from office. Less than a year later, a prophet named Jesus son of Ananias was arrested and whipped by "some leaders." When they turned him over to the prefect, Albinus, he let him go, thinking he was more to be pitied than feared. One exception to the Roman monopoly on execution involved the temple. The Jewish-Roman historian Josephus tells of inscriptions placed in the temple area in Jerusalem in Latin and Greek warning Gentiles against entering under penalty of death. Raymond Brown, *The Death of the Messiah*, 366, presents archaeological support for this statement by Josephus. According to Josephus (*The Jewish War* 6.2.4 #124–26) the Jewish authorities had been given the power by the Romans to carry this out. But it is a specific, limited situation: Gentiles passing into the parts of the temple reserved for Jews.

7. Asher Finkel, "Prayer in Jewish Life of the First Century as a Background for Christianity" in R. Longenecker, ed. *Into God's Presence: Prayer in the New Testament* (Grand Rapids: Eerdmans, 2001), 50.

8. Andrew Overman, *Matthew's Gospel and Formative Judaism* (Minneapolis: Augsburg Fortress, 1990), 1–71.

9. Frank Matera, "The Trial of Jesus," 10, indicated that Annas was high priest from 6 to 15 C.E. Five of his natural sons were high priest after him, and his son-in-law, Caiaphas was high priest from 18 to 36 C.E. Warren Carter in *Matthew and Empire: Initial Explorations* (Harrisburg, Pa.: Trinity Press International, 2001) gives evidence that the ruling elite was carefully protected by the Romans against the interests of *the many*. As such they had a great deal of personal interest in being in a cooperative relationship with the Roman prefect.

10. Andrew Overman, *Matthew's Gospel*, 8–9.

11. Warren Carter, *Matthew and Empire*, 148.

12. Gerard Sloyan makes this point in *The Crucifixion of Jesus: History, Myth, Faith* (Minneapolis: Augsburg Fortress Publishers, 1995), 27, 31.

13. John presents this episode years before Jesus' final visit to Jerusalem. We have to make a choice between his assertion and that of the other Gospel writers. Since John shows a tendency to move matters which the rest of the tradition seems to assert as being quite near the Passion to points earlier in his ministry (e.g., parts of the Last Supper are moved to John 6, and parts of the Jewish leaders' discussions of what must be done about Jesus are moved to John 11), it seems logical to most historians to accept Matthew, Mark, and Luke on the timing of the Temple Incident.

14. For a full presentation of this literary critical analysis see Robert R. Beck, *Nonviolent Story: Narrative Conflict Resolution in the Gospel of Mark* (Maryknoll, N.Y.: Or-

bis, 1996), 39–62. Not only did Matthew follow Mark in this presentation but nearly all modern presentations of the passion follow it too. We end up with Jesus being severely beaten by Jews and tried by Jews even before he is taken to the Romans.

15. See John Crossan's short discussion of the problem of the size and makeup of the crowd in "Crowd Control" in *The Christian Century* (23 March 2004): 18–22.

16. Matthew 27:25 has been enormously influential in Christian history. Until relatively recently it was pronounced *three times* at the great Passion play at Oberammergau in Germany. Many great figures within Christian history, including John Chrysostom and Augustine of Hippo, interpreted it as referring to Jews in their own time. Augustine's specific words in "Reply to Faustus the Manichean" (book 12 #9) were "the Church admits and avows the Jewish people to be cursed." This is precisely the kind of thing the council fathers of Vatican II meant to repudiate. See Edward Flannery, *The Anguish of the Jews*, 47–55, Mary Boys, *Has God Only One Blessing?*, 48–57, and Gerard Sloyan, *The Crucifixion of Jesus*, 72–97.

17. This view of Matthew has been forcefully challenged by Warren Carter in *Matthew and Empire*, especially 145–68. He sees Matthew as being quite critical of Roman abuses of justice. He cites the important work of Peter Garnsey, *Social Status and Legal Privilege in the Roman Empire* (Oxford: Clarendon, 1970).

18. R. Brown, *The Death of the Messiah*, 696.

19. See Warren Carter, *Pontius Pilate: Portraits of a Roman Governor* (Collegeville, Minn.: Liturgical Press, 2003), 6–10.

20. R. Brown, *The Death of the Messiah*, 704, near the end of a discussion of what we can know about the historical Pilate (693–705). He judiciously argues against Christianizing Pilate, as several early Christian writers did, or excessively vilifying him. For more on Pilate see Warren Carter, *Pontius Pilate*, especially his first chapter, "Would the Real Pilate Please Stand Up?" Both Brown and Carter think it wrong to present Pilate as anti-Jewish or especially prone to violence, but neither was he a secret Christian. He was something in the middle: a Roman career functionary from the business class (*equites*) with a military background.

21. Frank Matera ("The Trial of Jesus," 8) describes this analysis by Raymond Brown from *The Gospel according to John xiii–xxi* (Garden City, N.Y.: Doubleday, 1970), 857–59.

22. For a full discussion see Raymond Brown, *The Death of the Messiah*, 811–20.

23. Warren Carter (*Matthew and Empire*, 167) argues that the benefit Pilate would get from giving a crowd the chance to ask for Barabbas would be that Pilate could get a sounding as to how much trouble killing Jesus would bring him. This explains why after he was told they wanted Barabbas, he asked what he should do with Jesus. The words "seeing that he was getting nowhere" imply that he knew everything he wanted to know: there would be no rebellion over the death of Jesus. If this is what he intended, he was correct. There was no rebellion. In the meantime he had the chance to appear magnanimous to the crowd. If Barabbas were a real threat he could pick him up the next day. When the power imbalance is entirely in your favor, you have many options.

24. Gerard Sloyan, *The Crucifixion of Jesus*, 18.

25. In the ancient world *religious issues* were not separable from *political issues*. I am not sure that they are now, but we often like to act as if they are. In *Matthew and Empire*, Warren Carter makes a convincing case that the evangelists themselves are far more interested in political matters than most modern interpreters assume.

26. R. Brown, *The Death of the Messiah*, 391–97.

27. See Secretariat for Ecumenical and Interreligious Affairs, National Conference of Catholic Bishops, *Catholic Teaching on the Shoah: Implementing the Holy See's 'We Remember'* (Washington, D.C.: United States Catholic Conference 2001), 7, 9.

PART TWO

BIBLE

CHAPTER FOUR

~

Protestant Understandings
of the Passion

Walter Harrelson

"Christ died for our sins in accordance with the Scriptures" (1 Corinthians 15:3). No other biblical text better sums up a Protestant understanding of the Passion. Jesus' sufferings and death had in view the plight of sinful humanity. He died for *our* sins. Protestant explanations of the death of Jesus always have in view the concrete "benefits of His passion."[1] This perspective is pervasive in Protestant theology, ethics, liturgy, hymnody, and piety.

Equally important in Protestant thought is the understanding of the Passion as a sacrificial act, an act that "makes holy," the basic meaning of the term. Religious communities offer sacrifices in order to enter more closely, deeply, fully into the world and life of the divine. Christ's death was a sacrifice for the sins of the entire world, an offering that brought the world into closer, deeper, fuller communion with God. Sacrifices are costly; life itself is at stake.

Protestants divide sharply over the interpretation of Christ's sacrifice for the world's sins. Many self-designated evangelical Protestants interpret the biblical language and imagery along compensatory lines: divine justice demanded satisfaction; only a perfect sacrifice would suffice; Jesus' death was a cosmic necessity, planned before the foundation of the universe.

Non-evangelical Protestants, on the whole, have rejected such interpretations of Jesus' sacrifice for the world's sins. The biblical language must be understood metaphorically. To insist that God demanded the death of the Son as payment or satisfaction for earth's sins is a monstrous notion for many Protestants.[2]

43

Some Protestant interpreters of the sacrificial language of the New Testament suggest a polemical intention. The language of the Letter to the Hebrews may be polemical language against the temple authorities. No longer do they control access to God's mercy and forgiveness.[3] Christ died for all, and all now have equal access.

New Testament Understandings of Jesus' Death

In addition to presenting Jesus' death as a sacrifice for sin, the New Testament contains at least four other ways of understanding Jesus' death.

Execution. Early sermons in the book of Acts indicate that some Christians understood Jesus' death as an execution by the Roman authorities with the support of some Jewish leaders. God intervened, however, and raised Jesus from death, received him into heaven, and gave him a place of honor at God's right hand, all in accordance with the Scriptures (Acts 2–3).

Defeat of Cosmic Powers. Some early Christians saw Jesus' death as the result of cosmic forces of evil at work in the world, "the powers of this age" (Ephesians 6:12; see also Romans 8:38 and 13:1–7). That is, not only did Pilate and certain Jewish authorities put Jesus to death; forces of evil enshrined in the structures of society did their part. Some references to angels may also reflect this worldview (see 1 Corinthians 6:3 and 11:10). This understanding of social evil that inevitably accompanies the development of human societies makes much sense on the contemporary scene. Indeed, the very meaning of the Christian notion of "original" sin may best be seen as the accumulated effects of human misdeeds (alleviated by human positive achievements) over the centuries. Each individual and every generation is born into a world where the structures of evil and the forces for good are always present. Jesus' death, in this view, was both the product of societal structures of evil and voluntary acts of human beings.[4]

Imitation of the Cross. The New Testament also presents the death of Jesus as a pattern for the life of faithful followers. Jesus died as he lived: faithful to God's call, heeding the demand that one live out one's life in service to God and to others. The New Testament references to dying to the old life and rising to newness of life display this meaning of Jesus' death. The Christian life is a continued life of dying and being raised, following the pattern of Jesus' death and resurrection. On this view, Jesus' death is integral to his life, teaching, healing, and all the rest: Jesus died as he lived, rejecting the patterns and claims of the "old" age and affirming those of the "new" age (see Romans 6:3–11; 2 Corinthians 5:14–21; Galatians 2:19–20).

Divine Love. Even more powerfully does the New Testament speak of Jesus' death as due to and born of God's love for the entire world. The death of Jesus, inseparable from his incarnation, life, teaching, healing, suffering, and resurrection, is God's gift of love for humankind, for the world. God "gave" the Son (John 3:16) for the world's redemption. The author of 1 John underscores this divine love: "God's love was revealed among us in this way: God sent his only Son into the world so that we might live through him" (1 John 4:9).

None of these four interpretations denies the sacrificial import of Jesus' death, but the variety is an important reminder that Jesus' death was understood in many perspectives and that the understandings changed in emphasis and weight over time.

Protestants and the Bible

Protestants deal with this variety of biblical perspectives on the Passion in a number of ways, depending on how they understand and read the Scriptures. The many approaches to the Bible found in Protestantism may be grouped, perhaps, under the following four categories.[5]

There are those who approach the Bible literally and with little interest in its historical background, literary character, social setting, or ideological leaning. For them the Bible is God's Word, a source book of divine instruction and guidance for the Christian community and for each individual reader, under the Holy Spirit's guidance. Christians who read the Bible in this way will see all of the ways in which the Bible presents the Passion as equally true and equally important. By definition, there can be no weighting of the various perspectives on the Passion; each one is consistent with the others, and all are divinely given.

Other Protestants approach the Bible as divine revelation rooted in history and expressive of the culture of its times. Historical, literary, sociological, and cultural analyses are of critical importance, inasmuch as the message of the Bible, revealed by God, is received by fallible human beings and subject to misunderstandings as well as understandings. The Bible is not a heavenly book handed down to earth but the product of divine revelation received by generations of Israelite and Christian believers. These believers used their own languages, literary forms, and other cultural realities as they set down the divine revelation, and believers today do the same as they read the ancient texts.

Still other Protestants prefer to treat the Bible as one source of divine inspiration but by no means the only one. For these readers, the Bible should be read as any other text from the past is read: critically, but with an open mind; with appreciation of its insights and truths; but with awareness of its ideologies, limitations, and imperfections. For such readers, the language and imagery of the Passion narratives represent early efforts to interpret the mystery of divine love for sinners. Contemporary readers may find it necessary to discover other and more suitable metaphors and understandings to account for Jesus' death. The notion of Jesus' death as a sacrifice for sin may have little resonance or power for such Christians.

A growing number of Protestants place the Bible in the context of the Christian liturgy and sacramental worship. For them, the Bible has its chief setting in the worship of God. The ancient texts, like the creeds, confessions, theological writings, and moral and ascetic practices of the Christian life, are part of the holy Mystery of God's presence and guidance. Here, the Bible is a holy book but not in the sense of a set of factual/historical texts handed down by God but in the sense that it, like the liturgy, the hymnody, the art, and the prayers of the church, discloses and makes real the Mystery of God's presence and action in the world.[6]

Most Protestants probably approach the Bible in the first two ways, although there is surely a sizeable number for whom the third outlook fits, and (as suggested above) a considerable and growing number who approach Scripture in the fourth way.

Hymnic Presentations of the Passion

All Protestants, no matter which approach to Scripture they may take, have a common hymnic tradition that is of immense importance in understanding how the Passion has been comprehended and claimed through the years and centuries. What follows is a brief sketch of some hymns that seem to fit well under one of the four New Testament ways outlined above for understanding the meaning of Jesus' death.

A Blood Sacrifice

"Nothing But The Blood"

What can wash away my sins?
Nothing but the blood of Jesus.
What can make me whole again?
Nothing but the blood of Jesus.

O, precious is the flow
That makes me white as snow.

> No other fount I know,
>> Nothing but the blood of Jesus.

This Gospel hymn from the nineteenth-century hymn writer Robert Lowery indicates the enduring Protestant emphasis upon Jesus' death as a blood-sacrifice. Holy Week tells the story of God's providing a remedy for sin, a remedy available to all, but a remedy that must be claimed.

This remedy for sin is discerned in much of Protestant life and imagery in very concrete and morally oriented terms. Christ's death provides the means and also the power to overcome sin in one's life. Much of Protestantism is notoriously individualistic, and that applies to this remedy for sin.

One of the vivid illustrations of this viewpoint comes in the early twentieth-century hymn by Lewis E. Jones:

> "There's Power in the Blood"

> Would you be free from your burden of sin?
>> There's power in the blood,
>> Power in the blood;
> Would you o'er evil a victory win?
>> There's wonderful power in the blood.

An Execution

Jesus' death is also understood as an execution. Sometimes the hymn writers stress human enslavement to sin and its power. Sometimes they refer to Satan's control of a sinful world. In either case, human beings, trapped and unable to free themselves, find release, freedom, and a new life when the hold of cosmic powers is broken.

The opening stanza of the eighteenth-century hymn by Anne Steele has the following lines:

> "Enslaved by Sin and Bound in Chains"

> Enslaved by sin and bound in chains,
>> Beneath its dreadful tyrant sway,
> And doomed to everlasting pains,
>> We wretched, guilty captives lay.

Martin Luther speaks of:

> "A Mighty Fortress is Our God"

> The prince of darkness grim,
>> We tremble not for him;

His rage we can endure,
    For lo, his doom is sure:
One little word shall fell him.

A Model for the Christian Life

Prominent in all branches of Protestant hymnody is the presentation of Jesus' death as the path that His followers are to pursue. Here are a few of the hymn texts that picture the Cross in this way. We begin with a hymn by the nineteenth-century hymn writer Robert Lowery:

"Go to Dark Gethsemane"

Go to dark Gethsemane,
    You who feel the tempter's power;
Your Redeemer's conflict see,
    Watch with Him one bitter hour;
Turn not from his griefs away,
    Learn from Jesus how to pray.

Follow to the judgment hall,
    View the Lord of life arraigned,
O the wormwood and the gall!
    O the pangs His soul sustained!
Shun not suff'ring, shame, or loss
    Learn of Him to bear the cross.

Calv'ry's mournful mountain climb,
    There, adoring at his feet,
Mark the miracle of time,
    God's own sacrifice complete;
"It is finished!" Hear Him cry,
    Learn from Jesus how to die.

Widespread in contemporary Protestantism is this understanding of the Passion as an example for Christians to follow: live a life of prayer and intercession, calling on God to continue the work of redemption brought into stark relief in Jesus' death on the cross. Live a life of suffering love, placing the needs and concerns of the neighbor ahead of one's own, and above all, sharing in the world's sufferings just as Christ did and does. Live a life of principled fidelity to the will of God, no matter what the cost. A mere listing of familiar hymn titles makes the point: "Jesus, I My Cross Have Taken"; "The Way of the Cross Leads Home"; "In the Cross of Christ I Glory"; "Am I a Soldier of the Cross?" The number of such hymns in all branches of Protestantism is immense.

A Gift of Love

Perhaps an equal number of hymns underscore the love of Christ for unworthy sinners but do not emphasize either the necessity of the death or the centrality of Calvary's blood. One of the great Reformation hymns, based on a text from medieval times, is Paul Gerhardt's "O Sacred Head, Now Wounded." The hymn closes with the following lines:

> What language shall I borrow
>   To thank Thee, dearest Friend?
> For this Thy dying sorrow,
>   Thy pity without end?
> O make me Thine forever,
>   And should I fainting be,
> Lord, let me never, never
>   Outlive my love to Thee

Here, it is Jesus' suffering and death that bind the faithful to Christ with bonds of unbreakable love. Here also is that quality of Christian life found in Paul's assertion, "If anyone [is] in Christ, new creation!" (2 Corinthians 5:17). Another of Paul's assertions also reflects this mystic participation in the reality of the suffering, crucified, and risen Christ: "I have been crucified with Christ; and it is no longer I who live, but it is Christ who lives in me" (Galatians 2:19–20).

The mystic power of God's love, revealed in the Cross, is another aspect of hymnody portraying the cross as a gift of love. None is more memorable than the George Matheson hymn of the nineteenth century, "O Love That Will Not Let Me Go":

> O Love that will not let me go,
>   I rest my weary soul in Thee;
> I give Thee back the life I owe,
>   That in thine ocean depths its flow
>   May richer, fuller be.

Freedom from Enslavement to Sin

Protestant hymnody stresses other themes that are clearly understood as "benefits of His passion," to use the prayer book theme once more.

Other Protestant hymns stress the liberation that Calvary brings, not only from "original" sin but from the continuing assaults of Satan. Charles Wesley's great hymn, "O For A Thousand Tongues to Sing," is one of the most striking. One of the stanzas reads:

> He breaks the power of cancelled sin,
>> He sets the prisoner free;
> His blood can make the foulest clean,
>> His blood availed for me.

The hymn text clearly distinguishes between the cosmic act of Jesus' deliverance of the world (the universe) from the consequences, through the ages, of human failings and overt acts of sin against God, on the one hand, and Christ's breaking of the power of enslaving sin that continues even after one receives Christ's forgiving love for oneself. The theme of much Protestant hymnody is this liberation from Satan's power, personally experienced by the individual. The experience is often marked by wrenching and prolonged struggle to overcome the continuing power of various forms of addiction or the like.

The Cross as Gift of Joy

Many Protestant hymns affirm the joy that this liberation from the power of sin rightly brings. Not only does the hope of resurrection produce Christian joy; the cross does as well. The majesty of the cross is the subject of the nineteenth-century hymn writer John Bowring's well-known "In the Cross of Christ I Glory."

> In the cross of Christ I glory,
>> Towering o'er the wrecks of time;
> All the light of sacred story
>> Gathers round its head sublime.

The closing stanza underscores the joy and delight in the cross, emblem not only of Jesus' death but also of the benefits of his Passion:

> Bane and blessing, pain and pleasure,
>> By the cross are sanctified;
> Peace is there that knows no measure,
>> Joys that through all time abide.

The cross indeed becomes a metaphor for the divine presence in all its power, beauty, and mystery:

Beneath the Cross of Jesus
    I fain would take my stand,
The shadow of a mighty rock
    Within a weary land.
A home within the wilderness,
    A rest upon the way,
From the burning of the noonday heat
    And the burden of the day.

I take, O Cross, thy shadow
    For my abiding place,
I ask no other sunshine than
    The sunshine of his face;
Content to let the world go by,
    To know no gain nor loss,
My sinful self my only shame,
    My glory all the Cross.[7]

Understanding the Passion Today

As noted above, Christians understand the Bible in quite distinct and different ways today. Most Protestants view the Bible in either the first or the second of the ways mentioned above. They either consider it a sourcebook of divine truth without any historical or factual or doctrinal error or they look upon it as a revelatory book, foundational for Christian belief, but the product of fallible human beings responding to God's revelatory Spirit. For the first group, all reports concerning the Passion are treated as equally true, equally authoritative, no matter what the consequences of doing so may be. For the second group, the variety of perspectives on the Passion needs to be taken into account.

It is not surprising that most favorable viewers of Mel Gibson's *The Passion of the Christ* are evangelical Protestants and traditionalist Roman Catholics. Gibson's film does add many details to the several accounts of the Passion in the New Testament, but all of the themes known to evangelical Protestants are found, some with grotesque overstatement. And as noted above, some classical evangelical hymns lay great weight upon the theme of atonement by Christ's blood. It is also true that many non-evangelical Protestants, those who are accustomed to treat the Scriptures critically, have found inspiration in Gibson's film and speak of it warmly. That too should not be a surprise.

The biblical language and imagery provide, for both Protestant evangelicals and non-evangelicals, the primary texture for dealing with the mystery of faith. The very centrality of the Bible for Protestants probably makes this inevitable. All Protestants learn to distinguish between the language and imagery of the Bible and the language and imagery of their own day. They do not live in the biblical world but they wish to live by its tenets and insights. So, for instance, most evangelical Christians who take with great seriousness their belief that all the world is lost eternally apart from acceptance of Jesus as the Savior are still able to sleep at night and are not driven to frantic activity in behalf of the "lost." Likewise, those who are firmly convinced that the "rapture" is nearby are still able to live a normal life in a world not burdened by such a sense of doomsday.

Similarly with regard to the Passion, Protestants generally view Jesus' death as an act of self-giving love on the part of God, willingly done by Jesus. The biblical language is familiar and comfortable, but for most Protestants it is probably more conventional than essential. Controversy and debate over the Mel Gibson film probably has had a double effect: to tighten the hold of some Protestants on the conventional language and imagery and to cause other Protestants to evaluate these more critically.

For many Protestants, surely, Christ's sufferings and death are seen as consistent with his moral teachings, his acts of healing, his prophetic exposure of social and personal injustices, and his God-like love and compassion for struggling and suffering human beings. Jesus died as a result of what he *did*, what he *taught about the kingdom of God*, how he challenged some of the religious and political authorities of his day. From the viewpoint of the Roman authorities, he was a threat to public order and was executed on the charge of sedition. Those groups and individuals who underscore the above picture of the Passion may continue to use the conventional language, "Christ died for our sins." They do so, however, with an emphasis upon God's love for the whole universe, Christ's embodiment of that love, even unto death. It may well be that many within evangelical Protestantism will more and more be drawn to this position.

In my view, Jesus died as a result of his conviction that what Israel's prophets had promised—nothing less than the transformation of life on earth—was a reality in his own day. Although the concrete details of the promises of the prophets were not realized—no restored kingdom of David, no elevated Zion to which the nations marched in peace, no transformation of the physical and historical earth—that which the prophets promised was in substance finding realization. The poor were being addressed, the eyes of the blind were being opened, the outcasts were finding a place in society, the dominant powers of the world were being challenged and brought to account by their Creator and Sovereign. Neither Israel nor the gentiles need wait any longer for the transformations of the "latter days" to take place. God was actively present to realize these earlier prophetic promises, here and now.

On this view of the Kingdom, Jesus' death is the result of Roman charges of sedition and also of anxiety on the part of some Jewish authorities that Jesus and his message about the Kingdom threatened both the Temple and their leadership. His death was a consequence of his claiming too much: nothing less than the coming of the promised day of righteousness, blessing, and peace that Israel's seers of old had sketched. And on this view, God's raising Jesus from death, as the disciples and the Church affirmed, confirmed the authenticity of that claim. No society, no group, and no individual need wait longer to begin to live—and to die—as a member or citizen of the new creation (2 Corinthians 5:17), for "if we live, we live to the Lord, and if we die we die to the Lord; so then, whether we live or whether we die, we are the Lord's" (Romans 14:8).

It may well be the case that Protestant hymnody, much more than Protestant thought in general, best reflects both the range and the depth of Protestant understandings of the Passion. That may be a blessing, for Protestant believers are ready to grant poetic license to hymn writers—something that many Protestants have not been ready to grant to the biblical writers.

Notes

1. This is a familiar phrase from the Book of Common Prayer.

2. This is true for some Roman Catholics as well, of course. See, for example, Donald C. Maldari, "The Triumph of the Cross," *America* 190:8 (March 8, 2004), 8–11.

3. Marcus J. Borg, *The Heart of Christianity* (San Francisco: Harper, 2003), 94–95.

4. These cosmic powers are presented in the Dead Sea Scrolls; see the Manual of Discipline and especially the War Rule.

5. For this set of categories see Philip A. Cunningham, "Covenant and Conversion," in *Seeing Judaism Anew: Christianity's Sacred Obligation*, Mary C. Boys, ed., forthcoming from Sheed & Ward.

6. The comparative study of religion and religions, along with ecumenical and interconfessional studies, have contributed greatly to this approach to Scripture in recent decades.

7. The words are by the nineteenth-century hymn writer Elizabeth C. Clephane.

CHAPTER FIVE

~

Separating the True from the Historical: A Catholic Approach to the Passion Narratives

George M. Smiga

The Problem

One of the lasting achievements of the Second Vatican Council was its repudiation of the claim that the Jewish people were responsible for Jesus' death. In the now famous paragraph four of the Declaration on the Relationship of the Church to Non-Christian Religions (*Nostra Aetate*), the Catholic bishops of the world state:

> True, authorities of the Jews and those who followed their lead pressed for the death of Christ (cf. Jn. 19:6), still, what happened in his passion cannot be blamed upon all the Jews then living, without distinction, nor upon the Jews of today. Although the Church is the new people of God, the Jews should not be presented as repudiated or cursed by God, as if such views followed from the holy Scriptures.

This statement clearly forbids Catholics from believing that the Jewish people are cursed because of their involvement in Jesus' death. Moreover, the bishops insist that such a view should not be seen as if it "followed from the holy Scriptures."

Now, however, comes the problem. The immediate reading of several sections of the passion narratives appears to support just such claims for Jewish involvement and responsibility. Matthew 27:15–26 is an example:

> 27:15 Now at the festival the governor was accustomed to release a prisoner for the crowd, anyone whom they wanted. 27:16 At that time they had a notorious

prisoner, called Jesus Barabbas. 27:17 So after they had gathered, Pilate said to them, "Whom do you want me to release for you, Jesus Barabbas or Jesus who is called the Messiah?" 27:18 For he realized that it was out of jealousy that they had handed him over. 27:19 While he was sitting on the judgment seat, his wife sent word to him, "Have nothing to do with that innocent man, for today I have suffered a great deal because of a dream about him." 27:20 Now the chief priests and the elders persuaded the crowds to ask for Barabbas and to have Jesus killed. 27:21 The governor again said to them, "Which of the two do you want me to release for you?" And they said, "Barabbas." 27:22 Pilate said to them, "Then what should I do with Jesus who is called the Messiah?" All of them said, "Let him be crucified!" 27:23 Then he asked, "Why, what evil has he done?" But they shouted all the more, "Let him be crucified!" 27:24 So when Pilate saw that he could do nothing, but rather that a riot was beginning, he took some water and washed his hands before the crowd, saying, "I am innocent of this man's blood; see to it yourselves." 27:25 Then the people as a whole answered, "His blood be on us and on our children!" 27:26 So he released Barabbas for them; and after flogging Jesus, he handed him over to be crucified.[1]

How is a Catholic to read such a passage? Catholic teaching insists that the Jewish people are not cursed or responsible for Jesus' death. Yet here is a passage which Catholics believe is inspired by God, and it presents the Jewish crowd "as a whole" calling for crucifixion and saying that Jesus' blood might fall upon them! If the events of Matt 27:15–26 occurred as they are presented in this text, how can an educated reader deny Jewish responsibility for Jesus' death? If they occurred differently, how can one uphold the integrity and authority of the scriptures?

Moving Towards a Solution

It is possible to provide a context in which the teaching of the Second Vatican Council and the biblical passion narratives can be seen as complementary. Appreciating the complex process by which the gospels were formed and the particular characteristics of their literary style assist the interpreter in reading such passages as Matt 27:15–26 without deriving harmful conclusions regarding the Jewish people. Let us examine this context in three steps.

1. The Gospels Are Not Primarily Historical Accounts
Contemporary biblical scholarship and official Catholic teaching believe that the gospel writers did not see themselves as modern historians. Their chief aim was not to report what happened. Their overriding concern was to move their readers to faith—to encourage the belief that Jesus was the Mes-

siah, whom God had sent into the world. The evangelists were more concerned with presenting the *meaning* of Jesus' life, death, and resurrection than the exact details of *how* those events took place.

Is there historical information in the gospels? Clearly there is. Yet, in composing the gospels, the evangelists adapted the material which had been handed down to them. They added some things, left others out, emphasized one event over another.[2] Why did they feel such freedom? Because they judged that such use of the material would more clearly reveal the *meaning* of Jesus' mission. The gospels are not modern scientific biographies. They are creative works of evangelism, efforts to bring their readers to faith in Christ.

The nature of the gospels can be easily appreciated by readers of literature. Different literary works are held to different standards of historicity. If I am reading a modern biography of Abraham Lincoln, I expect everything in that book to be historically accurate. The biographer is not free to make up scenes or present his or her surmises as fact. If, however, I pick up a historical novel based upon the life of Lincoln, I understand that the writer has more flexibility. He or she can invent dialogue and create new scenes and characters. The gospels are closer to historical novels than they are to modern biographies. They do contain historical information, but not every aspect of them is historical.

2. The Historical Aspects of the Gospels Must Be Established

Because the gospel narratives are a mixture of historical data and artistic creation, a determination must be made as to which parts are historical and which are not. Simply because a character or scene occurs in the gospels does not guarantee its historicity.

An imaginary example may prove helpful. Say we wanted to write an accurate modern biography of Abraham Lincoln. However, somehow every source referring to him had been destroyed—except for one historical novel which miraculously was still available to us. We would know that the novel contained historical information. We would not, however, automatically accept every scene or character as historically reliable. Judgments would have to be made in each case whether a particular scene or character had the ring of historicity or whether it appeared in the novel because of the imagination and artistry of the novelist.

How would we go about making such judgments? One way (and this is a much used method in biblical research) would be to learn as much as we could about the culture, politics, and beliefs in the world in which the events happened. In our imaginary case of Lincoln, we would try to discover as much as we could about the culture and politics of the city of Washington during the Civil War.

Imagine that our novelist told us that Lincoln was shot and killed while watching a play, *Our American Cousin*, at Ford's Theater. We wonder. Is that what actually happened or is our author reshaping the facts? On one hand we might be suspicious. Being shot in a theater is an unusual way to die. Perhaps our novelist created this scene for dramatic effect. Yet, on the other hand, how likely would it be for the novelist to change something as fundamental as the manner of Lincoln's death? To resolve our doubts we would search diligently for any information to be found in sources outside the novel. Was there a Ford's Theater in Washington? Did it ever produce *Our American Cousin*? Can we document that any other presidents attended plays there? Asking similar questions concerning the background of the passion narratives can help to establish the historical reliability of the biblical accounts.

Yet questioning the historical accuracy of the biblical texts may surprise and upset some believers. Those who revere these inspired narratives may be left wondering whether the authority of the scriptures has been lessened. This concern leads to the third and final step.

3. There Is a Difference between Truth and History

The parts of the scripture which are not historical do not undermine their authority for believers. I write this chapter as a believing Christian and a Catholic pastor. I hold the scriptures to be the inspired Word of God. But I understand the gospels to function as a particular kind of literature. Because the gospels are not modern biographies, I recognize that the truth which they proclaim can in fact come from scenes and characters which are not historically accurate.

This leads to an essential insight: There are true things which are not historical. Some of the truest things ever written have come from works containing fiction. Shakespeare, Melville, Twain have presented us with truths which have shaped our lives. Therefore, even as Catholics believe that the gospels are the inspired Word of God, they are encouraged to understand that the authority of that truth is not diminished when it comes at times from scenes and characters which are not historical. In fact, some truths are so profound that they are best expressed in non-historical genres, such as poetry or psalms or parables, or in the form of narratives that convey religious truths dramatically. The only time that truth and history must correspond is in literary works which promise us such a correspondence. The gospels are not that kind of literature.

A Catholic Approach to Matthew 27:15–26

The three steps which have been outlined above provide an approach for a Catholic understanding of the passion narratives and indeed all of the scriptures. Although the claim that parts of the scriptures may not be historical may initially disturb the believer who has not previously examined the nature of the biblical narratives, once this insight is absorbed, clear benefits emerge. The freedom to accept certain aspects of the biblical accounts as non-historical allows the interpreter to reject the historical basis of some negative claims of the scriptures, such as the implication that the Jewish people as a whole are cursed or responsible for Jesus' death. At the same time the separation of what is historical from what is not allows the believer to appreciate more clearly the artistic intention of the evangelist and locate the particular truth which is valuable to faith. To illustrate these benefits let us return to the scriptural passage with which we began, Matthew 27:15–26.

What Is Historical in Matthew 27:15–26?

When we ask which parts of Matthew 27:15–26 should be accepted as historical, serious doubts emerge as to whether all aspects of the narrative occurred as presented.

After extensive historical research into the Roman and Jewish sources of the period, historians have been unable to confirm the existence of the custom of releasing a prisoner during Passover time as three of the gospels suggest.[3] If this custom were historical, we should expect some trace of it in contemporary writings. Pilate, of course, had the authority to pardon criminals if he wished. Therefore, we can ask, how likely would it be for Pilate to release a prisoner like Barabbas in the manner Matthew describes? Historically, this would be the last thing Pilate would choose to do.

To understand why this is the case, we must reconstruct the historical situation in Judea at the time of Christ. Palestine was occupied by Rome. The Jews deeply resented this, and it was widely known throughout the empire that a Jewish revolt against Rome could quickly develop. The ancient historian Josephus reports widespread revolts against Roman rule at the death of Herod the Great in 4 BCE. The commotion caused the Roman governor in Syria, Varus, to reduce the Galilean city of Sepphoris to ashes and to crucify two thousand of the insurgents.[4] Closer to the time of Jesus, Pilate had to deal with a number of popular insurrections as prefect in Judea.[5] This simmering resentment led in time to the Jewish War against Rome during which the temple was destroyed in 70 CE.

In light of this volatile situation, Pilate was sent to Judea in 26 CE with two clear objectives: to keep the peace and to collect taxes (precisely to keep the peace *so that* he could collect taxes). In order to meet these objectives Pilate was determined to nip any sign of disturbance in the bud. The most dangerous times of the year were the great Jewish festivals, especially the feast of Passover. Then the population of Jerusalem, which was usually about 30,000, would increase to 300,000.[6] In a city bursting with Jewish pilgrims, celebrating their liberation from the foreign domination of Egypt long ago and drinking wine, civil unrest was likely. Pilate, who normally resided in a seaside villa in Caesarea, would consciously come to Jerusalem during the festivals with additional Roman troops. Soldiers were stationed on the roofs of the temple colonnades with a clear purpose: to keep people moving, to stop crowds from forming. For if a disturbance began it could quickly spread. Such an eventuality would clearly be seen by the emperor as a failure on Pilate's part to keep the Jewish populace in line.

Therefore, historically the last thing which Pilate would desire is a crowd outside his residence. Should a crowd gather it is highly unlikely that he would invite them to decide who should live and who should die. The political situation of Judea in the time of Jesus renders major portions of Matthew 27:15–26 unlikely from a historical perspective. We should rightly question whether Jesus' trial took place in any public setting and certainly doubt the willingness of Pilate to give to any crowd a choice between Jesus and Barabbas. A much simpler historical scenario is likely. When it was reported to Pilate that there was a popular Galilean preacher in Jerusalem who was collecting crowds and who created a disturbance in the temple by overthrowing some tables, the prefect would act without doubt or hesitation. A perfunctory hearing would take place out of sight of the excitable Jewish pilgrims, and Jesus would immediately be sent to crucifixion.

With the historicity of the Barabbas scene in doubt, the notorious "blood curse" of the Jewish crowd loses its context. Although all four gospels know of the release of Barabbas, only Matthew tells us that Pilate washed his hands and the Jewish people took Jesus' blood upon themselves. This makes it likely that the "blood curse" is the result of Matthew's editorial activity rather than as a reflection of history.

If the choice between Jesus and Barabbas as presented in the gospels does not hold up under historical scrutiny, should we conclude that the scene is completely imaginary or can a historical substratum be identified? A tentative but responsible answer to this question has been suggested by Raymond E. Brown. It is evident even in modern translation that the man who the gospels say was released was not named simply "Barabbas" but rather "Jesus

Barabbas." Brown raises the possibility that two men with the name Jesus (Jesus Barabbas and Jesus of Nazareth) were historically brought before Pilate for judgment at different times but perhaps during the same Passover period. For some reason Pilate released Jesus Barabbas but condemned Jesus of Nazareth. Although they were judged separately and in private, the similarity of names struck the followers of Jesus as ironic. Their Jesus, who was clearly innocent, was found guilty by Pilate, whereas Jesus Barabbas was freed. By the time this irony was recorded in the gospels, the drama had been intensified by bringing both Jesuses together at the same moment before Pilate's tribunal. The addition of a crowd and paschal custom further increased the artistic impact of the scene.[7]

The likelihood that the presence of the Jewish crowd, the blood curse, and the choice of Barabbas over Jesus did not occur historically assists the Catholic interpreter in demonstrating how collective Jewish responsibility for Jesus' death does not flow "from the holy scriptures." Moreover, separating what is historical from what is not can also clarify the truth which a scripture passage offers to believers. It is to that truth that we now turn.

What Is True in Matthew 27:15–26?

When we ask whether some aspect of a narrative is historical, our intention is clear. However, what is intended when we ask whether a narrative is true? Terrence Tilley has suggested that a story is true when it re-presents our world or a part of it in a revealing way.[8] From this perspective the scriptures can be said to be true when they reveal something about our relationship with God as we experience it in our world.

A narrative is able to reveal more than one truth, and the variety of truths within a story emerge as new readers pose new questions to the text in differing circumstances. Unlike the historical, which either happened or not, the truth within a story can never be exhausted. The interpreter, therefore, must be satisfied in pointing to certain truths which the story reveals, knowing that other interpreters will discover different meanings as they approach the text. To the historically minded this wealth of truth is disturbing in that it cannot be "pinned down" to one particular result. However, to those who come to the scriptures seeking the mystery of God, the abundance of truth is a gift which keeps the Word of God alive and connected to the experience of believers from generation to generation.

Therefore, as we ask what is true in Matthew 27:15–26, it is impossible to be exhaustive. We must be satisfied in pointing to a few truths within the narrative. The task of identifying what is historical and what is not is helpful in this regard. For as we now examine this dramatic scene with an eye to its truth, the historical doubt of certain actions and characters impels us to question, why has the story been put together in this particular way? If the writing is historical, then the evangelist is simply reporting what happened. If the evangelist has amplified, altered, or created a scene or character, then it is in the very shaping of that material that the interpreter can search for the truth.

Allow me to present two truths which can be discovered within this passage: the depth of injustice and the responsibility for life.

The Depth of Injustice

The choice between Jesus Barabbas and Jesus of Nazareth heightens the injustice of Jesus' death. The reader of the gospel already knows Jesus' goodness and innocence. Therefore, any sentence of death would be clearly unjust. Yet situating that judgment in a circumstance where not only is the innocent one condemned but the guilty one released widens the scope of the evil. The reader recognizes that not only is evil present in our world but it also has power. Even when the right decision is obvious, the wrong decision can be made. Even though all sense and logic point in one direction, there is no guarantee that our choices will follow. There is no failsafe position. In any circumstance injustice can prevail.

The high likelihood that the evangelist is not simply reporting what happened but creatively shaping this scene around this cruel irony, only emphasizes its impact. We recognize the truth this scene reveals. Injustice flourishes. The poor suffer. The innocent die. The helpless are forgotten. Opportunities to correct what is wrong are overlooked. Chances to strike out in anger and violence are embraced. Evil is not to be dismissed or underestimated. We stand in sad recognition. Yes, that is the way our world is. The truth of the Barabbas scene is a bitter one.

Yet it is not a truth without hope. For the victim in the scene is the Messiah. As God's chosen he claims for himself no special privileges. If injustice holds sway in this world, it will have its way with him. Therefore, the cruel irony of the Barabbas scene dramatizes Jesus' full humanity and union with us. It further invites us to see his continued presence in our broken world. Those who discover the truth of this narrative will recognize that the ones who suffer injustice share a particular union with Christ.

The core of the Barabbas scene is a heavy truth. Neither Jesus' death nor his resurrection has been able to eliminate injustice from our lives. But until that day when Christ returns and every enemy is destroyed, we do not struggle on alone. For the One who was rejected in favor of Barabbas, the Savior, stands steadfast in our midst.

The Responsibility for Life

Pilate's washing of hands and the blood curse in this passage assert that life cannot be taken without responsibility. Together with Judas' suicide (27:3–10), another section found only in Matthew, the hand washing and the curse share a preoccupation with blood. Someone must claim responsibility for the innocent blood of Jesus. Judas does not want it; the temple authorities do not want it; Pilate does not want it. Yet the story cannot proceed until someone claims it. This happens when the whole people, together with their children, accepts it.

As long as we view this responsibility within a purely historical framework, the issue seems to be who killed Jesus. However, our previous discussion has established that the historical accuracy of the hand washing and the blood curse is dubious. This allows us to approach them on a different level. We are free to ask what truth emerges from Matthew's emphasis on blood. The question has deepened. Who is responsible for Jesus' blood? The Christian tradition has consistently answered, "We are." Jesus died for the sins of all people. However we determine the historical causes which led to his death, it is true to say that all who are human assume the blame for his unjust crucifixion.

Moreover, it would be an impoverishment to limit this truth only to Jesus. Any life which ends through human intervention entails responsibility. Every life has value and no life can be taken without the blood being shared by us all. As long as lives end because of the thirst for empire, the desire for wealth, or the impulse of revenge, as long as lives are subordinated to the maintenance of systems which enrich only a few and waste the gifts of our planet, we cannot limit the blame for such losses to only some among us. Innocent blood spreads. Hands cannot be kept clean. Whenever blood is shed, when a life is neglected, when a person is treated as a commodity, it is *our* problem. The words of the crowd are our words, "Let his blood be upon us and upon our children." The truth of this story is that we are responsible for each other. No one is free until all are valued. No one is absolved until all are protected.

Conclusion

By separating what is historical in the passion narratives from what is not, the Catholic interpreter seeks to remain faithful both to the teachings of the Second Vatican Council and also to the scriptures themselves. By recognizing the dubious historical basis for some scenes within the passion narratives, the interpreter can demonstrate how the holy scriptures need not be read as placing historical responsibility for Jesus' death on the Jewish people. More-over, this very process of identifying what is historical throws the artistic and theological creativity of the gospels into higher relief. What appeared at first to be a problem can now be recognized as an opportunity. Even as we defuse the negative historical claims which seemed to flow from the passion narra-tives, we can unearth the graced truths which lie within them.

Notes

1. New Revised Standard Version translation.

2. Note this description from the Second Vatican Council: the Gospel writers "se-lected certain of the many elements which had been handed on, either orally or in written form; others they synthesized or explained with an eye to the situation of the churches" (*Dei Verbum*, §19).

3. Raymond E. Brown, *The Death of the Messiah* (New York: Doubleday, 1994), 814–18.

4. Josephus, *The Jewish War* 2:55–75.

5. Josephus, *The Jewish War* 2:169–77; *Jewish Antiquities* 18:55–64, 85–89.

6. E. P. Sanders, "Jesus in Historical Context," *Theology Today* 50 (October 1993): 442.

7. Brown, *Death*, 819–20.

8. Terrence W. Tilley, *Story Theology* (Wilmington, Delaware: Michael Glazier, 1985), 188.

PART THREE

THE ARTS

~

CHAPTER SIX

The Depiction of Jews in Early Passion Iconography

Pamela Berger

Pictorial art has been a powerful means of teaching Christian beliefs since the second century of the Common Era. Along with sermons, liturgy, and theater, imagery has served to inform the faithful about the life of Jesus. The depiction of the scenes leading up to his Crucifixion is known in art history as the Passion Cycle. There are literally millions of images representing the events of that narrative. In this paper I will discuss a few of these images, primarily from before the sixteenth century.

Though the Gospels were the main source for Passion iconography, visual imagery was also influenced by non-biblical writings, folkloric accounts, and medieval theater. Sermons and liturgy likewise had an influence on the pictorial representations. In most cases the artists and their patrons depicted what the words reported or what their traditions told them was possible. However, the ways the artists or their patrons interpreted those words and those traditions differed greatly. In particular, some chose to emphasize the role of the Judeans as opposed to the Romans. Others did not. This essay explores how the cultural milieu of the patron and artist may have influenced the visual interpretation of the figures and the events.

During the first three centuries of Christian history no part of the Passion cycle was represented. When Jesus was depicted, it was as a simple shepherd gently carrying a sheep on his shoulders [Fig. 1], or as a healer touching a blind man, a paralytic, or a man possessed [Fig. 2]. The image of a suffering Jesus was not part of the Christian religious imagination in these early centuries.

Figure 1. Christ as Good Shepherd. Fresco. (1st–3rd c. CE) Catacombs of Saint Priscilla, Rome, Italy. Photo: Erich Lessing/Art Resource, NY.

When the cross was introduced [Fig. 3], it was shown not as an instrument of torture, but rather as a sign of victory over death. It was surmounted by a laurel wreath containing the Chi Rho, the first two letters of Christ's name in Greek. The cross in this image, with the small Roman soldiers at its base, is represented as a symbol of triumph, analogous to the Roman victory symbol, the tropaion [Fig. 4]. On the tropaion the enemy defeated by the Emperor was shown seated in the same place as Pilate's Roman soldiers guarding the tomb of Jesus on the Early Christian sarcophagi. The tropaion was known

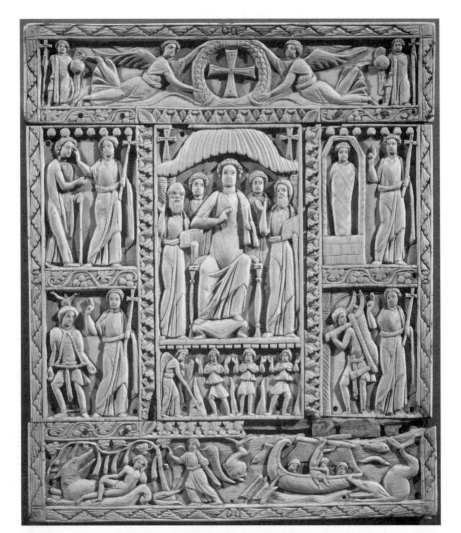

Figure 2. Christ with Saints: Healing scenes: On the left: Cure of the Blind Man, Cure of the Possessed; On the right: Raising of Lazarus, Cure of the Paralytic. Museo Nazionale, Ravenna, Italy. Photo: Scala/Art Resource, NY.

throughout the Roman world from coinage and served as a fitting model for the triumphal cross of Jesus, with soldiers at the base, "defeated" by his resurrection.

It was not until Christianity was firmly established in the fifth century that we see the first representations of the crucifixion of Jesus [Fig. 5]. The interpretation is clearly of a non-suffering, strong, and even proud figure. By this time, well after the council of Nicea in 325, Jesus' divinity had been

Figure 3.   Sarcophagus with cross and wreath of triumph. Museo Lateranense, Vatican Museums. Photo: Alinari/Art Resource, NY.

formally defined, and Christianity was the official religion of the Roman Empire. Debate continued among certain groups about whether Jesus suffered on the cross, but whether he did or not, the crucifixion was clearly viewed as a victory.

One of the earliest depictions of a cycle of scenes of the Passion is found on two pages of a Gospel Book from around the fifth century, the Rossano Gospels [Figs. 6–7]. The scenes are arranged to follow the sequence of readings during Lent.[1] The reading in the text accompanying the first image is from Matthew 27:1–2, "Early in the morning, all the chief priests and the elders of the people came to the decision to put Jesus to death. They bound him, led him away and handed him over to Pilate, the governor."[2] In this image we see that the chief priest and another Judean have brought Jesus before Pilate, who sits in the center. Pilate's court officials stand at the right. The officials are not mentioned in the Gospels, but they are part of an account in the apocryphal Gospel of Nicodemus.[3] Below, Judas has offered to return the silver to the chief priest, who has refused to take what he calls the blood money. In the lower right, Judas hangs himself.

The Passion imagery on the verso continues to follow the Matthew text, illustrating the crowd's preference for Barabbas and Pilate's washing his hands of responsibility for the crucifixion (Matthew 27:15–24) [Fig. 7].

Contemporary biblical and historical research is skeptical of the historical accuracy of this scene, especially given what is known from extra-biblical sources about Roman practices.[4] Therefore, one might ask *why* the Gospels recount Pilate's participation in these events in a way that appears to exonerate him. We can illuminate this question through the study of such visual imagery as this page in the Rossano Gospels. Here Pilate represents the Roman Empire. Since it was the Gentiles of the empire whom Christians sought to convert, a governor of the empire should not be cast as guilty of the con-

Figure 4. The Tropaion, depicted on a Bronze Sestertius, mint of Cologne, 260 CE. Heberden Coin Room, Ashmolean Museum, Oxford.

demnation of Jesus. Church officials sought to further the interpretation that Rome was not to blame in any way for the crucifixion. The blame had to be shifted from Pilate to others.

We see this exoneration of the Roman Empire and its governor, Pilate, through a study of Christian ecclesiastical imagery, and this manuscript provides us with a glimpse of that official imagery. If we look carefully at folio 8 v. we see that the crowd of Judeans agitating for Jesus' death is organized in a curved ascending line so that they form a semicircle. Art historians have discerned that this organization resembles the decoration of the conch of an apse.[5] Thus this depiction of angry Jews influencing Pilate may have been inspired by the décor of an apse of a fifth-century sacred site in Jerusalem, very

Figure 5. Crucifixion. Detail of wooden door of S. Sabina, 5th c. CE. Rome, Italy. Photo: Scala/Art Resource, NY.

likely the *Domus Pilati*, or The House of Pilate. Pilgrims came to Pilate's house to commemorate the Roman governor's attempt to stand up to the Jews. They celebrated Pilate; in fact, he became a saint in the Coptic Church. Though this small image in a manuscript would be seen by relatively few people, it is witness to a large, monumental wall painting or mosaic that would have been viewed by many of the thousands of visitors to Jerusalem. The House of Pilate was a major holy site, and with this vivid anti-Judean image supplementing the words of the Gospel, Rome, the governing authority, could remain innocent of the death of Jesus.

Let us go back to the Passion narrative in Matthew and to the image on folio 8v of the Rossano where Barabbas is being released at the exhortation of the gesticulating Jews: Pilate took water and washed his hands in front of the crowd. "'I am innocent of this man's blood,' he said. 'It is your responsibility.'

Figure 6.   The Trial of Christ; The Death of Judas. Codex Purpureus Rossanensis. Folio 8 r. Early 6th c. Painted purple vellum. 11″ x 10 1/4″. Biblioteca Arcivescovile, Rossano, Italy. Photo: Scala/Art Resource, NY.

Figure 7. Jesus before Pilate; From the Codex Purpureus Rossanensis. Folio 8v. Biblioteca Arcivescovile, Rossano, Italy. Photo: Scala/Art Resource, NY.

All the people answered, 'Let his blood be on us and on our children!' Then he released Barabbas to them. But he had Jesus flogged and handed him over to be crucified" (Matthew 27:24–26).

In 1965 the Second Vatican Council repudiated any interpretation of the phrase "Let his blood be on us and on our children!" that would conclude that Jews were collectively cursed for all time because of the crucifixion. The Vatican document reads, "what happened in His Passion cannot be charged against all the Jews without distinction then alive, nor against the Jews of to-day" (*Nostra Aetate*, 4). But until that declaration, the Matthean phrase, which placed the blame for the Passion on the heads of a group of Judeans, was widely understood by Christians to spread guilt to all Jews down through history. For nearly two thousand years the words were repeated sweepingly in sermons, in the liturgy, and in tracts, and were one of the main reasons for blaming Jews collectively for the crucifixion of Jesus. This widespread notion also shaped the way artists and patrons imaged the Passion.

However, we will see that the role of the Jews in the Passion narrative was interpreted differently during various periods. In the ninth-century Carolin-gian era, the Old Testament is illustrated more frequently than is the New Testament. And, apart from the Crucifixion, few scenes of the Passion nar-rative are found. When the Crucifixion is depicted, the role of the Jews is, for the most part, interpreted symbolically, through the representation of the personifications of Church (*Ecclesia*) and Synagogue (*Synagoga*) at the foot of the cross [Fig. 8]. Ecclesia collects the Blood of Jesus in a chalice, no doubt meant to allude to the cup he used at the Last Supper and the Eucharistic chalice. Meanwhile Synagoga turns her back on Jesus and walks away from him. But Synagoga is shown in a respectful manner, fully and modestly clothed, and the same size as Church. During this ninth century, Jews were fairly well accepted, at least in the areas that now make up France and Ger-many, and this relative 'climate of tolerance' is perceptible in the art from these regions.[6] During Carolingian times Christians visited services in syna-gogues, and discussions took place between priests and rabbis. Jews owned land and engaged in cultivating the vine. With Moslem physicians, they set up a medical faculty at Montpellier.

The first crusade, however, in 1096 was the impetus for a wave of hatred toward Jews, a hatred reflected in the Passion imagery of the Romanesque and Gothic periods [Fig. 9]. This page is from the Winchester Psalter, a Ro-manesque work from twelfth-century England. A Psalter during this time was the central prayer book, and certain psalms, especially Psalm 22, had been as-sociated with Christ since the Early Christian period.[7] The scene in the top register of this image is inspired by the account of the arrest of Jesus in the synoptic Gospels, for not one of those approaching Jesus appears to have the attributes of Roman soldiers mentioned in the Gospel of John. On the con-trary, they are easily identified as Jews, with large or hooked noses, misshapen mouths, pointed teeth, and heavy eyebrows. In the lower register, though Pi-late's raised hand implies that he has given the order, he does not have ex-aggerated features, and he is shown as being inspired by the winged demon whispering in his ear.

Figure 8.   Crucifixion. Ivory Plaque from Metz. 3rd quarter 9th c. H. 21 cm, w. 12 cm. Victoria and Albert Museum, London, Great Britain. Photo: Victoria & Albert Museum, London/Art Resource, NY

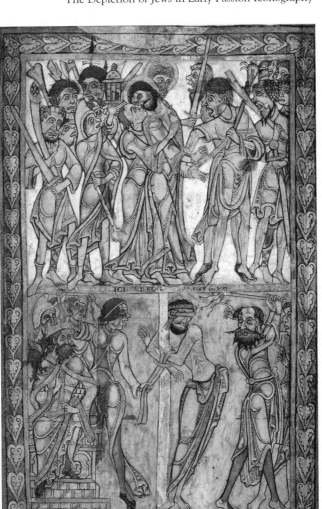

Figure 9. Arrest of Jesus and Flagellation. Winchester Psalter. England, mid-twelfth century. London, British Library, MS Cotton Nero C.iv, folio 21 recto. Photo: British Library.

The Gothic period continued the negative depiction of Jews. In some cases Jews were shown as monsters, as in "Jesus Brought Before Caiaphas" in this English Book of Hours [Fig 10]. The Jewish figures on the left, like the Jewish priest Caiaphas, wear pointed caps. All four Jews have mouths that look bestial, and the figures are shown in profile so that their hooked noses are emphasized. This interpretation of the scene distorts the figures into a

Figure 10. Salvin Hours, England, ca. 1270, British Library, London, Add. MS 48985, fol. 29. Photo: British Library.

surreal mode and connects Jews to demons, which are represented in a similar manner in the Middle Ages. We should also note that often, as in this scene, the Jews represented in the Passion sequences are dressed in contemporary garb. This means that the Jewish figures shown as harming Jesus have the same clothes as the Jews whom Christians saw every day.

The depiction of Jews as demons in some of these Passion scenes reflects extreme social tensions aggravated by and reflected in the sermons, tracts and law from the period, which stress how Jews are different and should be cast out. They did not eat pork, and they wrote and prayed in a strange language, Hebrew. From a Christian point of view, they were physically deformed, i.e., circumcised, and there was the folkloric belief that beneath their garments they concealed a tail or horns.[8] Christians observed that Jews had different headgear, and, after the Fourth Lateran Council of 1215, Jews and Muslims were made to wear identifying patches on their exterior garments. In some areas, Christians thought that Jews engaged in the grotesque acts of murdering children to acquire blood for Passover matzos. It is this hatred that comes out in the way some artists, particularly those in the northern lands, interpreted the story of the Passion.

Sometimes in the Passion imagery, Jews, and specifically Judas, are represented with red hair.[9] Though red hair is admired in our day, there was an aversion to red until the modern period. The Aramaic root of Iscariot (as in

Judas Iscariot) may be *sagor*, red. In Aramaic Judas *means* Jew, and the words sound similar in both Germanic and Romance languages. Thus Jews along with Judas may be represented with red hair because of this linguistic connection. The theme of Judas betraying Jesus for money also frequently makes its way into paintings. Jewish belief held that money could be lent at interest to Christians, but Christians defined money lending as usury, a sin, and Jews came to exemplify that sin. Often, when Jews lent, borrowers grew resentful and sought relief from their debts by attacking Jews. Well into the fourteenth and fifteenth centuries the attribute of Judas' money bag, highlighting his betrayal of Jesus for thirty pieces of silver, was probably connected in people's minds with Jews, specifically with Jewish moneylenders. Thus attitudes toward Jewish moneylenders were conflated with Judas' betrayal of Jesus for a bag of silver, a betrayal which led to Jesus' suffering and crucifixion.

The images I have cited were modeled on or served as model for other works of art. For instance, those appearing in books were used as models for wall paintings or stained glass windows. Though gestures and attributes are repeated, artists often included individual interpretive touches, and when they did, we will find that more of the images from the north inclined toward grotesque or exaggerated depictions of Jews than did the imagery from Italy, though Italy does have its share of anti-Jewish Passion iconography. The late thirteenth and early fourteenth centuries in Italy saw a strong interest in the suffering of Jesus. Saint Francis of Assisi had left a profound legacy of *imitatio Christi* and the stigmata that the saint suffered were interpreted as a supreme gift. Those who could emulate the life of St. Francis were invited to do so through deep contemplation of his life and especially his physical pain, a physical pain that he shared with Christ.

Some of the Italian Passion imagery was influenced by Byzantine art, especially scenes from the trial of Jesus before the Jewish priests. In this example from Giotto, however, the artist of the South does not depict Jews in the grotesque manner of the artist of the North [Fig. 11]. In this scene of the Mocking and Flogging of Jesus, Pilate is present on the right in a red gold-trimmed robe. The Jewish priests, likewise dressed in gold-trimmed garb, seem to be communicating with Pilate and pointing at Jesus. The figures in a circle around Christ are not dressed as soldiers, and so they have been interpreted as Jews. They are mocking, poking, pinching, and slapping the calm and dignified Jesus dressed in a shimmering gold robe. However, none of the Jews is treated as grotesque, or with particularly misshapen features. That Giotto could have painted imaginatively grotesque features is evident from the numerous devils he painted in his Last Judgment scenes in the same

Figure 11.   Giotto di Bondone, Mocking and Flogging of Jesus, Scrovegni Chapel, Padua, Italy. Photo: Alinari/Art Resource, NY.

chapel. Thus, as in so many other southern depictions, compared to the northern figures, Giotto's fresco of the floggers and mockers is relatively restrained. Though other artists such as Simone Martini include more nasty-looking Jews [Fig. 12], none of the work of the southern artists possesses the vitriol seen so commonly in the northern work.

One wonders what the reason is for this relative restraint. Perhaps it is the result of a general classicizing tendency found in Italian art, even in the medieval period. Or does this restraint reflect the social climate? This question is difficult to answer. The later Middle Ages in Italy was marked by the influence of the Dominican and Franciscan orders which, at times, preached violence against the Jews.[10] Though the papacy officially protected Jews,

Figure 12.   Simone Martini, Road to Calvary, Louvre, Paris. Photo: Réunion des Musées Nationaux/Art Resource, NY.

those who sought to practice medieval rabbinic Judaism were sometimes the victims of violence. The force of the newly formed Inquisition was felt after the 1230s, and condemnation of Jews and heretics grew more frequent and intense. (Jews were often linked with heretics, since inquisitors in some areas accused Jews of hiding them.) Nevertheless, the Italian art of this late medieval period does not demonstrate the vitriol present in so much of the art of the North.[11] Even in the most dramatic scenes, the emotions and gestures depicted are moderated. For instance, in the eight judicial scenes from Duccio's Maestà, the Jews generally have the same coloring and the same kinds of features as Jesus and the apostles [Fig. 13]. However, Duccio has used the damning iconography. He places the Jews in scenes of mocking and

Figure 13.   Duccio, Mocking of Jesus and Crowning with Thorns. Detail of Maestà Altarpiece. Siena, Italy. Museo dell'Opera del Metropolitana, Siena. Photo: Scala/Art Resource, NY.

scourging in Pilate's hall, for the figures flagellating Jesus do not wear the garments of Roman soldiers. So, even though there are no hooked noses or pointed caps, it would have been clear to the viewers that the torturers were Jews.

The late Middle Ages in the North saw the height of violent interpretations of the Passion. One example will suffice, "The Crowning with Thorns" attributed to Wolfgang Katzheimer the Elder and done around 1485 [Fig. 14]. Here Jesus' whole body is bloody and lacerated. The spikes of the thorns pierce his head. The figures involved in the torture are not dressed as soldiers,

Figure 14.   Crowning with Thorns. Wolfgang Katzheimer the Elder. Circa 1485. Wurzburg, Mainfrankisches Museum. Photo: Bayerisches National-museum.

and Pilate is off in the distance, under the archway of his palace. Right up front, and closest to the viewer, is a man whose garment has a border with Hebrew writing on it. That figure is also shown as diseased with a pock mark of some kind over his eye. He holds a pointed hat, a head covering so exaggerated that it could pass for a fool's cap. His long hooked nose is prominent, and he makes an obscene gesture with his right hand. Other figures torturing Jesus have hooked or grotesque noses and coarse features.

The turban on the figure to the left of Jesus designates him as a Muslim. Kufic writing, associated with Arabs, can be seen on a garment fluttering between him and the other coarse-featured figure behind Jesus. So we see that these torturers are meant to represent Saracens, the medieval term for the Muslims whom the Crusaders fought. From 1096 until the early modern period, Muslims were officially considered the enemy by Western Christendom, since, as an excuse for waging the Crusades, Muslims were characterized as having endangered the holy sites. Thus though wildly anachronistic, Saracens were included as among those mocking or flogging Jesus. In other examples sub-Saharan Africans came to be included among those torturing Jesus [Figs. 15 and 11]. Images such as these reveal that though most people in Western Europe had very limited exposure to dark-skinned people, they came to form part of a group seen as outcasts: the Jews, the Muslims who fought the Christians in the Crusades, and the Black person, and of course, the Heretic—all seen as "The Other." When people are seen as outsiders, by contagion they become assimilated with each other.

Contemporary scholars have used the tools of historical and literary criticism to understand more clearly the theological meanings, the apologetic and polemical purposes, and the historical events that lie behind the Passion Narratives. But exploring the Gospels in this way did not become commonplace until the early nineteenth century. Earlier artists and their patrons visualized the biblical material according to the traditions that had been passed down to them. Sometimes they conflated opposing details, ignored them, or outright contradicted them, as in depicting Jews as the scourgers of Jesus. Artists interpreted the Passion of Jesus in the light of tradition, their own social milieu, the style of their times, and, inevitably, by their own vision.

In the twenty-first century we can look to this scholarship. We can read and study the Greek, Latin, or modern translations of the Gospels. And, if we choose, we can use scholarly tools to contextualize these stories. In this way we can better understand the conditions that promoted hostility toward Jews, or indeed toward other groups considered outcasts. But some would question whether or not by bringing to bear textual, historical, or archaeological criticism we aren't corrupting a belief system. This is an important

Figure 15.   Crowning with Thorns. Prayer Book of Cardinal Albrecht of Brandenburg, illuminated by Simon Bening, MS Ludwig IX 19, folio 160 v. J. Paul Getty Museum, Los Angeles. Photo: Courtesy of the J. Paul Getty Museum.

question, for sometimes modern scholarship contradicts ancient sacred texts. This is not an issue only for Christians. Jews and Muslims could ask this question of their texts as well. Today, in our world in which interreligious conflict is rampant, an awareness of the vision of past centuries can challenge us to examine our own visions of the religious other, and ask, in what ways are ancient texts interpreted to incite hatred between peoples? And how does that hatred endanger us all in the modern world?

Notes

1. Herbert L. Kessler, "New Testament and Apocrypha," in *Age of Spirituality*, ed. Kurt Weitzmann (New York, Metropolitan Museum of Art. 1979), 492.

2. The English translations of the Greek used in this essay are from the *New International Version Study Bible*, 1985.

3. For the fourth-century *Gospel of Nicodemus*, also called *Acti Pilati*, see http:// www.earlychristianwritings.com/text/gospelnicodemus-roberts.html (accessed March 6, 2004).

4. See especially, Raymond E. Brown, *The Death of the Messiah: From Gethsemane to the Grave* (New York: Doubleday, 1994), 807–20.

5. William Loerke, "The Miniatures of the Trial in the Rossano Gospels," *Art Bulletin* 43 (3) (1961): 184ff.

6. Edward James, *Origins of France* (New York: St. Martin's Press), 102–4.

7. Kristine Edmondson Haney, *The Winchester Psalter* (Leicester University Press), 47.

8. Debra Strickland, *Saracens, Demons, Jews* (Princeton: Princeton University Press 2003), 122.

9. Ruth Mellinkoff, *Outcasts* (Berkeley: University of California Press), 150–53. See also Mellinkoff, "Judas's Red Hair and the Jews." *Journal of Jewish Art* 9 (1982): 31–46.

10. Jeremy Cohen, *The Friars and the Jews* (Ithaca and London: Cornell University Press, 1982), 242, 262.

11. Anne Derbes, *Picturing the Passion in Late Medieval Italy* (Cambridge: Cambridge University Press, 1996), 88, 78–9.

CHAPTER SEVEN

~

The Passion in Music: Bach's Settings of the Matthew and John Passions

Raymond G. Helmick

Within the heritage of Western music there are few treasures we value so much as the Passion settings of Johann Sebastian Bach. The St. Matthew Passion in particular has had more cultural impact, especially, of course, on Germans, than most things we can compare it with. When we hear these works questioned on the basis of antisemitism, it is rather like the situation I meet rather often, in dealing with Orthodox Christians, who can become very vehement in objecting to the inclusion of the *filioque* (the Holy Spirit proceeds from the Father *and the Son*) phrase in the Creed. They are right, of course. It doesn't belong there. The trouble is that all the great music has been written with that phrase included. But we should take the question of antisemitism very seriously, as the Christian treatment of Jews is not only a doctrinal question, though it is that, but one of basic humanity. Are the Bach Passions laced with antisemitism?

From very early in Western musical history it became the custom to chant the Passion accounts during the liturgy of Holy Week, the Passion according to St. John reserved for the Good Friday service, the St. Matthew on Palm Sunday and the others on the early weekdays. This accounts for the fact that the Matthew and John Passions received greater attention from musicians than those of Mark and Luke. Only in quite recent years, since the post–Vatican II amplification of the lectionary, have we had the three-year cycle of Sunday readings that gives us the three Synoptic accounts on the Holy Week Sundays of successive years.

The chant versions for the most part set only the actual words of the Gospel accounts, leaving any amplification or commentary to the Passion

Plays. It did become customary over the course of the Middle Ages to dramatize to the extent of assigning the words of Christ and of other individual speakers, and sometimes the crowd's exclamations, to different voices than the one that chanted the rest of the evangelist's text. By the late seventeenth century, in Germany, musical settings in the Baroque mode of the time began to displace the earlier chant. Dietrich Buxtehude has a particularly beautiful setting of the St. John Passion, for use in the Good Friday service, with a fluid and emotional musical line for the narrative, dramatic recitatives for the other voices, especially for the words of Christ, and colorful four-part choral settings for the interventions of the crowd, all this without instrumental accompaniment and only for the actual words of the Gospel text.

By Bach's time, early in the eighteenth century, musicians began to amplify the biblical texts with several kinds of supplementary material. These additional materials are of particular interest to the question of the potential for promoting antisemitism. In this era, the Passion receives a full Baroque orchestral setting. Solo voices, normally Soprano, Alto, Tenor, and Bass, other than those that take the parts of the Evangelist, Christ and the other persons of the narrative, add their commentary in the form of recitatives and *da capo* arias, representing the prayerful reflection and response of the individual soul. The chorus, besides dramatizing the often hostile cries of the crowd, adds its own impassioned statements of sympathy, of indignation, of resolve in the name of the entire Church. And at frequent strategic points in the narrative, familiar *chorales* are sung by the whole congregation to signify their own involvement in the drama of salvation as it unfolds.

This is what has given us the brilliant Passion settings of Johann Sebastian Bach and some other composers, which are really part of the Oratorio tradition of extensive dramatic musical compositions that were usually based on religious themes. The form is integral to the Pietist devotion of eighteenth-century German Lutherans. I've always felt, though, that it also resonates with the prayer forms of the founder of the Jesuits, St. Ignatius of Loyola, which Jesuits like me have inherited and cultivate. Ignatian prayer calls for an envisioning of the setting ("composition of place" in Ignatius' terminology), an imagining of the manner and sound of the voices of the characters who act in a Gospel narrative, meditation on the text (the recitatives in the Bach musical form), colloquies (prayerful personal addresses to Christ or the saints, corresponding to the arias in the Bach settings), identification of one's own private prayer with the prayer of the Church (the choruses), and then the communal recitation, in liturgy, of the familiar prayers of the congregation (the *chorales*)—all this makes for intense experience, and provides a good litmus test for our inquiry into the attitudes expressed.

The connections between the Ignatian practice of prayer and the Oratorio tradition to which Bach is indebted have their origins during the Renaissance in the work of Philip Neri and his Oratory in Rome. Neri was a close friend of Ignatius and acquainted with his way of prayer. That the musical performances the Oratorian Fathers presented in their Roman church had just this mix of scriptural text, reflection, commentary, and prayer in the way of recitative, aria, choral response, and familiar communal hymn points to a tradition of prayer that has analogies to that which Jesuits draw from the Spiritual Exercises of Ignatius.

Antisemitism, it should go without saying, was simply endemic to the period, unchallenged in the churches at large, Protestant or Catholic. There were people who would live by it and others who just never made it a part of their life. My finding is that Bach, especially in the whole structure of the St. Matthew Passion, went in an altogether different direction. This can readily be seen with Bach's treatment of the motif of the precious blood of Christ.

The blood of Christ, as a theme, has deep meaning for Christians for its Eucharistic dimension and for its role in the drama of salvation. The Bach Matthew Passion makes the shedding of Christ's blood a central theme from the very beginning, with the opening chorus—a very visually conceived "composition of place"—built dramatically around a traditional chorale, familiar to his hearers, *O Lamm Gottes, unschuldig* ("O Lamb of God, guiltless"). The blood of Christ shed on the cross is counterpoised from the start by the sacramental symbol, the sacrificial (paschal) lamb pouring forth the blood of the Eucharist. Two choruses converse, one crying:

> "Look!. . . Look!. . ."
> "See him!"
> "See whom?"
> "The bridegroom [Christ]."
> "See!"
> "How [is he seen]?"
> "He is seen as a lamb."

And with that other voices intone the words of the four-part chorale: "O Lamb of God, guiltless, slaughtered on the tree of the cross."

The antiphonal choruses continue their dialogue over the hymn:

> "See!"
> "What?"

"See his patience" while the chorale continues, its serene style contrasting with the profound anxiety of the other voices: "Found patient at all times, although you were despised."

"Look," continues the questioning dialogue.

"At what?"

"Upon our guilt;" but the hymn responds, "You have borne all our sin, otherwise we should have to despair."

The inquiring voices are by now calmed:

"See him, as from love and devotion he himself carries the wood of his cross!" and the hymn concludes:

"Have mercy on us, O Jesus."

The regular recurrence of this Lamb of God motif is structurally the most important feature here. That applies even more in the St. John Passion, which was the first attempt Bach made at an oratorio form on such an extensive scriptural text. It exists in two versions, the first presented at the Good Friday service in 1724, and a revised form for the same service in 1725. As a craftsman always engaged in preparing the music for a specific occasion, Bach had no concept of a musical work as a permanent monument for the ages. It remained open to reworking, and he had no scruple in cannibalizing material he had employed elsewhere, as in the case of the St. John Passion, many settings of the Latin *Agnus Dei*, or the *Lamb Gottes* hymn.

Bach made clear in the St. John Passion, even with that Gospel's repeated references to "the Jews," that Jesus was himself a Jew. This comes through most sharply in the Alto Aria *Es ist vollbracht*, "It is accomplished," elaborating on Jesus' final words at the moment of his death. The text reads:

> *Der Held aus Juda siegt mit Macht*
> *Und schliesst den Kampf.*
> *Es ist vollbracht!*
> The hero from Judah triumphs with power
> And ends the battle.
> It is accomplished!

In Bach's time there was a common libretto for many German Passions, a text from 1712 by Barthold Hinrich Brockes, *Der für die Sünde der Welt gemarterte und sterbende Jesus* ("Jesus, who for the sins of the world suffered and died"). Georg Phillip Telemann had first set it to music. The original had been a retelling of the entire Passion story that collated details from all the evangelists into one continuous story, rather than simply commentary material interpolated into one actual Gospel text. It was set, or recycled, by various composers, including Georg Friedrich Handel. Bach drew on it freely, but made significant changes.

One aria in each setting, Bach's and Handel's, comes directly after Pilate's question: "Shall I crucify your king?" to which the chief priests answer: "We have no king but Caesar," surely one of the passages most commonly taken as license for antisemitic interpretation. Handel takes the Brockes text unchanged, whereas Bach carefully removes the line that carries antisemitic content. The aria opens: *Eilt, ihr angefochtnen Seelen*, "Hurry, you besieged souls." But where Brockes (and Handel) continue: *Geht aus Achsaphs Mörderhöhlen. . . .* ("Leave the murder-dens of Achshaph"), Bach substitutes *Geht aus euren Marterhöhlen* ("Leave your dens of torture").

The difference is this. The city of Achshaph, Hazor in Joshua 11, was one of many cities the Israelites are shown as having destroyed in their battles to take over the Promised Land, "leaving none that breathed" (Joshua 11:11). Hence the Handel-Brockes line, "Leave Achshaph's dens of murder," portrays Jews as murderous by recalling the massacre in Joshua 11. But Bach's altered text instead alludes to the inner spiritual turmoil of Christians seeking refuge in Christ. Bach's primary focus is on the Christian hearers themselves.

The text goes on, in the Handel-Brockes version: *Kommt—Wohin?— nach Golgotha! Eilet auf des Glaubens Flügel; Fliegt—Wohin?—zum Schädelhügel. Eure Wohlfahrt blühet da.* "Come—where?—to Golgotha! Hurry to the wings of faith; fly—where?—to the hill of the skull. Your welfare blossoms there!" But Bach subtly changes it: *Eilt—Wohin?—nach Golgotha! Nehmet an des Glaubens Flügel; Flieht—Wohin?—zum Keuzeshügel. Eure Wohlfahrt blüht allda!* "Hurry—where?—to Golgotha! Embrace the wings of faith; flee—where?—to the hill of the cross. Your welfare blossoms there!" The difference? A theological shift that shows the care Bach actually devoted to his text. The passage is turned into a reference to Luther's famous notion that the Christian is at once both righteous and sinful, "*simul justus et peccator.*" The listeners are to *flee* (not "fly" as in Brockes) to the sheltering wings of the Savior, so that God will not reckon them as sinners on account of their undeserved gift of faith in Christ.

Why the change? Was it to obviate the Handel-Brockes gratuitous sideswipe at the Jews by equating the crucifixion with the massacre at Hazor? Or was it to facilitate the precise theological reference to the Lutheran doctrine of salvation that envisioned Christian souls fleeing to Christ for protection? I would judge that within the context of what Bach does elsewhere with these texts.

In another passage, at the mention of the scourging in John's Passion, Bach draws also on Brockes. The Arioso for Bass, *Betrachte, meine Seele, mit ängstlichem Vergnügen* ("Ponder, my soul, with anxious pleasure"), describes the suffering of Christ as the source of the listeners' salvation.

"Ponder, my soul, with anxious pleasure,
with bitter delight and half-uneasy heart,
in Jesus' agony your highest good;
how, for you, out of thorns that pierce him
the key-of-heaven flowers blossom!
You can break off much sweet fruit from his heartbreak (*Wermut*, 'wormwood').

At this point Bach breaks with the Brockes text, and concludes with a line not found in Brockes: *Drum sieh ohn' Unterlass auf ihn!* "Hence look on him without cease." This rather pallid line is Bach's very deliberate replacement for a tirade on the Jews which constitutes a second half of the Brockes text: "Look how his murderers (*Mörder*) plough his back, how deep, how cruelly they cut their ridges. . . .," explicitly identifying the soldiers (*Kriegsknechte*) as Jews whom Jesus had taught in their synagogues (for which, of course, there is no biblical basis).

That particular slander, which Bach rejects, attributing Jesus' scourging, unbiblically, to the Jews, appears in other vocal works, such as, in English, the nonliturgical passion carol "Woefully arrayed" by William Cornish (who died, pre-Reformation, in 1523). The opening verse contains the lines:

Unkindly treated, with sharp cord sore fretted,
the Jews me threatened.
They mowed, they grinned.
They scorned me. Condemned to death,
as thou mayest see,
Woefully arrayed.

Either of Bach's Passion settings is often taken to task for the way musical emphasis, repetition, and symmetry themselves constitute a type of commentary on the biblical texts. For example, Dagmar Hoffmann-Axthelm, in her "Bach and the Perfidious Jews: On the Symmetry of the Jewish Crowd in the Passion According to John,"[1] refers to the choral settings of the cries from the Jewish "crowd." In their symmetrical repetitions by which parallel series of phrases are inverted and reused, she sees "biblically sanctioned and thus religiously constituted, Luther-bolstered and textually and musically integrated hostility towards Jews." She contrasts the blindness, stubbornness, and impenitence of these settings with the suffering, love, and honor of Jesus and his followers as expressed in the chorales. Doubtless these terrifying repetitions of "Crucify, crucify" ring with great intensity in the ears of the listeners. I often have the same thought when, in our present-day churches, we have a simple prose reading of the Passion text in our services, with the congregation repeating those fierce words of the crowd.

It should be noted though, in my own assessment, that these declamations of the literal text itself do not have the same character of commentary as the recitatives, arias, chorales, and framing choruses that express the hearer's response to the narrative. They are all set in a musical form that would have been expected in the period for and interjection by a multitude of persons: the four-part fugue. The repetitions and inversions of the text follow necessarily from the character of this musical form, and would not have struck the listeners of the time as giving an especially hostile tone to the words. This fugal form for the crowd exclamations was present even in the Buxtehude St. John Passion I mentioned earlier, which confined itself simply to the Gospel text without any interpolations. Hoffmann-Axthelm is really upset, therefore, at the melodic dramatization of the scriptural narrative text itself, which Bach would not imagine altering.

The passage from Bach's Matthew Passion in which Pilate decides to offer the people a prisoner to be released, and asks whom they wish, Jesus or Barabbas, is important. Pilate receives his wife's warning that he should have nothing to do with this just man, Jesus, because of a dream she has had. Asking the people again which prisoner he should release, he receives their thunderous response: Barabbas. He asks: "What shall I do, then, with Jesus, who is called the Christ?" and they all say to him: "Let him be crucified."

The pattern Bach established of removing the patently antisemitic passages from widely used sources like Brockes holds true at this point in the Matthew Passion as well. Instead of commenting musically on "His blood be upon us and upon his children," and highlighting it, Bach simply proceeds with the Gospel text, not stopping to comment there at all. Instead his next Recitative-Aria sequence comes only after Jesus has been crucified, and the focus can be placed on his action, not on that of his executioners.

Where does this leave the basic underlying direction of the Matthew Passion? Blood, mentioned constantly as theme, does not call for a price in blood. Instead it is always and consistently the redeeming blood, the self-offering of his life for others by Christ. Where guilt and remorse are mentioned, as they often are, it is the guilt and remorse of the Christian hearers. The emphasis is not on pity for Christ suffering, but on gratitude for his gift of himself. And the mentions of blood and death and suffering are all subsumed into the sacramental imagery of the Eucharist.

Does this give us a useful model for handling these difficult texts of the Christian Gospels and their accounts of the Passion of Christ? I find it does.

There is a basic principle to follow when dealing with these passages, and Bach, even with the unhistorical biblical understanding of his time, follows it. Where blame is assessed, it is judgment on the community of faith. Blame must be the self-critical judgment of and on this community of faith present at the liturgical or preaching moment, not on anyone else. The attitude of Christ himself is always to be imitated, and it is one of forgiveness and self-giving, as symbolized in the sacramental life of the believing community.

Nowhere is this clearer than in the last aria before the concluding choruses of the Matthew Passion. The penitent soul seeks union with the now expired Jesus in the Eucharist. It is a peculiarly Lutheran and Pietist understanding of Eucharist, in which the dead body of Christ is itself buried in the person of the pious receiver:

> Mache dich, mein Herze, rein.
> Ich will Jesum selbst begraben.
>> Denn er soll nunmehr in mir
>> Für und für
>> Seine süsse Ruhe haben.
>> Welt, geh aus, lass Jesum ein!
>
> Make yourself clean, my heart.
> I will bury Jesus within myself.
>> So he should henceforth in me
>> Forever and ever
>> Have his sweet rest.
>> World, depart, let Jesus in!

And then the *da capo* return: "Make yourself clean, my heart. I will bury Jesus within myself."

Notes

1. Dagmar Hoffmann-Axthelm, "Bach und die *perfidia Iudaica*: Zur Symmetrie der Juden-Turbe in der Johannes-Passion" in *Basler Jahrbuch für historische Musikpraxis* 13 (1989): 31–54.

References

Notes to the Helmut Rilling recording of the *St. Matthew Passion*, Musical Heritage Society, Hänssler-Verlag, Germany, 1994, 1999.

Notes to the Smithsonian Collection recording of the St. John Passion, Smithsonian Collection of Recordings, Washington, D.C., 1990.

A. A. Clement, Ed., *Das Blut Jesu und die Lehre von der Versöhnung im Werk Johann Sebastian Bachs*, Proceedings of the International Colloquium: The Blood of Jesus and the Doctrine of Reconciliation in the Works of Johann Sebastian Bach, Royal Netherlands Academy of Arts and Sciences, 1995.

Michael Marissen, *Lutheranism, Anti-Judaism, and Bach's St. John Passion*, Oxford University Press, New York, Oxford, 1998.

Don O. Franklin, Ed., *Bach Studies*, Cambridge University Press, 1989, esp. Eric T. Chafe, "The St. John Passion: theology and musical structure," 75–112.

Other Passion settings:

Georg Philipp Telemann, *Matthäus-Passion*, 1746, recorded by Ulrich Stötzel, Collegium vocale des Bach-Chores Siegen, Barock-Orchester "La Stravaganza" Köln, for Hänssler Classic Exclusive Series.

Sofia Gubaidulina, *Johannes-Passion*, 2000, recorded by Valery Gergiev, St. Petersburger Kammerchor. Chor und Orchester des Mariinsky-Theaters, St. Petersburg, for Hänssler Classic Exclusive Series.

Arvo Pärt (b. 1935), Johannes-Passion, 1982, recorded by the Candomino Choir/Tauno Satomaa, for Finlandia Records.

Wolfgang Rihm, *Deus Passus*, St. Luke Passion, recorded by Helmut Rilling, Gächinger Kantorei, Bach-Collegium Stuttgart, for Hänssler Classic Exclusive Series.

Osvaldo Golijov, *La Pasión según San Marcos*, recorded by Maia Guinand, Orquestra La Pasión, Schola Cantorum de Carácas, Cantoría Alberto Grau, for Hänssler Classic Exclusive Series.

CHAPTER EIGHT

~

Oberammergau:
A Case Study of Passion Plays

A. James Rudin

Mel Gibson's controversial film, *The Passion of the Christ*, has reminded many of the centuries-old tradition of dramatizing the death of Jesus in performances known as "Passion Plays." This is not only because of its focus on the final hours of Jesus' life, but also because of the way it combines and embellishes the New Testament in its depiction of Jewish characters.

Indeed, Passion Plays and their almost universally negative portrayal of Jews and Judaism have been flashpoints in Christian-Jewish relations for centuries. The fallout surrounding *The Passion of the Christ* was not surprising because films reach hundreds of millions of people and play a major role in shaping cultural, political, and in this case, religious attitudes. Added to the mix in the case of this particular film were the long-standing problems vis-à-vis Jews and Judaism that are a basic part of Passion Plays.

Passion Plays as we know them began in medieval Europe and were a dramatic way to tell the story of Jesus' death and his resurrection (in most Plays) without the necessity of an audience or congregation reading a text. They evolved from semi-theatrical readings of the Gospel passion narratives in churches during Christian Holy Week observances to the outdoors in town squares, involving many people and moving far beyond simple recitations of the New Testament texts. Unfortunately, the traditional Plays, as they emerged in Christian communities in Europe, transmitted harshly negative images of Jews and Judaism: a bloodthirsty people intent on killing Jesus, and a religion that was outmoded, legalistic, brittle, and without love. These were easy and convenient targets to portray in medieval staged dramas or in preaching inside churches. It must be remembered that the idea "the Jews" had been cursed by God for the crucifixion of Jesus and doomed to homeless wandering was a widespread presupposition in Christian culture. New Testament verses that in this or that Gospel were negative about Jewish characters were combined into a more anti-Jewish presentation than found in any single New Testament work. Extra-biblical elements were also added. Thus did Passion Plays incorporate and spread the belief in Jewish accursedness.

One of those productions that has survived into the twenty-first century is the Oberammergau Passion Play, performed once every ten years in Germany. The Play remained in relative obscurity until the late nineteenth and early twentieth centuries when it was "discovered" by some visiting English Anglicans and travel agencies. In 1899, a new railroad line connected the once remote Bavarian village of Oberammergau with the rest of Europe. The rail link made the Play accessible for international tourists as well as for German visitors.

The Play, however, began much earlier. During the Thirty Years' War in 1633, Oberammergau, nestled in the Bavarian mountains south of Munich, narrowly escaped the lethal bubonic plague. In gratitude to God for their deliverance, the townspeople presented a Passion Play the following year. In 1680 the Play, a huge undertaking for a small village, began to be performed once every ten years.

The Oberammergau Passion Play was one of many such theatrical depictions of the death of Jesus that were presented in numerous European Christian communities. The German language Oberammergau version that began in the seventeenth century traces its roots to earlier twelfth-century dramas that were presented in Latin and not in the vernacular.

At one time, Passion Plays were performed in hundreds of European communities. Between the fourteenth and sixteenth centuries, over 300 villages in Germany and Austria had their own theatrical versions of the classic Passion story.

As a direct result of the anti-Jewish elements within Passion Plays, European Jews were often physically attacked following a performance, especially during Christian Holy Week. In 1338, the councilors of Freiburg banned the performance of anti-Jewish scenes of that town's Play; because of the anti-Jewish representations in its Play, the Frankfurt Jewish ghetto was protected in 1469; and in 1539 a Passion Play was forbidden in Rome because of the violent assaults against the city's Jewish residents in previous years.

Many of those earlier Passion Plays are no longer performed, but Oberammergau's Play endured. Today it is considered the "Grandparent" of all modern Plays, including Gibson's film.

During the six-month performance season of 2000, more than 500,000 people from all parts of the world came to Oberammergau to attend the Play. Visitors from the United States, frequently traveling in tour groups, were the single largest group, surpassing in size tourists from Europe and Canada. Interestingly, Germans constituted a small percentage of the total audience.

In 2000, the Oberammergau Play earned in excess of $30,000,000. In earlier years the production lasted nine hours, but by 2000 the production was reduced to six hours plus a long intermission for lunch. The Play is produced, directed, staged, and performed solely by Oberammergau residents.

As is typical in all Passion Plays that originated in Europe, from the outset Oberammergau contained many anti-Jewish stereotypes and caricatures. The Play portrayed the Jews as bloodthirsty and eager to kill Jesus. The Jewish priests, clad in sinister costumes, led by Caiaphas, the High Priest at the time of Jesus' death, were shown to be especially venomous.

And although the New Testament speaks only of a Jewish "crowd" of unspecified size, the Oberammergau Play presented a cruel howling "mob" on its massive outdoor stage located in the shadow of the Bavarian Alps. The classic cry of the shrieking Jewish mob, "Crucify him! Crucify him!" was an important and indispensable staple of the Oberammergau production.

The fact that first-century Judea was occupied by the Roman Empire was minimized in the Play. Roman prefect Pontius Pilate's decisive role in the execution of Jesus was lessened or softened. Even the historical reality that crucifixion was a well-documented Roman method of capital punishment was barely highlighted and even omitted in some productions. For centuries, decade after decade, Oberammergau unambiguously made clear to its huge rapt audiences that the enemies of Jesus, and by inference of Christians and Christianity, were the Jewish people.

German Chancellor Adolf Hitler was present at a 1934 performance of the Oberammergau production that marked the three-hundredth anniversary of the Play. The Nazi leader praised the Play, calling it a "precious gift" in the fight against Jews. He declared, "Never has the menace of Jewry been so convincingly portrayed." Ironically, in a 1998 visit to Oberammergau, I happened to stay in the same hotel as Hitler.

The defeat of Nazi Germany in World War II and the horror of the Shoah [Holocaust] forced many Christian and Jewish leaders to demand significant, even radical changes in the Oberammergau Passion Play. However, the U.S. occupation authorities led by High Commissioner John J. McCloy approved the restoration of the traditional Play in 1950. The Americans believed the resumption of the Oberammergau Passion Play would help restore a sense of stability to defeated Germany.

McCloy attended the opening performance on May 18, 1950. Sir Brian Robertson, the British High Commissioner, Federal Republic President Theodor Heuss, Chancellor Konrad Adenauer, Bavarian Minister-President Hans Erhard, and other dignitaries joined him.

In an interview thirty years later with historian Saul S. Friedman, McCloy recalled that in the middle of the Play, Adenauer was upset with the anti-Jewish elements in the production and said: "Das war zuviel!" ["That was too much!"]. McCloy added: "I had the feeling myself."

The 1950 production was nearly identical to earlier productions including the 1934 version. For Oberammergau, it was "back to normal" for its world-renowned Play, a production filled with many anti-Jewish elements.

But unlike the pre–World War II period, Oberammergau's critics grew more vocal in their calls for reform. They were strengthened in their demands by the historic teachings of the Second Vatican Council and especially its declaration *Nostra Aetate* on Catholic-Jewish relations. Under attack were the Oberammergau Passion Play's script, music, costumes, and staging, all of which, critics charged, transmitted a toxic and inaccurate picture of Jews and Judaism.

The demand for reform grew stronger in 1985 when Pope John Paul II declared:

"We should aim, in this field, that Catholic teaching at its different levels. . . presents Jews and Judaism, not only in an honest and objective manner, free from prejudices and without any offenses, but also with full awareness of the heritage common [to Jews and Christians]."

In 1988, the Bishops' Committee for Ecumenical and Interreligious Affairs of the National Conference of Catholic Bishops in the United States published "Criteria for the Evaluation of Dramatizations of the Passion." In it the Bishops taught that:

[E]xtra liturgical depictions of the sacred mysteries conform to the highest possible standards of biblical interpretation and theological sensitivity. . . . The greatest caution is advised in all cases where "it is a question of passages that seem to show the Jewish people in an unfavorable light."

A general principle is if one cannot show beyond reasonable doubt that the particular gospel element selected or paraphrased will not be offensive or have the potential for negative influence on the audience for whom the presentation is intended, that element cannot, in good conscience, be used. (Vatican Guidelines, 1974)

Christian and Jewish critics who attended Oberammergau performances in the years following 1950 grew insistent that significant changes were necessary. They asserted the Oberammergau Play was a transmitter of anti-Jewish images and stereotypes that severely retarded Christian-Jewish relations.

Critics pressed their concerns in public conferences, the general and religious media, scholarly publications, from church and synagogue pulpits, and by making personal visits to the village itself to express dismay about the Play's anti-Jewish elements. Their message was that the Passion Play in Oberammergau conveyed the false and pernicious belief that the Jewish people are collectively responsible for and guilty of Jesus' death. Because of their alleged culpability, Jews must receive an eternal punishment from God.

Oberammergau critics also charged the Play was supersessionist: the religious belief that with the arrival of Jesus, Christianity and the Church had spiritually vanquished Judaism and the Synagogue, rendering them obsolete.

In the Oberammergau Passion Play, Jesus and his followers were falsely removed from their Jewish roots and religious tradition. The Jews, the opponents of Jesus, were carefully staged negative stereotypes, while Pontius Pilate was exonerated. Such dramatic depictions, the critics charged, significantly distorted historic reality and the sacred teachings of both the Hebrew Bible and the New Testament.

In the years following World War II, two leading American Jewish organizations, the American Jewish Committee (AJC) and the Anti-Defamation League (ADL), became centrally involved in attempts to achieve reforms in the Oberammergau Passion Play. Working at first with the prominent Christian and Jewish scholars, the AJC and the ADL made a series of specific recommendations for changes to the Oberammergau authorities.

At first these efforts were rebuffed, but beginning in the late 1970s the Oberammergau officials including the mayor, Play director, and others entered into a long-term joint process that included conferences, consultations, and symposia—all centered on reforming the Play and eradicating anti-Jewish elements from the production.

Over time, the Oberammergau Play officials agreed their traditional production did, in fact, contain anti-Jewish images, caricatures and stereotypes. After viewing the 1984 production, I publicly called the Oberammergau Passion Play "fundamentally flawed" in its negative presentation of Jews and Judaism.

As the acknowledged "grandparent" of other Passion Plays, Oberammergau exerts an influence on similar productions throughout the world. By the late 1980s it was clear the traditional anti-Jewish orientation of the Oberammergau production had become a major obstacle to building constructive Christian-Jewish relations.

I was both stunned and angered by the many anti-Jewish elements that were present in the 1984 production including a Moses figure with ugly horns growing from his head. Particularly vicious was the judgment scene when 250 men, women, and children shouted in unison for Jesus' death by crucifixion and uttered the New Testament (Matthew 27:25) curse: "We take his blood upon us and upon our children." Although that chilling verse appears only in Matthew, it has been a major scriptural justification for religious anti-semitism.

Perhaps the worst anti-Jewish moments in the 1984 production came when Caiaphas, the High Priest, and his cohorts urged the assembled Jewish mob to reject the "tempter" [Jesus] and obey the laws of Moses:

ANNAS: And may the Galilean die. . . .

NATHANIEL: Let us demand his death.

PEOPLE: Away to Pilate! The Nazarene must die!

CAIAPHAS: He corrupted the law. He despised Moses and the Prophets. He blasphemed God.

PEOPLE: To death with the false prophet! The blasphemer must die. Pilate must have him crucified.

CAIAPHAS: He will pay for his misdeeds on the cross.

PEOPLE: We shall not rest until the sentence is spoken. . . . We demand the conviction of the Galilean! The Nazarene must die!

In that climactic scene, Pilate appeared at the Praetorium in Jerusalem:

PEOPLE: Judge him! Sentence him!

PILATE: See what a man!

HIGH COUNCIL [The Sanhedrin]: To the cross—

PILATE: Cannot even this pitiful sight win some compassion from your hearts?

PEOPLE: Let him die! To the cross with him!

PILATE: So take him and crucify him, for I find no guilt in him.

CAIAPHAS: Governor, hear the voice of the people of Jerusalem. They join in our accusations and demand his death.

PEOPLE: Yes, we demand his death.

PILATE: Lead him down and let Barabbas be brought here from prison.

ANNAS: Let Barabbas live. Pronounce the death sentence on the Nazarene.

PEOPLE: To death with the Nazarene.

Later in the scene Pilate asks the "People," in reality a howling mob of Jews, whether Jesus should be released. They respond in a loud chorus: "Kreuzige ihm! Kreuzige ihm!" ("Crucify him! Crucify him!").

Toward the end of the twentieth century the town residents voted to em-power two Play reformers, Otto Huber and Christian Stuckl, to direct and rewrite the 2000 Passion Play. Oberammergau's mayor, Klement Fend, supported them in these efforts. One persuasive argument for revising the traditional script was the historical fact that in the mid-nineteenth century the Play script had been rewritten by Othmar Weis (1769–1843) and further developed by his student, Alois Daisenberger (1799–1883). While many people believed the "traditional" Oberammergau script originated in the eighteenth century, the so-called "Daisenberger text" actually replaced an earlier version. The Play's orchestral musical score also stemmed from the nineteenth century and was composed by Rochus Dedler (1779–1822). Before Dedler, most of the Play's music consisted of Gregorian chants and vocal arias. Reformers were thus able to argue that because the Daisenberger text was of relatively recent origin there was a precedent for making significant changes in Oberammergau scripts.

Sadly, the 2000 Oberammergau Passion Play contained some of the same problematic features as earlier versions. This is because Huber and Stuckl did not create an entirely new script from the Gospel narratives but instead built upon the foundation of Weis and Daisenberger by making revisions, deletions, and additions. Some of the anti-Jewish problems of the nineteenth-century script thus lived on in the 2000 revision.

However, one tangible result of the joint consultations with the Oberammergau authorities was the removal of the Matthew blood curse from the 1990 and 2000 productions. Play officials promise it will not appear in future performances.

Other 2000 revisions highlighted the dynamic and pluralistic Jewish religious world of ancient Judea at the time of Jesus. Pilate, the cruel Roman governor of the occupied Jewish province, was correctly presented to audiences as the venal official responsible for the death of Jesus.

In the 2000 performance Jesus is called "Rabbi" and he intones a Hebrew prayer that accentuates the Jewishness of both himself and his religious milieu. That important fact was either minimized or omitted in earlier Oberammergau productions.

The murderous Jewish "mob" of past performances was replaced in 2000 with a nuanced representation of the myriad of divisions extant during the Second Temple period.

The religiously radioactive word "Pharisee" (made so by centuries of distorted use by Christian teachers) was absent from the 2000 Play. Pharisee means "religious separatists" in Hebrew, but it became a term of derision that was often employed by anti-Jewish elements inside the Christian Church to defame and delegitimize Jews and Judaism. The fact that the Pharisees are scarcely mentioned in the New Testament passion narratives had not impeded their prominent presence in earlier versions of the Play.

The Judas figure, usually garbed in cowardly yellow in most Passion Plays, the same color as the Star of David that Jews were compelled to wear during the Holocaust, was radically recast in 2000 as a tragic complex figure. He ceased to be the wretched "traitor" of past productions.

Even though constructive and important changes were incorporated into the 2000 Oberammergau Passion Play and more are promised for 2010, much work needs to be done. I believe the Oberammergau production is still flawed and an anti-Jewish bias remains.

That contention was supported by a group of eight prominent American scholars of religion, including three Roman Catholics, three Jews, and two Protestants, who systematically studied the 2000 script line by line. Each of the eight scholars, acting alone, raised important, often similar criticisms of the Oberammergau Play's script.

The American Christian and Jewish scholars were cognizant of the positive changes introduced into the 2000 production. However, they were dissatisfied because, in their collective judgment, the Oberammergau Play still represented biblical, theological, and historic inaccuracies and distortions vis-à-vis Jews and Judaism. Though some minor changes were made in response to the scholars' suggestions, the final production still suffered from the more structural weaknesses that they had noted.

A few examples illustrate some scholars' overall concerns about the revised 2000 script.

Dr. Eugene J. Fisher, the Director of Catholic-Jewish Relations for the National Conference of Catholic Bishops, said:

> There have been revisions which have improved the text. The townspeople involved worked hard to get them and should be congratulated. But Jewish and Christian scholars in this country who have looked at it [the proposed 2000 script] find serious problems remaining that have to do with the way the play is structured and not simply a phrase here or there that can be fixed in time for 2000. Indeed, Catholic biblical scholars who have gone over the text have expressed keenest disappointment with it.

Another scholar was the Rev. John T. Pawlikowski of Chicago's Catholic Theological Union. Pawlikowski saw the 1984 production, and he wrote of his "deep disappointment" in the 2000 text. He called it "significantly flawed," noting that the 2000 text is a:

> [F]ictionalized account . . . that fails to take into account what biblical scholars are saying today . . . [the Play has] little or no scholarly sensitivity for the complexity of the gospel accounts . . . the Jewish priests are portrayed as totally

wicked and ultimately responsible for Jesus' death. Pilate appears as a somewhat reluctant accomplice . . . all in all I do not feel the 2000 version of the Play should be supported. While one can detect some effort to make it more acceptable to the current canons of the Christian-Jewish relationship, it is far too minimal. Christian visitors deserve something better.

Dr. Norman A. Beck of Texas Lutheran University in Seguin, Texas, compared the 1980, 1990, and 2000 texts:

The 2000 edition of the Oberammergau Play is not less but somewhat more supersessionist and viciously anti-Jewish than was the 1980 edition. A concession was made with regard to Matthew 27:25 [the blood curse], but lines were added elsewhere that more than compensated for the non-use of the Matthew text. . . . Unless and until those who write and produce Christian passion plays . . . have the desire and the motivation to this issue, we shall continue to see what we still see in the 2000 edition of Oberammergau.

Dr. Franklin Sherman, who formerly taught at the Lutheran Seminary in Chicago and is currently the Evangelical Lutheran Church in America's Interfaith Relations Associate, was somewhat more positive:

On the whole, the improvements to the traditional text are impressive, and go a long way toward eliminating the elements of 'the teaching of contempt' that marred the previous versions. The elements that remain are, unfortunately, in the New Testament text, and hence difficult to remove.

However, Sherman was still critical of the 2000 script. His chief concern was the strongly supersessionist tone that appears in the Play's opening verses that "skip from the banishment from Eden to the cross of Christ, without any mention of God's redemptive work in between [e.g., the election of Israel, the rescue from Egypt, etc.]." This "immediately establish[es] a supersessionist framework . . . underlying the whole text."

Dr. Amy-Jill Levine, a New Testament Professor at the Vanderbilt Divinity School, was also critical of the 2000 script:

the Play fails to overcome its negative depictions of Jews and Judaism. The text reinforces negative stereotypes of Jews as greedy, bloodthirsty, misanthropic, and vindictive. . . . The biblical accounts of the Passion can be found to be anti-Jewish. Yet a sensitive selection of materials from the biblical texts combined with both historical and biblical information on the role of the priests and the Roman governor and the concern for Jesus' growing political reputation could produce a Passion Play that would not give anti-Jewish impressions. This version fails to do so.

Another Jewish scholar, Dr. Alan Mittleman of Muhlenberg College, said, "the Play is a vast improvement of prior versions, particularly the text of the 1984 version, which I saw performed in Oberammergau. Gone are the blood curse, the invidious portrayal of the Pharisees, the implicit whitewashing of the Romans and the damning of all the Jews." But he added, "there are areas which could use improvement. The evil characters, Caiaphas and the other priests, are driven by envy, malice, a hint of worry about possible insurrection and Roman retaliation, but mostly by savage hatred of Jesus. They are really dark, unredeemable characters . . . their hatred is wrapped in religious sanctimoniousness." Despite some of the negative aspects of the 2000 text and the "structural anti-Jewish dimensions" of the New Testament, Mittleman believed the "present text demonstrates good will and shows the spirit of dialogue."

Sister Mary C. Boys, a professor at Union Theological Seminary in New York City, was concerned by the 2000 text's "extraordinary emphasis on the people's resolve that Jesus be put to death." While the Matthew blood curse had been eliminated in the Oberammergau Play, Boys was highly critical of these particular lines: "We demand his death. . . . The Nazarene shall die. . . . We demand the death of the Nazarene. . . . Crucify him. . . . Death for the Nazarene . . . Out toward Golgotha . . . Away! Away to Golgotha! On the cross with him. On the cross!"

She agreed with other colleagues that the revised script removed:

> some of the malicious stereotypes of past productions—Jews as bloodthirsty sinners wearing hats in the form of devil's horns—nevertheless it is an oversimplified presentation. . . . In view of the publicity accorded to its revisions, it may be that the Play is even more problematic than previous versions: audiences may believe that at long last it accurately portrays first-century history. It does not. . . . Were I in the audience, I would hold the Jewish authorities and "all the people" entirely responsible for the death of Jesus.

Dr. Michael J. Cook, Professor of Judeo-Christian Studies at Hebrew Union College-Jewish Institute of Religion in Cincinnati, noted that while "improvements, some cosmetic, some more substantial" have been made to the 2000 production, he is "not convinced that the audience will necessarily be in a position to grasp this [the changes from earlier texts]."

He was concerned by the "little sense of any fundamental rethinking which can exorcize the anti-Jewish conceptual structure of the presentation . . . since some party [in all Passion Plays] must personify Evil, that function came to devolve solely upon the Jewish authorities and the Jews as a people—now the foil against which the purity and innocence of Jesus can be juxtaposed in stark contrast."

Cook sees the Oberammergau Play as a "dreadful" drama in which the Jews and their religion remain defamed and belittled. The Hebrew Union College-Jewish Institute of Religion scholar worries that "Regardless of the subtle changes introduced by this year's editors, the inference by the new audience will be essentially no different from that in previous years . . . the end result will still be negative since the audience will never perceive the improvements."

Cook's concern, and one that is shared by other critics of the Oberammergau Passion Play, is that audiences will continue to assume that what they see in Bavaria is historically accurate and religiously sound. Audiences will experience the production, not as a carefully staged theatrical drama, but rather as an extraordinary spiritual experience, the same kind of experience described by many who saw the Gibson film in 2004.

For many people, and especially for those who actually saw either the Oberammergau Play or the Gibson film, both productions are perceived as the "gospel truth" about the life, trial, and death of Jesus. Despite that perception, both the stage and film versions transmit to their audiences pejorative perceptions and attitudes toward Jews and Judaism.

Those who seek improved Christian-Jewish relations must confront the continuing issue and problem of Passion Plays, whether medieval or modern. That is because the Passion story, so central to the Christian message and Christian self-understanding, is familiar to hundreds of millions of people throughout the world. When Passion Plays emit anti-Jewish images and stereotypes to audiences, positive Christian-Jewish relations suffer.

Despite its long history of transmitting such negative images, the Oberammergau Passion Play offers a useful model for those involved in other Passion Plays. For too many years, defensive, sometimes hostile Oberammergau leaders, including some who were Nazi party members in the 1930s and 1940s, were locked into a harshly anti-Jewish production. Because of the town's conservative religious tradition, the strong anti-reform sentiment within the Oberammergau community, and the community's fear of losing lucrative tourist revenue, little effort, even after World War II, was made to remove anti-Jewish elements from the world-famous Play.

It required extraordinary time and talent by concerned Christian and Jewish leaders to first develop a scholarly and religious critique of the Play. Next came the task of building of human bridges of mutual respect and understanding between the Play's critics, led by the AJC and the ADL, and the Oberammergau officials directly responsible for the Play.

Once a bond of mutual trust was established, and once the people of Oberammergau voted for Play reform, changes became possible. But even then, based on my personal experiences, reform came slowly in Oberammergau. While the 2000 production was a welcome and notable change from previous productions, the Oberammergau Passion Play still remains fundamentally flawed. Further substantive reform is needed.

Yet, Oberammergau, "warts and all," illustrates what can be achieved when both sides work together. The result of that effort is not only a more accurate, less toxic anti-Jewish Passion Play, but it is also a significant achievement in the vitally needed area of positive Christian-Jewish relations.

CHAPTER NINE

~

Celluloid Passions

John J. Michalczyk

The Byrds' 1960s' song, "Turn, Turn, Turn," based on the biblical text Eccle-
siastes 3, noted in a secular and at the same time spiritual way, that there was
a season and time for every purpose under heaven. Mel Gibson's *The Passion
of the Christ*, released in a flurry of controversy on Ash Wednesday, 25 February 2004, raises the question: is *this* the right time for a vividly "realistic"
and potentially divisive film based on Jesus Christ's last days?[1]

In the history of dramatizations of the Passion, each century and each
decade brings its values, cultural sensitivity, and current technology to bear
when a play, film, or TV miniseries is produced. Our era is no exception. All
producers of Passion dramas have to make decisions that will, wittingly or
not, determine whether their production will promote animosity toward
Jews. These include the portrayal of such characters as the high priests Annas and Caiaphas, the Jewish council, Pilate, and the Jewish people in general. A brief historical overview will demonstrate the visual and at times controversial evolution of the Passion in film.

The Passion on celluloid is more than a century old. In 1898, just three
years after the birth of cinema in Paris with Auguste and Louis Lumière's
screening of the famous "Train Arriving at LaCiotat" and "Baby's Breakfast,"
the Passion was first filmed in a memorable way. *The Life and Passion of Jesus
Christ* (1898), in a primitive, condensed version of the biblical story, inspired
directors with a basic vision of how to depict the last days of Christ in terms
of sets, costumes, and staging. In the same year, *The Passion Play of Oberammergau* was produced on film. The original stage production had been

undertaken by a German town and performed each decade since the on-slaught of the plague in 1634. Its controversial history illustrates the challenges that confront Passion dramatists in whatever medium. After his 1934 visit to the Oberammergau play, Adolf Hitler declared, "It is vital for the Passion play to be continued at Oberammergau: for never has the menace of Jewry been so convincingly portrayed as in this presentation of what happened in the times of the Romans. There, one sees Pontius Pilate, a Roman racially and intellectually so superior that he stands out like a firm, clean rock in the middle of the muck and mire of Jewry."[2]

In the wake of the earliest filmed versions of the Passion, Italian film-makers created elaborate costume dramas with the exaggerated gestures that were typical of the silent era films.

Notably, many movies from this point on displayed some care in handling characters and scenes that could have sparked hostility to Jews. D. W. Griffith's *Intolerance* (1916), for instance, presented the sufferings of "The Judaean" (Jesus) rapidly and from afar with Jewish characters minimally present.

Cecil B. DeMille's silent epic *The King of Kings* of 1927 helped standardize the world's visual conception of the New Testament. He saw his film as a fulfillment of Jesus' command to take His message throughout the world. The film opened with this statement: "This is the story of JESUS of NAZARETH . . . He Himself commanded that His message be carried to the ends of the earth. May this portrayal play a reverent part of that great command."[3] De-Mille was sensitive to the danger of visually suggesting that the Jewish people collectively were responsible for the death of Jesus. DeMille's Jewish crowd unbiblically exclaims, "Nay, ye shall not crucify him! The High Priest speaketh not for the people!" Guilt is focused on Caiaphas when he declares to Pilate in a private exchange with no Jewish crowd present, "If thou, imperial Pilate, wouldst wash thy hands of this man's death, let it be upon me and me alone!" (an adaptation of Matthew 27:25)

Within a decade, there were several other epics that made a significant impact upon Christian audiences, some set during the Passion, and others afterwards with references back to this important moment of Christian salvation history. Although commercial ventures, they were filmed to offer inspiration to the viewer, enlarging upon the basic details of the gospels in a fictional manner. In 1951, Mervyn LeRoy directed *Quo Vadis*, based on Peter's encounter with Jesus (John 13:36), "Quo vadis, Domine?" (Where do you go, Master?). Two year later director Henry Koster adapted the 1942 novel *The Robe* into a moving drama with Richard Burton as the Roman soldier Marcellus who converts and then dies for his faith in the crucified Jesus. In 1961, Nicholas Ray directed *King of Kings* and in the following year,

Richard Fleischer and Dino De Laurentiis' production of *Barabbas* focused on the later life of Barabbas, the murderer released at the time of Jesus' execution in the puzzling gospel scene (see pp. 59–61).

Of these epics, Samuel Bronston's 1961 production of *King of Kings* was most noteworthy for the critics' harsh reaction to it. Critic Moira Walsh in *America* criticized both the weakness of the production as well as its theological content, calling it "the logical culmination of a gigantic fraud perpetrated by the film industry on the movie-going public."[4] In fairness, the film did attempt to move beyond stereotypical images of Jews and Romans and supplied some of ancient history with an eye to modern sociopolitical issues such as the Holocaust and Arab-Israeli tensions. The fictional character of Lucius, a Roman military commander serving in Palestine, was created for continuity throughout the film. At the conclusion of the film he comes to understand fully at the crucifixion that "Jesus is the Christ." Nicholas Ray responded to the vocal critics who considered the film long and tedious by saying, "They are not hip enough with the times of Jesus!"

George Stevens' epic *The Greatest Story Ever Told* (1965), in pre-production while *King of Kings* was being launched, received horribly negative reviews: "God is unlucky in *The Greatest Story Ever Told*. His only begotten son turns out to be a bore, the photography is mainly inspired by Hallmark Cards . . . as the Hallelujah chorus explodes around us stereophonically and stereotypically," wrote *New York* magazine critic John Simon.[5] The original theatrical release was four hours, twenty minutes long, but later was pared down to a bit more than two hours. A tender scene ensued between Max von Sydow as Jesus and Telly Savalas as Pilate in order to show Pilate as reluctant to execute Jesus. Pat Boone, Charleton Heston, John Wayne, Sal Mineo, and even Sidney Poitier got a chance to "act" in what was seen as a grievous offense against the Passion story. In this Hollywood, stylized version of the Passion at the close of the film, the crowd is very split; some cry out, "Release this man!" while others demand Jesus' crucifixion. Not only is Caiaphas absent from the scene before Pilate, but once the Roman governor passes sentence on Jesus a narrative voiceover intoned the phrase from the Nicene Creed, ". . . suffered under Pontius Pilate, was crucified, died and buried . . ."

Pier Paolo Pasolini's *The Gospel According to St. Matthew* in 1966 was dedicated to the pope who convened the Second Vatican Council that led to the repudiation of centuries of Christian antisemitism.[6] The film began, "To the dear, joyful, and loving memory of John XXIII." Trapped in his room in Assisi in October 1962 during John XXIII's visit to the city, Pasolini had nothing better to do but go through the Bible which he found in the drawer. He was overwhelmed by the richness of Matthew's text and wished to bring it to the screen. Ultimately, Pasolini depicted a rough-hewn, Semitic-looking Jesus who is a strong, charismatic, and passionate preacher. Very tellingly, the Matthew 27:25's blood curse on the Jews "His blood be on our children" is uttered by one unidentified Jewish voice and is barely noticeable in the handful of other voices that speak simultaneously in the small alleyway in which the scene of Jesus' judgment occurs in Pasolini's movie. In this stark, grainy, black-and-white film, Pasolini gave a profound sense of realism and a cinéma-vérité version of the life and death of Jesus. With the haunting desert landscape of southern Italy (Matera) and the ethereal music of Bach and Mozart, ironically, this controversial Marxist filmmaker created one of the most successful spiritual interpretations of the biblical narrative.

Two musical films in the next decade captured the ethos of the "love" or "hippie generation"—Godspell and Jesus Christ Superstar, both produced in 1973. David Greene's Godspell developed the camaraderie of a Jesus who wears a "Superman" shirt and a heart emblazoned on his forehead. The film highlighted the "flower people" who were attracted to this likable, charismatic figure. After a very tender Last Supper, Judas betrays Jesus with a kiss and is responsible for his death. The Jewish council and Pilate scenes are eliminated from the piece. The film concluded with a very moving musical number in which Jesus' followers bearing his dead body disappear into the New York City crowd singing, "Long Live God/Prepare Ye the Way of the Lord!"

Norman Jewison's Jesus Christ, Superstar also vividly recorded the fashionable rock tones of the times. For some it was schlock for the plebes, while for others it was an attempt to infuse the ancient texts with contemporary meaning. The crucifixion scene gives way to exotic sets and an anachronistic rock number in hopes of engaging and entertaining film audiences with the challenging question, "Jesus Christ, Jesus Christ, who are you? What have you sacrificed?"

In 1977, Franco Zeffirelli's Jesus of Nazareth was the fulfillment of a dream for the director. Like Pasolini, Zeffirelli was very moved by the Second Vatican Council and its decree, Nostra Aetate, that rejected notions of collective Jewish culpability for the death of Jesus. The Italian director set out to create a fresh new vision of the life and death of Jesus. Although on the surface the film appears to be a romanticized, soft-focus, televised epic of Jesus' life, it bears the print of someone keenly aware of religious sensitivities. He described his personal goal: "The point I wanted to make was that Christ was a Jew, a prophet who grew out of the cultural, social, and historical background of the Israel of his time."[7] Jesus is portrayed as a Jewish teacher and healer, engaging occasionally in pleasant conversations with scribes and Pharisees.

In the discussions within the Jewish council about Jesus' fate, the members are hotly divided. A very vocal group wishes to negotiate with Jesus to tone down his "activism," which may be seen as too political to the Romans. The others, led by high priests Annas and Caiaphas, wish to deliver him to Pilate. They win out. However, the fictional scribe, Zerah, is the one who actually orchestrates Jesus' demise.

The Last Temptation of Christ created quite a stir upon its release by Martin Scorsese in 1988. Although the film opened with a disclaimer that it was not based on the biblical Gospels, many Christian groups judged the movie blasphemous. Jerry Falwell called for a boycott of the film. Ink was thrown at the theatre screen at one showing and a protestor walked across the lawn of the producer carrying a cross. In essence, the film was a very visual adaptation of the work by the Greek novelist Nikos Kazantzakis (*Zorba the Greek*). In his prologue to the novel, Kazantzakis wrote: "The dual substance of Christ—the yearning so human, so superhuman, of man to attain to God or, more exactly, to return to God and identify himself with Him—has always been a deep inscrutable mystery to me."[8] The dilemma of the film is Jesus' desire to be human, to marry and be a husband and father. *America* critic Richard Blake, S.J., viewed "the temptation" as something not sexual in the prurient sense of the term, but as a natural and human desire to choose earth over the things of the spirit.[9] It is Judas (Harvey Keitel) who dissuades Jesus from this and tells him he must follow the mission of the Father. The bloodied Jesus (Willem Dafoe) dies upon the cross, fulfilling His Father's wish. Pontius Pilate (David Bowie) perceives Jesus as yet one more Jewish troublemaker and needs no urging from any Caiaphas, who never appears in the film at all.

Like Pasolini in *The Gospel According to St. Matthew*, producer John Heyman decided to focus on one Gospel, in this case Luke's, in his *Jesus* (1979). The Lucan gospel features a very human, compassionate Jesus who extends his mission "to all the nations, beginning from Jerusalem" (Lk 24:47). *Jesus* was made in conjunction with the *Campus Crusade for Christ* to serve as an educational, evangelizing vehicle throughout the world in a myriad of languages. The seven-minute commentary at the close of the film is a direct evangelical appeal to follow Jesus. Parallel to the positive results of the Vatican Council, however, the film does not implicate all Jews in the execution of Christ and gives Pilate more active responsibility for his death than some other Passion films.

In a more contemporary version of the Passion narrative, Denys Arcand's *Jesus of Montreal* (1989) depicts a group of very committed players following a modern-day charismatic leader, as they prepare to perform a Passion play. At the heart of the drama are Jesus' words to Pilate, "Greater love hath no man than to lay down his life for his friends" (Jn 15:13). These words of Jesus spoken at the Last Supper, used here as a quasi-flashback to the final Passover meal shared with his disciples, serve as a microcosm of his teaching. Responsibility for the crucifixion is placed squarely on Pilate's shoulders; he doesn't need much persuasion to accept Caiaphas' arguments from political expediency. Brian D. Johnson of *Maclean's* sums up the film: "Arcand reinterprets Christianity with agnostic wit. Although the director penetrates to the heart of the Gospel, his hero remains a secular savior."[10]

And now enter Mel Gibson's *The Passion of the Christ*. Although dependent on some earlier movies for a few visualizations, the movie is most indebted to the writings of Anna Katherina Emmerich, an eighteenth-century Benedictine nun whose visions of the Passion were published posthumously.

Like previous dramatizations, Gibson blends elements from all the gospels, but he adds distinctive materials from Emmerich, such as the presence of Satan, demons, and Pilate's wife, who actually provides Jesus' mother with burial linens. However, in a very Catholic act of piety, these linens are used by Mary to soak up pools of Jesus' blood left from his excruciatingly graphic scourging. Unlike previous movies, *The Passion of the Christ* evidences little sensitivity toward the issue of how Jewish characters are portrayed. Other than glimpses of protesting or compassionate Jews here and there and the heroic depiction of Simon of Cyrene, Jews other than Jesus' mother and disciples seem implacably and inexplicably hostile. The presence of Satan among Jewish figures, a flashback to Jesus defending the woman caught in adultery by literally drawing a line in the sand against his scribal opponents, demons disguised as Jewish children, and the destruction of some portion of the Temple upon Jesus' death (an idea from Emmerich) contribute to the movie's extremely negative image of Jewish leaders and institutions.

As noted above, in "Turn, Turn, Turn," the Byrds say that there is a time for everything under heaven. Is now the time for a movie that departs from the care shown by many of its predecessors in how Jews are portrayed? After four decades of building more sensitive Christian-Jewish relations, could this film today be seen as more divisive than inspirational? Or could it be a way of reconnecting both communities through the acknowledgment of free speech and an honest evaluation and discussion of the impact of the Scriptures today on all audiences? Time will tell!

Notes

1. This is an expanded version of "Jesus Christ, Cinema Star," *Boston Sunday Globe*, 22 February 2004, N1, 16.

2. James Shapiro, "Updating (and Retouching) an Old Passion Play," *New York Times*, 14 May 2000, A7.

3. W. Barnes Tatum, *Jesus at the Movies* (Santa Rosa, CA: Polebridge Press, 1997), 45.

4. Moira Walsh, "Christ or Credit Card?" *America*, 21 October 1961, 71.

5. Quoted in John Walker, ed. *Halliwell Film & Video Guide* (New York: Harper Perennial, 1997), 324.

6. For a more detailed development of the film see John Michalczyk's chapter, "Pier Paolo Pasolini," in *The Italian Political Filmmakers* (Cranbury, NJ: Associated University Presses, 1986), especially 80–84.

7. Franco Zeffirelli, *The Autobiography of Franco Zeffirelli* (New York: Weidenfeld & Nicholson, 1986), 275.

8. Nikos Kazantzakis, *The Last Temptation of Christ* (New York: Simon & Schuster, Inc., 1960), 1.

9. Richard A. Blake, S.J., "The Universal Christ," *America*, 27 August 1988, 99–102.

10. Quoted in Tatum, *Jesus at the Movies*, 187.

PART FOUR

THEOLOGY

CHAPTER TEN

~

What Does It Mean to Be Saved?

Clark Williamson

The purpose of this essay is to discuss some of the many understandings of the term "salvation" in the New Testament scriptures and the Christian tradition. Other terms such as "redemption," "reconciliation," and "sanctification" must also be taken into account. All these expressions are important if we are to understand the many ways in which the gracious love and loving grace of God save human beings and, indeed, the entire creation from destruction.

The thesis of this essay can be stated in a few propositions: first, that salvation is always both salvation *from* some situation that is so dire that God's grace and power is required for deliverance from it. Second, salvation is always *to* some new and transformed situation to which God promises to deliver us. Third, there are, therefore, as many meanings of salvation as there are understandings of the kinds of situations from which we need to be delivered and to which we will be brought.

It will be helpful to give some examples of this thesis. Let us do so by considering how we encounter the grace of God. God's grace is: God's empowerment of our salvation; God's seeking and saving us as the lost ones; God's benevolent disposition toward and action on behalf of people trapped in evil; God's forgiveness of sins; God's reassuring us as to God's reality and meaning when damnation takes the form of meaninglessness; God's placing us in a community of redemption and reconciliation when abandonment and isolation is the form of human hurt; God's supply of strength when weakness is characteristic of human effort; God's yes in the gospel to every no of the world within, the world among, and the world around; God's presence to us as eternal in the midst of the temporal; God's promise and power of life at the moment or in the fear of death; God's free and unconditional love of all and calling of us to love all others as we love ourselves, particularly when we clearly do not love all others. All these and more point us to the many-splendored meanings of the apparently simple term "salvation."

Salvation as Redemption

One of the oldest meanings of salvation in the scriptures is that of redemption. The meaning of "redemption" is *buying back*. It derives from simple commercial transactions, as when we use something that we have, typically money, to trade it for something else that we would rather have, such as groceries. Biblically, the term was used to refer to situations in which a person or a society was in slavery or under some other kind of oppression, as when a nomadic people had moved from the desert into a settled society because there was a drought in the desert and their flocks and their lives were at risk. But then in the settled society they were on the bottom of the social and economic heap and reduced to hard labor under severe conditions or sold into slavery. It took on the connotations of "ransom," as in "buying back" a prisoner of war or a slave and buying that person's freedom.

This was exactly the experience of the people Israel in Egypt: "the Lord has brought you out with a mighty hand and redeemed you from the house of slavery, from the hand of Pharaoh king of Egypt" (Deut 7:8). "Redemption" came to be the most fitting term to refer to the liberation of the people Israel from its slavery in Egypt. So the scriptures refer to God's action in saving Israel from bondage: "the Lord your God—who brought you out of the land of Egypt and redeemed you from the house of slavery" (Deut 13:5). In turn, when the people Israel were later taken into exile to Babylon, the prophetic declaration of hope focused on the claim that God is the Redeemer: "with everlasting love I will have compassion on you, says the Lord, your Redeemer" (Isa 54:8). Isaiah 43:3 proclaimed that God ransomed Israel from captivity: "For I am the Lord your God, the Holy One of Israel, your Savior. I give Egypt as your ransom, Ethiopia and Seba in exchange for you." God is the redeemer (*go'el*) of Israel.

Redemption is liberation *from* bondage and *to* freedom. It is a key meaning of salvation in the scriptures of the early church. Paul in Galatians 5:1 proclaims: "For freedom Christ has set us free. Stand firm, therefore, and do not submit again to a yoke of slavery." The letter reminds its Gentile addressees that "formerly, when you did not know God, you were enslaved to beings that by nature are not gods" (4:8). Again, redemption is from slavery, to freedom. As God redeemed Israel from Egyptian slavery to a life of freedom with God and neighbor in the land of promise, so God redeems Gentiles from slavery "to beings that by nature are not gods."

In the New Testament the terms "redeem" and "redemption" occur about twenty-two times and "ransom" three times. Acts 20:28 tells of Paul's writing to Ephesus and saying: "Keep watch over yourselves and over all the flock, of which the Holy Spirit has made you overseers, to shepherd the church of God that he obtained [*periepoiēsato*, 'purchased'] with the blood of his own Son." The gospels say that "the Son of Man came not to be served but to serve, and to give his life a ransom for many" (Mark 10:45; Matt 20:28).

One primary meaning of salvation, hence, is redemption. To live in faithfulness to God is to live in freedom. We can best understand this claim if we think of ourselves as always and again being presented with the gift and demand, the call and claim, of God. The only adequate way in which we can understand ourselves, in any ultimate sense, is in terms of God's love for us and for all others. God's love is the only ultimate ground of the being and meaning of our lives. Faith is freedom *from* all finite and relative things as the only definers of the ultimate meaning and destiny of our lives. It is freedom from idolatry. We are under no compulsion to find the meaning of our lives in anything other than the all-inclusive love of God. At the same time, faith is freedom *for* everyone else as worthy of our love and help: "you were called to freedom, brothers and sisters . . . through love become servants to one another. For the whole law is summed up in a single commandment, 'You shall love your neighbor as yourself'" (Gal 5:13–14).

In short, redemption means that God loves us into being free and frees us to love. Redemption means that we are cleansed from the guilt and power of sin, of alienation from God, from our fellow human beings, and from indifference to God's good creation. 1 John 1:7 says: "if we walk in the light, as he himself is in the light, we have fellowship with one another, and the blood of Jesus his Son cleanses us from all sin . . . he who is faithful and just will forgive us our sins and cleanse us from all unrighteousness." As Paul states it: "God proves his love for us in that while we were yet sinners Christ died for us" (Rom 5:8). Christ has "set us free from the present evil age, according to the will of our God and Father" (Gal 1:4). We are liberated from sin and evil and liberated to love the neighbor.

Salvation as Reconciliation

Reconciliation of human beings with God and with one another is a major theme of the biblical witness to God's saving activity. Reconciliation is distinctively the activity of God and we are the objects of it, the ones who need to be reconciled both with God and with each other. While it is persons who are to be reconciled with God, with themselves, and with each other, reconciliation in the New Testament also has to do with the relationships between groups of people, particularly with reconciliation between Jews and Gentiles. For example, the letter to the Ephesians accurately depicts the situation of us Gentiles prior to the revelation of God in Christ: "remember that at one time you Gentiles by birth, called 'the uncircumcision' by those who are called 'the circumcision'. . .—remember that you were at that time without Christ, being aliens from the commonwealth of Israel, and strangers to the covenants of promise, having no hope and without God in the world. But now in Christ Jesus you who once were far off have been brought near by the blood of Christ. For he is our peace; in his flesh he has made both groups into one and has broken down the dividing wall, that is, the hostility between us" (2:11–14).

As a result of God's action in Christ we Gentiles "are no longer strangers and aliens, but . . . citizens with the saints [the people Israel] and also members of the household of God" (Eph 2:19). In Romans, Paul asks: "Is God the God of Jews only? Is he not the God of Gentiles also? Yes, of Gentiles also, since God is one; and he will justify the circumcised on the ground of faith and the uncircumcised through that same faith" (Rom 3:29–30). We should notice that according to both Ephesians and Romans we Gentile followers of Jesus are not the "only" members of the reconstituted household of God. Far from it, we are "also" citizens "with" the people Israel. Paul uses the term "justify" (*dikaioō*) to mean "set right." God's reconciling activity in Christ "sets right" the relationships not only between us and God but between us and the people Israel. For Paul this means that all humanity ("Jews and Gentiles" is scripture's way of referring to everybody) is reconciled with itself. "Salvation," Jesus said to the Samaritan woman, "is from the Jews" (John 4:22).

Whereas we Christians often wonder how Jews can be included in God's salvation, the New Testament is concerned with making it clear how we Gentiles have been co-included in the household of God with the people Israel, how God's "peace" has come to replace the "hostility" that formerly governed our relationships with each other. "In Christ God was reconciling the world to himself" (2 Cor 5:19) and, as Paul makes abundantly clear, also to itself. He insists that Christ became "a servant of the circumcised on behalf of the truth [faithfulness] of God in order that he might confirm the promises given to the patriarchs, and in order that the Gentiles might glorify God for his mercy" (Rom 15:8–9). He quotes Isaiah: "The root of Jesse shall come, the one who rises to rule the Gentiles; in him the Gentiles shall hope" (Rom 15:13).

Our culture is so dominated by individualism, the view that only separate individuals are real and that everything is to serve the needs and interests of individuals, that even our understanding of Christian faith and particularly of salvation falls prey to being interpreted as merely individualistic. We think of ourselves as being saved, one by one, as though any of us could be saved in isolation. But we are all part of each other and no one is ever finally saved until all are saved. And individuals cannot live a life of blessing and well-being, that to which we are saved, unless we can manage to do so together with each other. So Simeon, in Luke's gospel, sings praises at the birth of Jesus: "my eyes have seen your salvation, which you have prepared in the presence of all people, a light for revelation to the Gentiles and for glory to your people Israel" (Luke 2:30–32).

Colossians makes this understanding of salvation utterly explicit: "through him [Christ] God was pleased to reconcile to himself all things, whether on earth or in heaven, by making peace through the blood of his cross. And you who were once estranged and hostile in mind, doing evil deeds, he has now reconciled . . . so as to present you holy and blameless and irreproachable before him" (Col 1:19–22). Reconciliation is not only individualistic, although individuals should be reconciled with themselves, but a matter of corporate and universal importance. God seeks to reconcile to Godself "all things, whether on earth or in heaven." We cannot claim to be reconciled to God if we are not reconciled with one another. We Gentiles cannot claim to be reconciled to the God of Israel if we are not reconciled with the Israel of God. Nor can men and women, or different cultures and ethnicities, claim reconciliation with God apart from reconciliation with one another.

Reconciliation is also freedom—emancipation from hostility and indifference and freedom to love our neighbors as we love ourselves.

Salvation as Sanctification

The scriptures speak frequently of salvation as sanctification. Sanctification refers to the process of becoming a new and transformed person, that is, of becoming what God gives and calls us to be—people who love God with all their selves and their neighbors as themselves, and who do this intelligently and courageously. Sanctification has to do with ethics and the development of Christian character. It is not, however, moralism; it is, rather, responding to God's gracious gift with a grateful devotion.

"Sanctify" means to "make holy" (*sanctus*). We should note several important points about how the scriptures speak of holiness and becoming or being made holy. First, holiness belongs appropriately to God alone; only God is holy. "Let them praise your great and awesome name. Holy is he" (Ps 99:3)! God's name is holy and we Christians pray as Jesus taught us, "hallowed be your name." When persons are referred to as "holy," this is always a derivative holiness; we are not holy in ourselves but can become holy by virtue of God's gracious reconciliation of us to God. Because God is holy, holiness has a personal connotation and therefore moves in ethical directions. But because holiness is derivative from our relation to God, it is something neither that we achieve by effort nor that we simply have naturally. It is granted, by grace, as God's gift and call.

Second, although holiness is a gift, it is a gift that keeps on giving—it has to unfold in the continual deepening of our lives, the widening of our perspectives, the more universal our communion with all of God's creatures. Holiness has about it the character of a goal that is ahead of us. Paul speaks of "making holiness perfect in the fear [awe] of God" (2 Cor 7:1). It is helpful to think of sanctification as a practice or exercise; properly speaking, it is what Christians should mean when they talk about spirituality—the practices of the Christian faith by which we increasingly learn to pay attention to how we lead our lives. Worship, for example, is an occasion for Christians to practice themselves, that is, to practice becoming the kind of persons they have been given and called to become.

When Paul wrote to the Corinthians he distinguished between "spiritual people" and "infants in Christ" (1 Cor 3:1). This is not an invidious distinction; infants can grow up and become mature, which is Paul's point. He urges his readers not to be "conformed to this world," but "transformed by the renewing of your minds" (Rom 12:2). Transformation is what sanctification is all about. The knowledge of God is a transformative knowledge; it does not leave us in the condition in which it found us. Growing up in grace is possible by God's grace; God asks nothing of us that God has not previously empowered us to become.

Being transformed means growing up in our understanding of the gospel of Jesus Christ, coming to an ever deepening discernment of what faith involves and a more complete commitment to it. Theology, as the tradition has said, is simply "faith seeking understanding." This is because God's grace continues to work in our lives and calls us to engage in the struggle for a mature faith. Being transformed means growing up in Christian freedom, learning the fuller dimensions of what it means to be freed to love the neighbor and the stranger; it means coming to "fulfill the law of Christ" (Gal 6:2). Being transformed means arriving at a keener awareness of the death-dealing powers that shape so much of our life on this earth. Only if we are adequately aware of all that crushes both human and nonhuman life on our planet, life with which we are involved in a covenant of moral obligation, can we intelligently live out our faith in the web of relationships in which we find ourselves. Being transformed means living in an ever widening circle of communion and loyalty, solidarity, with all of those other people whom God loves.

In short, salvation as sanctification means that the God who calls us forward into the future that God has in mind for us, as God called Abraham and Sarah and as Jesus called his followers, is a God who is never finished with us. Nor are we ever finished with God who is the ground of all possibilities and ever calls us forward into a future of blessing and well-being.

Salvation as Everlasting Life

Salvation from death, from being utterly forgotten, from final meaninglessness and salvation to life everlasting with God is a crucial dimension of Christian understandings of salvation. If the final consequence and destiny of our lives, and of the lives of all others, is the graveyard, then on us and all human beings the slow, sure doom falls pitiless and dark. And the final truth of our lives is that they are ultimately insignificant. The proclamation that we are saved to life everlasting in the presence of God, however, claims that we and our lives are ultimately meaningful because we matter to and are enfolded in love by the One who is ultimate.

We should not make the mistake of downplaying the significance of our lives in this world, however, in our talk about salvation to everlasting life. Rather, we should see that the promise that our lives are ultimately meaningful should strengthen our commitment to live authentically Christian lives in this world. We do this, not somehow thereby to earn salvation, but out of a joyous and grateful response to the faithfulness of God who created us, who re-creates us in redemption and reconciliation, and who seeks the consummation of our life in the fulfillment of life with God.

Sometimes this aspect of salvation is talked about as "immortality," but the scriptures are utterly clear that we are not immortal: "you are dust, and to dust you shall return" (Gen 3:19). Plato expressed the classical Greek conception of the immortality of the soul, according to which the soul is inherently immortal (it cannot die) and continues in being after the death of the body. The scriptures, however, could not think of life after death as a disembodied existence. Instead, life after death is a renewal of the close union of body and soul which is human life. We do not possess immortality; only God does (1 Tim 6:16). Rather, we receive everlasting life as the gift of God

(1 Cor 15:53–54). Salvation, in every one of its aspects, is always God's gracious gift and initiative.

When we ask the question as to what is the ground for Christian belief in life after death, the standard answer is: the resurrection of Jesus Christ of whom 2 Timothy 1:10 speaks as having "abolished death and brought life and immortality to light through the gospel." But this explanation overlooks the fact that Jesus and his disciples likely already believed in the resurrection of the dead prior to Jesus' resurrection. Isaiah 26:19 says: "Your dead shall live, their corpses shall rise. O dwellers in the dust, awake and sing for joy." The slaughter of the righteous martyrs by Antiochus Epiphanes led Daniel to say: "Many of those who sleep in the dust of the earth shall awake, some to everlasting life, and some to shame and everlasting contempt" (12:2). By the time of Jesus the idea that God must one day vindicate God's faithful servants was widely held among Jews.

It seems to be the case, then, that Christians believe in life after death for more reasons than we typically give. One is that Jesus in the gospels believes it and teaches it; a number of parables and stories set the frame of our lives in the context of the life to come and encourage us to take account now of this ultimate situation. In the parable of the rich man and Lazarus (Luke 16:19–31), failure to do so was the rich man's problem.

Another reason focuses on the understanding of God's steadfast love for God's children. God loves us and in saving us seeks to lead us to the perfection or consummation of our relationship with each other and with God. God is lovingly related to each and every one of us and so will cherish us in that relationship beyond the bounds of our short span of time on earth. A loving God would not tolerate the fact that so many of God's children live lives that are short and brutish and that unfold in conditions that are devastating to human well-being. A visit to a cemetery where slaves were buried, or to a military cemetery near a battlefield, such as Gettysburg or Omaha Beach, makes it excruciatingly clear that if salvation is merely this-worldly it is a joke. And a bad one.

Finally, Christians do indeed believe in life after death because of the resurrection of Jesus Christ, for here we find disclosed with utter clarity what many Jews, Jesus included, had already come to believe about who God is—a God of steadfast love for all God's children whose love will not finally be defeated.

Is Salvation Universal?

Standard Christian thought for a long time has held that human beings face a dual destiny: some go to heaven (life with God) and the rest go to hell (life in alienation from God). Some agree with Paul that "just as one man's [Adam's] trespass led to condemnation for all, so one man's [Jesus'] act of righteousness leads to justification and life for all" (Rom 5:18). Paul's view is that salvation is universal—"for all." This position holds that because the cross is a "full, perfect and sufficient sacrifice for the sins of the world," salvation must be universal. As Paul also put it: "as all die in Adam, so all will be made alive in Christ" (1 Cor 15:22).

Of course, other texts can be cited to the contrary, as this example from the parable of the Last Judgment shows: "Then he will say to those at his left hand, 'You that are accursed, depart from me into the eternal fire prepared for the devil and his angels" (Matt 15:41). Other texts that seem to deny universal salvation include Acts 4:12: "There is salvation in no one else, for there is no other name under heaven given among mortals by which we must be saved." Paul, however, would not disagree with this; he would simply note that salvation in the name of Christ is all-inclusive. John's Gospel, however, clearly denies universal salvation: "Those who do not believe are condemned already, because they have not believed in the name of the only Son of God" (3:17).

Clearly the scriptures can be quoted pro and con on this issue. Yet we should note that 1 Peter 3:18–20 claims that after Christ was crucified "he went and made a proclamation to the spirits in prison," that is he descended into hell to preach to the "spirits in prison." The later Christian tradition would talk of Christ's "harrowing" hell, despoiling it and freeing its captives. This tradition is concerned with the issue of theodicy—showing that God is just and loves all God's creatures—and asserts that God would not condemn those who had no opportunity on earth to place their faith in Christ.

Similarly, the book of Revelation (wrongly thought to be all about doom and gloom) tells us in apocalyptic imagery that "Michael and all his angels . . . defeated" Satan and that the salvation of God has won out over Satan's opposition. Satan and his angels were "conquered . . . by the blood of the Lamb" (Rev 12:7–12). And later it claims that "Death and Hades" were themselves "thrown into the lake of fire" after having given up "the dead that were in them" (Rev 20:13–14).

The point of the book of Revelation is simply that God's intentions that all God's creatures be reconciled with God and with each other cannot finally be defeated—"the gates of Hell will not prevail." This, too, is universal salvation.

Finally, however, the issue comes down to a simple one: if salvation is by God's grace, then all are saved. If we save ourselves by being good enough to be worthy of salvation, then some will indeed go to hell (actually, all would since none are perfect), but if we think this way we have in effect denied that salvation is by God's grace. If salvation is granted to some and denied to others for reasons that we can never comprehend because God's will is impenetrable, then God is not the God of steadfast love of whom the scriptures speak. So, if salvation is by God's grace, it is all-inclusive. If it is not, then we either save ourselves by works-righteousness or cannot utterly trust and rely on God because God's will is capricious and unreliable. That is hardly the God proclaimed by Jesus Christ.

~

CHAPTER ELEVEN

Why Is the Death
of Jesus Redemptive?

Louis Roy

Numerous people concerned with spirituality or religion reject Christianity's claim—particularly forceful in the Letters of St. Paul—that Jesus is the universal Savior. They find incredible the suggestion that his death had a decisive impact for the whole of humankind. Hesitancy in the face of such a claim is normal; indeed it is a sign of intelligence. Unfortunately, this Christian dogma is often misunderstood. Thus I would like to present it in a way that may make its meaning clearer. If one purifies this doctrine of certain unfortunate interpretations acquired in recent centuries, the classic view of salvation maintained by Catholicism may be helpful for the twenty-first century. Insights into this Catholic conception can also aid interreligious dialogue.

Causes and Effects of the Death of Jesus

Modern theology, both Catholic and Protestant, has focused upon the *effects* of the death of Jesus, that is, upon what his passion merited for humankind. This position risks suggesting that the Father demanded that reparation be made by his Son as a precondition for his forgiveness. Since it can be inferred that God directly willed the suffering of Christ, one is likely to overlook the factual, human factors that brought about his passion.

In reaction against this inattentiveness to history, biblical scholarship of the past fifty years or so has emphasized the actual *causes* that led to the arrest and condemnation of Jesus. By uncovering the sources of the conflict between Jesus and the Jewish and Roman authorities of his time, this research helps us realize that the violence he endured was a consequence of his prophetic activities. The life of Jesus explains his death. By making this clear, biblical scholarship underscores the social origin of this drama.

While such attention to the causes of the death of Jesus is indispensable, still we must not overlook the effects that this death has had for the life of humanity.[1] Contemporary theology should explore the question: according to the Christian view, what unique outcome has Jesus' death entailed for the human race? How does it surpass the significance of the death of a Socrates, of a Gandhi, or of a Martin Luther King, Jr.?

A Movement Coming from God

An adequate response to this question requires that we envision the entire existence of Jesus as more than a mere earthly episode subsequently ratified by God. Indeed, it is as a movement coming from God to begin with. In the latter case, it is the eternal Son of the Father who becomes incarnate and who brings about a saving effect with universal impact. In the former case, it is a matter of the tragedy of an admirable but purely human life, which terminates not in Good Friday, but rather in the Friday of the great failure. As with Socrates, Gandhi, and Martin Luther King, the death of Jesus, when taken as a tragedy, constitutes an expression and a symbol of that profundity to which certain individuals can attain when their conduct is inspired by faith and love. From this perspective, Jesus appears praiseworthy in terms of congruence and courage. He certainly proves to be a great model, but one cannot very well see why the New Testament proclaims him Savior of the world.

However, if it is understood that it is the eternal Son of the Father who becomes incarnate and who died, then it is more evident why his death brings about a saving effect with universal consequences.

The theological alternatives, therefore, are the following: either Jesus is essentially a human being whom God recognized as exemplary by raising him from the dead; or Jesus is the concrete face of the transcendent mystery, the human nature personally assumed by the eternal Son, whose love, manifested in his earthly existence, exercises a universal impact. In other words, it is his divinity that makes his life, death, and resurrection actually change the course of history. As Anselm of Canterbury stated, the divinity of Christ ensures the effectiveness of redemption, while his humanity constitutes the free response and collaboration of the human being. As the Head of his Body (a metaphor for the Church in the Letter to the Ephesians), he unites all believers in his saving work by sharing with them his Holy Spirit, who enables them to love as Christ loves. At the time of his resurrection, he bestows on them this Holy Spirit who inspires their commitment and elevates them to the dignity of true cooperators in the work of salvation.

In the Christian view of things, although such great figures as Moses, Gautama, or Muhammad wielded a vast influence by their example and their teaching, Christ accomplished something more decisive. Being both God and man, he alone brought about an astonishing reversal: the transformation of evil into good, from a desperate situation to a situation of hope. Only he had the divine-human power to straighten out the downward path of oppression espoused by sinners, and to make it an upward trail. Thanks to him, the descending movement of disobedience, of fleeing God, was converted into an ascending movement of obedience, of being orientated toward God. By willingly entering into the free fall that had resulted from fear and hatred, Jesus traveled a trajectory that became a curve, a loop culminating in Jesus being lifted up and drawing all people to himself (John 12:32). As God incarnate, Jesus alone was able to use suffering as the vehicle of a definitively victorious love, once and for all.

In the case of Jesus Christ, the liberating movement commences with God and is completed with humanity. The Father sends the Son and the Spirit in order to save the world. The liberating dynamic originates from the Father and is concretized differently in the Son and in the Holy Spirit. The Son accomplishes "objective" salvation: a new situation is created for the human race. The Holy Spirit accomplishes "subjective" salvation: grafted into Christ, each individual can enter freely into this new situation.

In each of these two stages, what is achieved is not the result of mere human forces, but rather the result of divine initiative. First of all, Christ, the author of our liberation, is the Son equal to the Father; he assumes a concrete human nature by which means he infuses his love into the emptiness caused by evil. Secondly, in the reconciliation with God, it is not the spirit of the sinner that changes itself; only the Holy Spirit can transform weakened wills and darkened intellects.

Has God Willed the Passion of Jesus?

The French thinker René Girard has shed much light upon the scapegoat mechanism by which societies endeavor to minimize and control the damage brought about by violent rivalries. Unfortunately, he always understands sacrifice in terms of the scapegoat mechanism. Consequently, he interprets the New Testament's accounts of the passion and resurrection as a rejection and a total dismantling of the sacrificial system.[2] All the same, in a recent work, Girard recognizes that the New Testament never resorts to the term "scapegoat" but speaks of the "Lamb of God." Still, he maintains that although the latter word is better than the former, there is no significant semantic difference between them.[3] I'll explain this difference later.

Girard realizes that those who understand the significance of Jesus' resurrection move out of the infernal cycle of violence that plagues the human race. He insists that God would have shown himself to be a violent agent, had he approved of the crucifixion of Christ perpetrated by the Roman authorities. But this is an ambiguous assertion, which both means: (1) God did not directly will (and did not actively orchestrate) the death of Christ; (2) God did not even permit it. I think we should accept the first statement and reject the second.

To say that God permitted the passion in no way amounts to saying that God absolutely wanted it and ordered Jesus to march toward it in a self-immolating way. How could we not see as barbaric a god who would command such a thing? Therefore, in accord with Girard, we ought to resist the suggestion that Jesus' sufferings changed God's stance and caused his willingness to save. As if a transaction was needed by which God's disposition toward the human race would have been turned around! Nevertheless, we must take into consideration the New Testament's statement that Jesus was put to death "according to the definite plan and foreknowledge of God" (Acts of the Apostles 2:23).

One of Girard's followers, Raymund Schwager, gives us a very helpful analysis of the various biblical trends regarding sacrifice. He reminds us of an important fact: the prophets of Israel not only criticized sacrificial rites unaccompanied by justice and righteousness, but they even asserted that they were not at all indispensable. He points out that we cannot readily situate Jesus in the framework of cultic sacrifice, since the Letter to the Hebrews portrays Jesus as the high priest who *abolishes* the Temple's sacrificial provisions.[4] Notwithstanding my positive interpretation of the temple worship in Israel (which will be proposed further on in this essay), I agree that we do find a certain discontinuity between the First and the Second Testament regarding sacrifice.[5] Yet I must add that there is also an analogical continuity, since there are numerous texts in the New Testament—culminating in the Letter to the Hebrews—that suggest a sacrificial construal of Christ's death.[6] Unfortunately, Girard and Schwager set up an exaggerated opposition between a generic notion of sacrifice (which they observe in most religions, including Judaism) and what happened in the passion of Jesus.

I would submit that we ought to think of the passion of Jesus analogically, on the model of what self-sacrifice means in ordinary life. First, in an obvious and somewhat superficial manner, we sacrifice when we give up something for the sake of a higher good. Sacrifice is the renunciation that occurs whenever choosing x entails renouncing y. Any choice involves sacrifice. Second, the word "sacrifice" acquires a more profound meaning when a commitment requires voluntary suffering. For example, parents give up much for their children. Third, we observe the phenomenon of heroism, for instance, if a son throws himself on his mother's attacker at the risk of being killed.[7] Jesus' self-sacrifice takes on its deep meaning as the highest degree on this scale. He sacrificed his life and offered it to God for the sake of all human beings, whom he loved as his brothers and sisters.

The Seriousness of Sin

Secular thought offers partially valuable but not fully penetrating explanations for human failings. Those explanations do not reach the deepest level: poverty, social inequalities, ignorance, inattention, distrust of oneself and of others, false perceptions, fears, ambition, greed, rivalry and retaliation, etc.

In the Bible, on the contrary, one notes a profound recognition of sin and of its consequences. Our ancestors in the faith discovered that infidelity to the covenant with God damages the bond between the people of Israel and their Creator. They established a connection between this damaged bond and the harm done to others. Every distortion in interhuman relationships entails a distortion in the relationships with God.

A person who has not experienced genuine love cannot but have an inadequate apprehension of sin. The gravity of sin is unveiled at the same time as the seriousness of love. So long as one has not perceived the beauty of love, it is possible to ignore the negative effects of one's actions. It is not by chance that chapters 13 to 17 of the Gospel of John present at once the reality of the love disclosed in Jesus and in the community, and the fact of hatred on the part of the world. The extraordinary overture of Jesus brings into full contrast the rigid closing-off of human hearts.

Meditating on the New Testament, the Christian tradition has equated sin with self-idolatry, namely, a search for complete autonomy in regard to the conditions of life, other people, and God. There is in sin a refusal of limitations and of mortality. In order to protect this artificial independence, individuals or groups are ready to affirm themselves by any means. The logic of this disposition leads to the injuring of human beings, by taking from them their goods, their health, their honor, their human relationships, and sometimes their physical lives. In this manner, one also does the greatest wrong to oneself and one accentuates a discontentment, even a disgust of oneself that reinforces the tendency to destruction.

Interestingly, a theologian like Raymund Schwager links the theme of universal salvation in Jesus with the declaration, based on Psalm 2 and Acts 4:25–26, that all human beings allied themselves against God and his representative.[8] He attributes this universal attack on God and on Jesus to the deeply set resentment we feel against God because of the evil that afflicts us. Such ambivalence toward God, which is usually unconscious, has been uncovered by the Book of Job. Schwager's insight highlights humankind's hidden hatred for God, epitomized in the execution of Jesus and overcome because of Jesus' identification with all sinners and because of his resurrection.[9] We have here a twofold universality: of enmity and of reconciliation.

Otto Semmelroth beautifully expresses the reversal: "Christ's being killed on the cross only became a sacrificial action because what was intended in a totally different sense by his executioners was transformed into a sacrificial action in the heart of Jesus, which his words express."[10] In the heart of Jesus, the intention of total self-giving perfectly coincided with the Father's will.

The Divine Solution: Sacrifice

Properly understood, the notion of sacrifice helps us to grasp how many Christians came to envision the death of Jesus as the ultimate solution to the mystery of evil. We start from an analogy found in interpersonal relationships. When we have caused sorrow or done wrong to someone who is dear to us, we have the possibility of speaking to her or to him and expressing our sincere regret. But in addition to words, we feel the need to compensate the offense by making a gesture which goes beyond what we would ordinarily do. Such a gesture signifies our resolution to do better in the future. In this way, reconciliation can express itself in the offer of a gift or in an activity likely to please the person we love.

The biblical idea of sacrifice is not unlike this human reflex. At the temple of Jerusalem, people offered sacrifices of communion and of expiation in order to symbolize the continuation or the restoration of the covenant. As they immolated animals they would signify that all life—represented by the blood—belongs to the Creator. These sacrifices, which would eventually help his followers understand the gesture of Jesus, should be sharply distinguished from the rite of the scapegoat, which was burdened with the sins of the people and expelled into the desert. The New Testament never presents Christ as a scapegoat. Rather, it construes him as the slain lamb.

On the one hand, the scapegoat should not be understood as representing Jesus, because there is a total separation between the scapegoat and the people. One substitutes the scapegoat for the people by heaping upon it the sins of all. It is lamentable that quite a few Christians view Jesus as a scapegoat, since this image in no way reflects the collaboration between him and them in the work of salvation.

On the other hand, the metaphor of the slain lamb is also not without its problems. It easily suggests a passive acceptance, on the part of Jesus, of being treated as a pure victim, irrespective of his basic religious goals.

Still, what is important to retain from it is the fact that Jesus does not resist the evil that is done to him. If, at the Mount of Olives, he does not flee to avoid being arrested, it is because he is convinced that his Father will make sense of his passion by using this non-resistance. The religious intention of Jesus, his obedience to the Father, his consent to the divine plan, constitutes an interior action, a "yes," an engagement. As a contemporary theologian sums it up, "Handed over, he hands himself over."[11] In the exterior passivity of Jesus, we discern an entirely voluntary commitment, an amazing activity.[12] This is the most perfect form of self-gift: he freely offers his life. In the complete outpouring of blood and water (John 19:34), he unleashes his Spirit into the world.

The extent to which Jesus may have seen his death as a source of salvation is a much disputed matter among exegetes and theologians.[13] But Jesus' conviction that his death had a meaning in God's design is, to my mind, incontrovertible. Such meaning has to do with the manner in which evil must be reversed. This is exemplified in texts such as Matthew 5:39 ("Do not resist an evildoer. But if anyone strikes you on the right cheek, turn the other also") and 5:44 ("Love your enemies and pray for those who persecute you"). In the light of those and similar texts, I would make the following twofold contention: As a human being Jesus did not fully understand nor thematize exactly why and how his imminent passion made sense; he nevertheless possessed sufficient apprehension of meaning to be able to maintain that his passion was part of a drama in which God would provide a resolution to the problem of evil.

We should not underestimate the fact that the suffering of Jesus on a cross was a rather banal affair. For the Roman soldiers, this execution was but another one among the hundreds that had taken place. It must have been extremely humiliating and demoralizing for "a prophet mighty in deed and word before God and all the people" (Luke 24:19) to be crucified by a group of soldiers in a perfunctory way, and then slowly to suffocate in a shameful public display before all passersby. Far from being an important event in the history of Israel, the death of Jesus looked exactly like the capital punishment undergone by hundreds of rebels and criminals in the Roman Empire. Jesus' fate shares in the apparent insignificance of all those men and women crushed by the strong and powerful. Its banality was a case of annihilation, as suggested by these words: "He emptied himself, taking the form of a slave . . . and became obedient to the point of death—even death on a cross" (Letter to the Philippians 2:7–8).

What saved the world was not the material sacrifice of Jesus, which was an ordinary episode, however awful, and which did not involve the greatest amount of suffering. Surely his suffering was intense; and yet it was short, if we compare it with cases of torture which last for weeks and which involve extreme psychological torments. What saved the world, then, was rather the love with which he consented to give his life—his self-offering, the spiritual and yet embodied sacrifice.[14] Thus Thomas Aquinas writes, "[Christ's] satisfaction would not be efficacious unless it proceeded from charity."[15]

Neither the Father nor Jesus directly willed the passion. By stopping the hand of Abraham when he was about to sacrifice his son Isaac, God made known his rejection of human sacrifices (Genesis 22:12). Nonetheless, given sin and its deadly character, the divine compassion did not shun the ultimate form of presence that involves total solidarity with the victims of evil. By undergoing the extreme consequence of sin, the inseparably victimized and forgiving Son of God could break the logic of hatred.

In this sense, Christ did not come on earth directly in order to die; but he accepted death as coming *from humans* (not from God) and as a means (used by God) for loosening hardened hearts. Christ's direct intention was to free humanity, and this goal entailed his non-resistance to evil. Confronted with the damage caused by humans, Jesus offered a loving and liberating response. What the Father and Jesus directly willed was not the sin culminating in the execution of Jesus, but the love-in-suffering which vanquished sin.

The passion of Jesus calls us to recognize the consequences of sin. Complicity with evil introduces a grave distortion in relationships among humans and with the Creator. Taking account of this fact, the divine mercy does not propose a superficial solution, which would consist in letting bygones be bygones, in cleaning the slate with a quick brush. Such a gesture of pardon would be artificial, because it would not enlist human beings in their own religious rehabilitation. On the contrary, the Savior acts like a physician whose surgical action is followed by the prescription of exercises to be performed each day by the patient. The paschal mystery constitutes a divine-human operation in which all believers collaborate.

If it was "necessary that the Messiah should suffer these things" (Luke 24:26; see also 9:22 and 17:25), this was not in order to appease the wrath of an irate Father. Its purpose consists in working out a solution to the mystery of evil, a solution that contains an inexhaustible wisdom. Jesus is not punished *in the place of* others. In fact, God does not punish: humans are those who, by sinning, punish one another. We routinely sacrifice one another. The Father permits that in the passion Jesus be punished and sacrificed *by* and *with* the others. The "satisfaction" that he accomplishes derives from the love with which he reverses the sinful movement of punishment by making it a movement of blessing. "Satisfaction" literally means "to do sufficiently," that is, to exert the divine-human power that enables love to rise up even in the innermost depths of hatred. Such an achievement, on the part of Christ, has nothing to do with what one could call a "satispassion," namely, brute suffering that would have been unjustly inflicted upon Jesus—himself substituted for others—by a Father concerned to avenge his offended honor.[16]

Saved for What?

It is important to take sin seriously in order to be able to answer the question: *from what* are we saved? However, the answer to this fundamental question depends on the answer given to a question still more fundamental: *for what* are we saved? In other words, religious liberation can certainly be formulated in negative terms: we are saved *from* sin. Yet, more profoundly this experience is a positive reality: we are saved *for* God. Christ renders us capable of living fully, because he puts us in relation with each Person of the Trinity.

Reflection upon the passion of Jesus—the way of the cross—is an entry into the divine mystery. A step toward conversion is taken as soon as one discerns in the passion a love concerned to reach out to every human person. Jesus looked his death in the face; inside himself he knew the destiny which was imposed upon him from outside, and he saw in it the ultimate occasion to love in the deepest way. The friendship offered by Jesus who forgives is for us Christians the sole absolutely indefectible friendship. Confronted with betrayal, his faithfulness reaffirms solidarity and community. In the course of his last meal, the abiding covenant is symbolically renewed in two gestures expressing complete self-gift. His body broken, soon to be put to death, becomes the bread of life; his blood poured out, soon to exhaust his last strengths, becomes the wine which fills us with joyful energies.

For Christians, this historic episode exhibits not only a human love, but also a divine love. More than a human being, it is the Son equal to the Father who undergoes the passion. In this way, Jesus' movement of love is identical to the movement of the eternal Son. He constantly gives back to the Father everything he receives from him. This offering is not only that of the man Jesus, but inseparably that of the eternal Son. And all human beings can be associated to this mutual donation: by participating in the paschal mystery, they obtain and hand over to the Father the life that he imparts to them. In the Eucharist they follow the curve of the loop: with Jesus Christ they receive "every generous act of giving, with every perfect gift, . . . from above, coming down from the Father of lights" (James 1:17) and as they lift up their hearts, they offer it back to God in a loving exchange.

The Father is the source. He gives himself entirely to his Son and he gives us his incarnate Son as well as their mutual Spirit. The Son returns this gift without reserve. With Christ, the Christians make this offering, inspired and animated by the Holy Spirit. On such a representation, what salvation makes accessible is participation in the Trinitarian life. Believers are intimately associated in the exchanges that take place between the divine Persons. In this context of love, everything that a person experiences, joyous or painful, can be gratefully received as grace.

Notes

1. For this distinction between the causes and effects of Jesus' death I am indebted to Anthony Akinwale, a former doctoral student at Boston College, now a professor of theology at Ibadan, Nigeria.

2. René Girard, *Things Hidden since the Foundation of the World*, trans. Stephen Bann and Michael Metteer (Stanford, Calif.: Stanford University Press, 1987), Book II, chap. 2.

3. Girard, *I See Satan Fall Like Lightning*, trans. James G. Williams (New York: Orbis, 2001), 155–56.

4. Raymund Schwager, *Must There Be Scapegoats? Violence and Redemption in the Bible*, trans. Maria L. Assad (San Francisco: Harper & Row, 1987, reprint in New York: Crossroad, 2000), 82–91 and 200–4; *Jesus in the Drama of Salvation: Toward a Biblical Doctrine of Redemption*, trans. James G. Williams and Paul Haddon (New York: Crossroad, 1999), 177–86.

5. In *Foundations of Christian Faith: An Introduction to the Idea of Christianity*, trans. William V. Dych (New York: Crossroad, 1978), 282–83, Karl Rahner, while maintaining the notion of sacrifice, raises relevant critical questions regarding its various senses and implications.

6. I cannot list them here, for lack of space. See Rudolf Schnackenburg, "Sacrifice," B. "New Testament," in *Sacramentum Verbi: An Encyclopedia of Biblical Theology*, ed. Johannes B. Bauer (New York: Herder and Herder, 1970), 803–7.

7. See Louis Roy, *Self-Actualization and the Radical Gospel* (Collegeville, Minn.: The Liturgical Press, 2002), 53–56.

8. See Schwager, *Must There Be Scapegoats?*, 188–89. Schwager draws attention to these two biblical texts in the German edition of 1978. Girard does the same later in *Je vois Satan tomber comme l'éclair* (Paris: Grasset, 1999), chap. 8; for title of English translation, see note 4.

9. See Schwager, *Must There Be Scapegoats?*, 183–200; *Jesus in the Drama of Salvation*, 169–172.

10. Otto Semmelroth, "Sacrifice," III. "Sacrifice of Christ," in *Encyclopedia of Theology: The Concise Sacramentum Mundi*, ed. Karl Rahner (New York: Seabury Press, 1975), 1492–95, at 1493.

11. Jean-Noël Bezançon, *Dieu sauve* (Paris: Desclée de Brouwer, and Montreal: Bellarmin, 1985), 64.

12. See Louis Roy, "The Passion of Jesus: A Test Case for Providence," *New Blackfriars* 79 (1998): 512–23.

13. See John Galvin, "The Death of Jesus in Contemporary Theology: Systematic Perspectives and Historical Issues," *Horizons* 13 (1986): 239–52.

14. This is worth stressing, given the enormous importance that Mel Gibson ascribes to physical suffering, without any historical context, in his film *The Passion of the Christ*.

15. *Summa Theologiae* III, q. 14, a. 1, ad 1.

16. See Charles C. Hefling, Jr., "A Perhaps Permanently Valid Achievement: Lonergan on Christ's Satisfaction," *Method: Journal of Lonergan Studies* 10 (1992): 51–76, esp. 60–61.

PART FIVE

THE PASSION OF THE CHRIST

～

CHAPTER TWELVE

A Challenge to Catholic Teaching

Philip A. Cunningham

Mel Gibson's movie *The Passion of the Christ* projects a world in which demonic powers and evil, faithless humans blow by blow and wound by wound gradually destroy the body of Jesus of Nazareth. As David Elcott has observed, the film prompts viewers to take sides in a war of good vs. evil, of belief vs. the powers of darkness. One is either a follower of Jesus or a pawn of Satan. For some this dualism seems to reach out from the screen into reactions to the movie. A viewer either praises the film or is aligned with the sinister forces that oppose it. Fans of the film pillory critics of this Hollywood production as enemies of the New Testament.

The dualistic world projected by the movie is one in which forgiveness is talked about but is not always operative even on the side of the forces of light. The God to whom Jesus prays seems quite unforgiving. Bare moments after Jesus prays to his Father to forgive his ignorant crucifiers, a raven descends from the heavens to peck out the eye of the presumably ignorant crucifixion victim who has taunted Jesus. Seconds after Jesus dies, a divine teardrop from heaven triggers an earthquake that destroys the heart of the Jewish Temple. Neither scene is found in the New Testament. The increasingly severe tortures inflicted on Jesus suggest that only endless pain can put things right with God.

Unbiblical Scenes

The film is filled with non-biblical elements. In principle there is nothing wrong for a screenwriter to augment the rather meager Gospel narratives.

Indeed, choices such as staging, lighting, costuming, etc. make the supplementing of the biblical texts inevitable. In Gibson's film these unbiblical features are so interwoven with scenes from one Gospel or another that the unwary viewer, already experiencing sensory overload because of the film's vivid brutality, is unlikely to detect them or ponder their significance. The extra-biblical materials shed light on one of the sources of the movie's polarized "us vs. them" world. A partial list, excepting flashbacks, includes:

- Satan tempts Jesus in the garden of Gethsemane. "Who is your father? Who are you?" an androgynous, hooded figure asks. "No one man can carry this burden of sin, I tell you." [N.B. In Mark and Luke, demons are well aware of Jesus' identity as God's Son.]
- Jewish arrestors throw Jesus shackled in chains off a bridge on his way to his encounter with the Jewish high priests. Demonic creatures lurk beneath. Among other injuries, one of Jesus' eyes becomes swollen shut.
- Agents of the high priests pay money to other Jews to assemble at the high priest's courtyard to demand Jesus' death.
- Mary Magdalen entreats Roman soldiers to help Jesus. "They are trying to hide their crime from you," she pleads. An organizer of the assembling Jews tells the Roman that it is merely an internal affair over someone who broke the Temple laws.
- In his encounter with a council of Jewish priests, Jesus is physically assaulted by a crowd of dozens of Jews, many wearing prayer shawls. Although the site had earlier been described as the high priest's courtyard, the immense size of the place suggests that this scene actually occurs within the Temple, a suspicion partially confirmed by the destruction that befalls the Temple when Jesus dies.
- While awaiting his meeting with the Roman prefect Pontius Pilate, Jewish captors shackle Jesus to a wall in a chamber beneath the site of his encounter with the Jewish council. His mother Mary somehow senses his presence below.
- An aide tells Pilate that trouble is brewing "within the walls. The Pharisees apparently hate the man." [N.B. The Pharisees are almost totally absent from the Gospel passion narratives.]
- Judas is driven to suicide by (Jewish) demon-children.
- Pilate sums up the Jewish abuse of Jesus by asking the priests, "Do you always punish your prisoners before they are judged?"
- Pilate offers Jesus a drink, which is refused.

- Pilate confesses to his wife that he fears the Jewish high priest will lead a revolt against Rome if he does not yield to Jewish demands to crucify Jesus. Pilate and his aides decide they need reinforcements because an uprising has already begun.
- The high priests and Jesus' mother are among the spectators at Jesus' scourging. Satan drifts among the priests, at one point carrying a demon-baby.
- Jesus struggles to his feet after a first round of scourging, apparently inviting further punishment with more destructive implements. The Roman torturers oblige, including scourging him frontally (yet vulnerable vital organs are not ripped out by scourges that expose Jesus' ribs).
- Pilate's wife gives the mother of Jesus linens with which to bury Jesus.
- Jesus' mother, with Mary Magdalene, tries to soak up the pools of blood left after the scourging.
- Pilate, a Roman governor, is shocked by the appearance of Jesus after the scourging.
- Jesus carries an unusually large, complete cross. One of those to be crucified with him taunts, "Why do you embrace your cross, you fool?"
- The Roman execution squad is drunk and continues to so abuse Jesus that it is doubtful if he will make it alive to Golgotha.
- The executioners flip the cross with Jesus affixed to it face down in order to bend back the protruding nail points. Inexplicably, he is not crushed beneath its weight but is somehow suspended above the ground (or the earth has withdrawn from beneath him).

As this list makes clear, the extra-biblical scenes help divide the characters into friends and foes. While there are certainly dissenters (Nicodemus calls the council proceedings "a beastly travesty," voices in the crowd call Jesus a holy man, Simon of Cyrene almost carries Jesus as well as the cross), the film gives the strong impression of implacable and murderous Jewish hostility to Jesus. The portrayal of the high priests and the destruction of portions of the Temple visually situate Jewish institutions, and perhaps Judaism itself, on the side of the unbelieving dark forces.

Roman figures are handled differently. There are brutal and vicious scourgers and executioners who are sadistically wicked. But Pilate and his wife and some close aides come across as reasonable decent people who strive to save Jesus from death. The wife's gift of linens to Mary associates her character with some Christian traditions that considered Pilate and his wife to have been inchoate believers and eventually saints.

An Ahistorical Mixing of the Gospels
in Violation of Catholic Teaching

Catholic teaching understands that the diversity among the Gospels reflects four complementary inspirations that each present one facet of the jewel that is the mystery of Jesus Christ. Or to use another metaphor, "the New Testament authors, precisely as pastors and teachers, bear witness indeed to the same Christ, but with voices that differ as in the harmony of one piece of music."[1]

The Catholic magisterium also teaches that the Gospels contain insights and information from three different historical "stages": (1) the ministry of Jesus; (2) the post-resurrection preaching of the apostles; and (3) the time of the composition of the Gospels.[2] One consequence of this teaching is that debates over Jesus' divine identity that arose after the resurrection influenced the narratives of his ministry and crucifixion. As one Vatican document has put it, "The Gospels are the outcome of long and complicated editorial work. . . . Hence it cannot be ruled out that some references hostile to the Jews have their historical context in conflicts between the nascent church and the Jewish community. Certain controversies reflect Christian-Jewish relations long after the time of Jesus. To establish this is of capital importance if we wish to bring out the meaning of certain Gospel texts for Christians today."[3]

What does this mean for contemporary dramatizations of the passion of Christ from a Catholic perspective? Unless they decide simply to present the passion according to Mark or one of the other evangelists, all authors of passion dramas have to choose elements from the four different Gospel narratives of Jesus' death in order to shape a coherent narrative. This leads to the question: what principles of selection will guide the composition of a particular passion script? In addition, how will the drama of the death of Jesus deal with the later theological insights that are embedded in the Gospel texts? If this question is ignored, a script will anachronistically present theological debates that had not yet occurred during Jesus' lifetime as realities at the time of his death.

In *The Passion of the Christ*, one can readily discern the Gospel sources behind various scenes. The principles for their selection and arrangement are not so evident. Excluding flashbacks, this is a partial list of the Gospel sources employed:

- In Gethsemane, Jesus prays for the cup to pass him by [Synoptics].
- Jesus asks the arresting party whom they are seeking and then identifies himself to them [John, but omitting the Johannine element of the arrestors swooning when Jesus says, "I am he."]

- Judas kisses Jesus to identify him [Mark, Matthew].
- Jesus heals the ear of an arrestor [Luke].
- Jesus is brought before a Passover night meeting of the Sanhedrin. During the proceeding he is asked if he is the Son of God or the Son of the Blessed [Mark, Matthew].
- When brought to Pilate, Caiaphas accuses Jesus of various crimes [a combination of Luke, John, and extra-biblical material].
- Pilate's wife warns him of her dreams about the righteous Jesus [Matthew].
- Pilate tells Jesus that his own leaders have handed him over [John].
- Pilate sends Jesus to Herod for judgment. He refuses to get involved [Luke].
- Pilate orders Jesus scourged in a vain attempt to elicit pity from the Jewish mob [John].
- Jesus tells Pilate that the one who handed him over to the governor bears the greater sin [John].
- Pilate washes his hands of responsibility before the Jewish mob [Matthew].
- Simon of Cyrene is coerced into carrying Jesus' cross [Synoptics].

One effect of this arrangement is to heighten "Jewish" guilt. This is especially evident in the pivotal confrontation between Pilate on the one hand, and Caiaphas, the priests, and the Jewish mob on the other.

Gibson has chosen to follow the Gospel of John in having Jesus scourged as an effort by Pilate to placate the bloodthirst of the Jewish crowd. In Matthew and Mark, Jesus is scourged only *after* Pilate pronounces his sentence, i.e., as part of the normal Roman crucifixion process. Luke doesn't present it at all. John's is the only Gospel in which a crowd of Jews is unmoved by the sight of the scourged Jesus.

In the film, Pilate presents the flayed Jesus to the Jewish crowd, saying "Behold the man" [John]. Caiaphas leads the crowd in chanting "Crucify him!" [all four Gospels, but at this point only in John]. Pilate, gesturing to the bloody Jesus, asks. "Isn't this enough?" [extra-biblical]. The crowd is unappeased. "Shall I crucify your king?" asks Pilate. Caiaphas declares ironically, "We have no king but Caesar" [John]. Pilate turns to Jesus, seeking some escape. "Speak to me. I have the power to crucify you or to set you free." Jesus reassures him, "He who delivered me to you has the greater sin" [John]. If there is any doubt about to whom this refers, Caiaphas immediately exclaims, "If you free him, governor, you are no friend of Caesar's" [John, adapted]. Violence breaks out between the crowd and the soldiers. A riot appears imminent [Matthew]. Pilate summons a servant to bring him a bowl of water. Dramatically lifting his hands, Pilate announces, "It is you who want him crucified, not I" [extra-biblical]. He washes his hands. Caiaphas, angrily pointing to Pilate, exclaims in Aramaic (not in subtitles), "Let his blood be on us and our children!" [Matthew, adapted]. Pilate commands his aide, "Do as they wish" [extra-biblical].

This combination of the Johannine scourging as Pilate's effort to free Jesus with Matthew's scene of Pilate washing his hands of responsibility results in a depiction of Jewish hostility that is more relentless, implacable, and evil than either Gospel on its own conveys. The 1988 words of the U.S. Bishops' Committee on Ecumenical and Interreligious Affairs are pertinent: "It is not sufficient for the producers of passion dramatizations to respond to responsible criticism simply by appealing to the notion that 'it's in the Bible.' One must account for one's selections."[4]

There were other choices that could have been made that would have been equally faithful to the Bible but would have produced a substantially different combined narrative. These include:

- Because Jesus is popular with the people at large, he is arrested clandestinely at night to avoid a riot (Mk 14:2).
- Caiaphas fears that a riot could provoke the Romans to destroy the Temple (Jn 11:48). [N.B. the opposite of the film's claim he could lead a revolt.]
- Jesus is arrested by Temple guards *and* Roman soldiers (Jn 18:3).
- Jesus is questioned by Annas and Caiaphas about his disciples and his teaching and then taken to Pilate (Jn 18:19, 24, 28). [N.B. no Sanhedrin "trial" or question of Jesus' divinity]
- Pilate was known to use violence to enforce Roman rule (Lk 13:1).
- Jesus was scourged as part of the Roman crucifixion procedure (Mk 15:15, as against Jn 19:1–8 ff.).
- "A great multitude of the people" (Lk 23:27) and "all the multitudes" (Lk 23:48) of Jews are sorrowful about Jesus' crucifixion.
- Jesus' execution was done in haste (Mk 15:25; Jn 19:31).

Moreover, *The Passion of the Christ* completely ignores the fact, which also happens to be authoritative Catholic teaching, that the Gospel narratives convey post-resurrectional theological understandings. Given the film's use of ancient languages (although the Latin should have been Greek), viewers are even more inclined to accept the movie as a historical reproduction. They are likely, therefore, to come to the ahistorical and erroneous conclusion that Jewish characters wanted Jesus dead because he claimed to be the

Son of God. From there it is easy to slip into thinking that Judaism itself is aligned with the dark forces that oppose Jesus, a notion reinforced by the destruction in the Temple at the film's end.

Catholics who take seriously the legacy of Pope John Paul II are obliged to ask the following questions about *The Passion of the Christ*:

Is it acceptable for a filmmaker—even though he regularly repeats the teaching of the Council of Trent that Christ died for the sins of all humanity—to so combine elements from the four Gospel accounts and to add many scenes not found in the New Testament with the result that the wickedness of Jewish characters is magnified? Can such directorial choices simply be overlooked because they occur in a movie about Christ?

In a church whose highest leadership has prayed for God's forgiveness for exactly those sins over the past millennium and whose teachings repudiate such practices, the answer can only be "no."

Why has Gibson chosen to select and combine in the way he did? What is the source of the extra-biblical material in Gibson's film?

There is an author at work who ought to have received a screenwriting credit for the film. Indeed, it is obvious upon close examination that Gibson has actually created a cinematic version not so much of the Gospels but of Anne Catherine Emmerich's purported visions of the death of Jesus.

The Passion According to Anne Catherine Emmerich

Anna Katherina Emmerich lived between 1774 and 1824. An Augustinian nun in Westphalia, Germany who was renowned as a mystic and stigmatic, her dreams or visions of the life of Christ were collected after her death and published. Living when Christians simply took it for granted that Jews were collectively cursed for the crucifixion of Jesus, her narratives emphasize Jewish evildoing.

Probably the most disturbing indication of Emmerich's attitude toward Jews is found in a reported vision that occurred in 1819. A recently deceased Jewish widow takes Emmerich's spirit on a journey to a distant Jewish city:

> The soul of the old Jewess Meyr told me on the way that it was true that in former times the Jews, both in our country and elsewhere, had strangled many Christians, principally children, and used their blood for all sort of superstitious and diabolical practices. She had once believed it lawful; but she now knew that it was abominable murder. They still follow such practices in this country and in others more distant; but very secretly, because they are obliged to have commercial intercourse with Christians.[5]

Given this matter-of-fact repetition of the "blood libel," followed by racist descriptions of Jews with "hooked noses" (whose degree of bend indicates their degree of evilness),[6] it is not surprising that Emmerich's account of Jesus' passion prominently features negative images of Jews, including a close association with the demonic:

> At the same moment I perceived the yawning abyss of hell like a fiery meteor at the feet of Caiaphas; it was filled with horrible devils; a slight gauze alone appeared to separate him from its dark flames. I could see the demoniacal fury with which his heart was overflowing, and the whole house looked to me like hell. [. . .] I remember seeing, among other frightful things, a number of little black objects, like dogs with claws, which walked on their hind legs; I knew at the time what kind of wickedness was indicated by this apparition, but I cannot remember now. I saw these horrible phantoms enter into the bodies of the greatest part of the bystanders, or else place themselves on their head or shoulders.[7]

While Gibson did not include this scene, its worldview of a cosmic battle between demonic powers and Jews against the forces of believers in Christ certainly permeates his film. Indeed almost all of the film's extra-biblical scenes mentioned above are derived from Emmerich. To them one could add the picture of Herod as effeminate, of Barabbas as bestial (which makes the Jewish crowd's preference of him even more vile), and of Jesus' arm being dislocated by his crucifiers in order to line up with pre-drilled holes in the cross. The film's arrangement of the different Gospel elements is also indebted to Emmerich. *The Passion of the Christ* is a filmed version of Emmerich's imaginative interpretation of the Gospels. The film is so dependent on her that it could have been aptly titled *The Passion According to Emmerich*.

It is thanks to Emmerich's influence, for example, that the film exaggerates Gospel passages that describe Jesus as struck by Jewish individuals and turns them into a severe assault upon Jesus. All the Gospels describe some violence being inflicted on Jesus when he is brought before the high priest. In the synoptics, he is spat upon, blindfolded, struck on the face, and slapped (Mt 26:67–68, Mk 14:65; Lk 22:63–65), although in John, a single soldier only strikes Jesus once with his hand (Jn 18:22). However, in Emmerich, Jesus is brutally abused at this juncture, a scene that is clearly echoed in the film:

> [A] crowd of miscreants—the very scum of the people—surrounded Jesus like a swarm of infuriated wasps, and began to heap every imaginable insult upon him. [. . .] [They] pulled out handfuls of his hair and beard, spat upon him, struck him with their fists, wounded him with sharp-pointed sticks, and even ran needles into his body; [. . .] around his neck they hung a long iron chain,

with an iron ring at each end, studded with sharp points, which bruised and tore his knees as be walked. [. . .] After many many insults, they seized the chain which was hanging on his neck, dragged him towards the room into which the Council had withdrawn, and with their sticks forced him in, [. . .] A large body of councilors, with Caiaphas at their head, were still in the room, and they looked with both delight and approbation at the shameful scene which was enacted, [. . .] Every countenance looked diabolical and enraged, and all around was dark, confused, and terrific.[8]

Gibson has been quoted as saying that Emmerich "supplied me with stuff I never would have thought of."[9] He also carries what he considers to be her relic, which he showed during a television interview shortly before the film's opening.[10] This raises the possibility that Gibson has relied so heavily on Emmerich because he believes she was gifted with a historical vision of the first century. Whether this is true or not, Gibson stated in the same television interview that he saw nothing antisemitic in her writings. However, from a Catholic perspective it seems undeniable that both Emmerich and Gibson have failed to "avoid absolutely any actualization of certain texts of the New Testament which could provoke or reinforce unfavorable attitudes toward the Jewish people."[11]

Historical Errors

The Passion of the Christ's filming in ancient languages gives the film the veneer of historical verisimilitude that may mislead some viewers into thinking they're watching a documentary. And despite claims that the film is the most accurate portrayal of the death of Jesus ever filmed, *The Passion of the Christ* contains many historical errors and omissions. For instance, although graphic and bloody, the movie shows Jesus carrying a complete cross and not simply a crossbeam; the nails are driven through his palms, not his wrists; and the addition of a footrest to the cross, which is unattested in Roman literature or archaeological studies, instead of a projecting seat.[12] It is also noteworthy that those crucified with Jesus are not scourged, even though that was the standard Roman procedure. The film's depiction of the mechanics of crucifixion is more derived from traditions of Christian art than from historical knowledge. An artistic judgment is also evident in the scourging scene where, although Jesus' flesh is torn to ribbons so that his ribs are visible, his loincloth is amazingly resistant to the whips.

More importantly, the film totally reverses the relationship of Pilate to Caiaphas. It is an undisputed historical fact that Caiaphas was dependent on the Roman prefect, Pontius Pilate, to retain his position as high priest. Since

Caiaphas held the high priesthood throughout Pilate's eleven-year tenure as prefect, but was quickly removed when it ended, it seems clear that the two collaborated closely. There was surely no possibility that Caiaphas could even imagine revolting against Roman rule, as the film contends. The result of this historical fantasy is that the Jewish leader is made the driving force behind Jesus' execution.

Also significant is the historical fact that the Passover festival was an especially volatile time since it celebrated freedom from foreign domination. Jerusalem overflowed with Jewish pilgrims from around the Empire, and it was the usual practice for Roman governors to station soldiers in the Temple precincts to prevent any uprising.[13] The inflamed mood of the Jewish populace at Passover probably explains why Pilate was in Jerusalem, instead of at his headquarters in Caesarea Maritima, when Jesus arrived in the city a few days before the festival and caused a disturbance in the Temple.

Given this enflamed setting, it is not difficult to discern why a Roman prefect might want to execute Jesus. Jesus came from the Galilee, the homeland of earlier foes of Roman rule; he had been proclaiming the dawning of the Kingdom of Israel's God, which would result in the overthrow of Caesar; he had spoken of the Temple's destruction and caused a disturbance there; he had been coy about the question of tribute to Rome; and he had arrived in Jerusalem with followers in the incendiary Passover season. The quickness with which Jesus was executed after his surreptitious arrest, and the fact that he was publicly crucified (not quietly assassinated) as a seditionist "king of the Jews" as a warning to all malcontents, makes it all but certain that it was Pilate who chose to make an example of him. None of these historical considerations influenced Gibson's Emmerich-driven storyline.

This makes the movie deficient according to Catholic teaching since "a guiding artistic vision sensitive to historical fact and to the best biblical scholarship are obviously necessary"[14] in composing passion dramatizations.

Theological Concerns

Finally, the film's graphic, persistent, and intimate violence raises theological questions from a Catholic perspective. It closely resonates with an understanding of salvation that holds that God had to be satisfied or appeased for the countless sins of humanity by subjecting his son to unspeakable torments. This sadistic picture of God is hardly compatible with the God proclaimed by Jesus as the one who seeks for the lost sheep, who welcomes back the prodigal son before he can even express remorse, or who causes the rain to fall on the just and unjust alike.

One wonders why it was necessary to communicate God's love by scenes of unremitting torture. None of the Gospel writers felt obliged to go into gory details and yet they have communicated God's love for two millennia. Is it a sign of some cultural pathology that some people were delighted by the feeling of being actually present at the scourging and crucifixion?

Moreover, one cannot properly understand the meaning of the cross without pondering the meaning of the resurrection, as 1 Corinthians 15 and Philippians 2 make clear. By focusing on his torments, the film minimizes the central and defining reality of the resurrection for Christian faith.

Conclusion

The Passion of the Christ is a powerful cinematic experience that has been emotionally moving to many viewers. Whether this emotion is the result of the trauma of seeing someone graphically tortured to death or a genuine spiritual encounter or some combination of the two is difficult to assess. Grief, guilt, and shock do not automatically produce or deepen Christian faith. Moreover, simply because some viewers do not personally experience feelings of hostility to Jews after seeing the film does not excuse the unbiblical intensification of Jewish culpability that the film, like its Passion Play forebears, conveys.

The movie's problematic aspects outweigh some positive features. For example, many Catholics will appreciate the prominence given to the mother of Jesus, even though in the New Testament she only silently appears briefly at the foot of the cross in just one Gospel (John). Likewise, the visual Eucharistic allusions are praiseworthy, although they depict the Mass only in sacrificial terms and minimize its fellowship meal dimensions.

The controversy over the film has brought to light the most disturbing claim that to criticize the movie is to criticize the New Testament. For example, Paul Lauer, Mel Gibson's publicist, declared:

> Are some people going to make the argument for anti-Semitism [in the film]? Maybe. But to do that, they would have to call the New Testament gospels anti-Semitic, which, as you know, some people do. You can't change the story told in the gospels any more than Steven Spielberg could be expected to change the history of the Holocaust to avoid blaming the Germans.[15]

This argument has been echoed by admirers of a pre-release version of the film, including some Catholics, who, frankly, ought to have known better.

According to one commentator, "[t]o take issue with this movie is, essentially, to take issue with the Gospels, to take issue with the Christian faith and to take issue with a monumental artistic achievement by a filmmaker of increasing stature."[16] Another opined, "I really don't think all the liberal cat-erwauling is going to hurt the movie. For some people, the Gospels them-selves are anti-Semitic. There's nothing we can say to convince them other-wise, no matter how hard we try."[17] And Archbishop John Foley stated, "There's nothing in the film that doesn't come from the Gospel accounts. [!] So if they're critical of the film, they would be critical of the Gospel. It was very faithful to the Gospel."[18]

Honesty demands the recognition that Christians have used (and abused) the New Testament over the centuries to claim that "the Jews" were cursed for rejecting and crucifying Jesus. As Cardinal Edward Idris Cassidy has put it, "preaching accused the Jews of every age of deicide."[19] Beginning in the late Middle Ages, the deicide charge was especially dis-seminated every Holy Week in connection with the proclamation and preaching of the Johannine passion narrative and through performances of passion plays. These dramatic reenactments regularly inspired violence against Jews. In 1539, Pope Paul III banned the annual passion perfor-mance in the Coliseum because it had routinely caused the ransacking of the Jewish ghetto, and examples could be multiplied. The history of Chris-tian-Jewish relations in Europe makes it undeniable that the New Testa-ment can be put to antisemitic purposes.

This is a different question from whether the New Testament is intrin-sically antisemitic. To affirm the latter, it seems to me, would require mak-ing a case that the New Testament authors, many of whom were themselves Jews, had a racist antipathy toward Jews. Given the intramural nature of the polemics used by the biblical authors, such a case is difficult to sustain. But at all events the real issue is the proper *interpretation* of the New Tes-tament, not whether to apply to it, anachronistically, the term "antise-mitic." Later, when the separate "books" of the New Testament had been assembled into one canon, and were read in very different social contexts by an all-Gentile church, the potential grew for combining and construing them with hostility to Jewish outsiders. To ask, then, whether a particular dramatization of the New Testament passion narratives might promote hos-tility to Jews does not imply any judgment on the alleged antisemitism of the New Testament itself. Rather, to repeat, it is to ask how the passion narratives are being interpreted—a question morally demanded by past an-tisemitic interpretations.

For Gibson's fans to polemicize that the film cannot be critiqued without rejecting the New Testament is to ignore history and to trivialize decades of official Catholic teaching on biblical interpretation. In some ways the movie is a direct challenge to that teaching. It also rejects the Holy Father's solemn commitment at the Western Wall in 2000 to do penance for past Christian sins against the Jewish people by "seeking genuine fellowship with the people of the covenant." Such fellowship cannot possibly rest upon the endorsement of a film that perpetuates hoary anti-Jewish images.

Notes

1. Pontifical Biblical Commission, *Instruction on the Bible and Christology* (1984), 2.2.2.

2. Pontifical Biblical Commission, *Sancta Mater Ecclesia*, Instruction on the Historical Truth of the Gospels (1964), 6.2–10; Second Vatican Council, *Dei Verbum*, The Dogmatic Constitution on Divine Revelation (1965), 19.

3. Pontifical Commission for Religious Relations with the Jews, *Notes on the Correct Way to Present Jews and Judaism in Preaching and Teaching in the Roman Catholic Church* (1985), 21.

4. Bishops' Committee on Ecumenical and Interreligious Affairs, *Criteria for the Evaluation of Dramatizations of the Passion* (1988), C, 1, c.

5. Carl E. Schmöger, *The Life and Revelations of Anne Catherine Emmerich* (Rockford, IL: Tan Books, 1976), I: 547–48.

6. Ibid., 549–50.

7. Anne Catherine Emmerich, *The Dolorous Passion of Our Lord Jesus Christ*, Chapter VIII, §156. Because there have been various published editions of this book, all citations will provide chapter and section numbers as found in an online edition at: www.emmerich1.com/DOLOROUS_PASSION_OF_OUR_LORD_JESUS_CHRIST .htm.

8. Emmerich, *Dolorous Passion*, Ch. IX, §158–60.

9. Peter J. Boyer, "The Jesus War: Mel Gibson's Obsession." *The New Yorker* (Sept. 15, 2003): 71.

10. Diane Sawyer, "From Pain to *Passion*: A *Primetime* Event" (Feb. 16, 2004).

11. Pontifical Biblical Commission, *The Interpretation of the Bible in the Roman Catholic Church* (1993), IV, A, 3.

12. Martin Hengel, *Crucifixion* (Philadelphia: Fortress Press, 1982; J. F. Strange, "Crucifixion, Method of," *The Interpreter's Dictionary of the Bible* (Nashville: Abingdon Press, 1981), V, 199–200.

13. Josephus, *Wars* 2.12.1.

14. U.S. Bishops, *Criteria for the Evaluation of Dramatizations of the Passion* (1988), C, 1, c.

15. Carol Eisenberg, "Stirring Passions: Gibson's film about Jesus raises Jews' fears," *Newsday*, July 22, 2003.

16. Joseph Farah, *WorldNetDaily.com*, July 23, 2003.

17. Deal Hudson, *Crisis Magazine* e-letter, July 31, 2003.

18. Christopher Claire, "Vatican Praises Gibson's film on life of Jesus despite fears of Jewish groups," *The Scotsman*, Sept. 14, 2003.

19. Edward Idris Cardinal Cassidy, "Reflections: The Vatican Statement on the 'Shoah'," *Origins* 28/2 (May 28, 1998): 31.

CHAPTER THIRTEEN

~

Gibson's Passion in the Face of the Shoah's Ethical Considerations

John T. Pawlikowski

A contemporary film on Christian antisemitism describes this centuries-long social disease as a "shadow" over the cross. Recent Catholic documents have spoken in even stronger language. In 1989, the Pontifical Commission for Justice and Peace insisted that "harboring racist thoughts and entertaining racist attitudes is a sin."[1] And it clearly placed antisemitism high on its list of continuing manifestations of racist ideologies that fall into the sinful column. In point of fact, it termed antisemitism "the most tragic form that racist ideology has assumed in our century."[2]

Pope John Paul II has provided decisive leadership in the effort to raise the consciousness of the global community regarding the fundamental sinfulness of the social disease we call antisemitism. During a visit to Hungary in 1991, conscious of the post–Communist era resurgence of antisemitism in certain parts of Central and Eastern Europe, John Paul II spoke of the urgent task of repentance and reconciliation. "In face of a risk of a resurgence and spread of antisemitic feelings, attitudes, and initiatives," he said, ". . . we must teach consciences to consider antisemitism, and all forms of racism, as sins against God and humanity."[3] In his book *Crossing the Threshold of Hope*, the Pope repeated this indictment of antisemitism, calling it "a great sin against humanity."[4]

Many Protestant church statements have followed in this same vein regarding the basic immorality of antisemitism. The 2001 comprehensive document on Christian-Jewish relations issued by the Fellowship of Reformation Churches in Europe quotes a number of documents from its member churches, which clearly condemn antisemitism. The statement from the Synod of the Evangelical Lutheran Church in the Rhineland (Germany) issued in 1980 is highlighted as is a 1998 declaration from the General Synod of the Evangelical Lutheran Church in Austria which insists that the Christian churches must share responsibility for the Shoah (the Holocaust) and are duty bound "to resist any form of social or individual anti-Semitism."[5]

In my own writings on the Shoah I have insisted that we cannot view Nazism as simply the final and most gruesome form of classical Christian antisemitism. Hitler and his cohorts took antisemitism to a new level by setting it within a biological framework that totally dehumanized Jews, thereby making them into vermin. Unlike the Christian version which aimed at marginalizing Jews and making them perpetually miserable as a supposed reminder of what happens to people who reject Christ, the Nazi version of antisemitism aimed at the total annihilation of the Jewish community worldwide. Both forms of antisemitism are fundamentally immoral. But a distinction needs to be maintained.

Though I have steadfastly maintained over the years that we cannot draw a simple straight line between the anti-Jewish attitudes within the Christian tradition beginning with the Church Fathers and the Nazi form of antisemitism, any effort to disconnect the two totally is equally in error. This is a tendency one even finds in the 1998 Vatican document on the Shoah, We Remember. I have critiqued We Remember at length on this point.[6] In point of fact much of the support by baptized Christians for the Nazi program was motivated by the classical outlook toward Jews and Judaism within the churches. We Remember speaks of "wayward members" of the church being responsible for Christian antisemitism. The problem is that most of these "wayward members" likely thought they were following church teaching in their negative attitudes because of what they heard continually in sermons and the depictions they saw in Christian art. The famous facade of the medieval cathedral in Strasbourg, France, with its depiction of the vibrant Church and the bedraggled and blindfolded Synagogue is a striking illustration of how deeply antisemitism became embedded in the popular religious culture of the period.

There is need to recognize that the widespread acquiescence and even collaboration with the Nazi effort to exterminate Jews was influenced by the antisemitic legacy of Christianity. This legacy provided what I like to term "an indispensable seedbed" for the growth of Nazism. Nazi ideologues drew upon classical anti-Jewish church legislation in developing the laws by which they dispossessed Jews of property and civil rights, and they exploited Christian-based cultural entities such as the Oberammergau passion play to promote Nazi ideology among the masses.

In light of the very real involvement of classical Christian antisemitism with the Nazi onslaught against the Jews we Christians have a moral obligation in the post-Holocaust era to wipe out any remaining vestiges of this cancer embedded in the institutional church. We very much need a spiritual chemotherapy in this regard. Regrettably *The Passion of the Christ* moves us in the opposite direction. It has become a carrier of traditional antisemitism even though it may not bring about antisemitic attacks on the Jewish community. Its fundamental storyline of a Jewish cabal pursing Jesus relentlessly until its members could intimidate a weak-kneed Pilate into ordering his execution, the interjection of the blood libel curse from Matthew 27:25 (arguably the most toxic New Testament text historically in terms of supporting Christian antisemitism), the use of devil imagery in connection with the Jews and the total fabrication about the destruction in the Temple at the time of Jesus' death are all repetitions of classical antisemitic themes which Mel Gibson has brought back to the forefront. This is particularly troubling if the film is to be marketed as a DVD for use in Christian education. It has the possibility of undermining the more than forty years of detailed work on revising textbooks within Catholicism and Protestantism. This causes great concern at this time when the rise of antisemitism has been amply documented by the European Union and in a recent Pew Research Center Survey in which the number of people attributing responsibility for Jesus' death to the Jews has increased.[7]

Church leadership now faces a significant moral challenge. Clearly, institutional Christianity generally failed its membership in perceiving and making clear the return to classical Christian antisemitic themes in the film. There were a few notable exceptions to this record such as the statements from the Evangelical Church in Germany, the strong statement from the French Catholic Episcopal Conference, and a joint statement by leaders of the Catholic and Lutheran churches in Germany. There were some strong statements as well by leaders of Orthodox Christianity but they tended to focus on distortions of Christian theology in the film. But by and large, church leadership failed to expose *The Passion of the Christ* as a carrier of classical Christian antisemitism. In light of the experience of the Holocaust there was need for a clear-cut repudiation of the film in this regard. What was required in terms of post-Holocaust morality was the honest language of the 1997 French Bishops' document on the Shoah: "Too many pastors of the Church by their silence offended both against the Church and its mission. Today we confess that this silence was a grievous offense." Those words unfortunately are somewhat applicable to the situation surrounding the release of the Gibson film. Silence, and even outright support of the film, dominated Christian institutional responses despite the fact that many scholars and sensitive lay people did clearly raise the issue of the film's antisemitic potential.

A committed moral response to the Holocaust requires zero tolerance for antisemitism (or any other manifestation of racism). Gibson's reseeding of Christian consciousness with the traditional antisemitic imagery must be identified for what it is—a basic violation of post-Holocaust morality. It has been disturbing to me as person intensely involved with the discussion of the film for over a year to see how few church leaders seem aware of Christianity's antisemitic legacy. The minister of the megachurch in the Chicago area who interviewed Mel Gibson on stage in connection with one of the final pre-screenings never raised a word about this legacy in his lengthy interview. But an evangelical Christian scholar with whom I shared an extended radio interview did admit, to his credit, that the evangelical Christian community had failed to raise the issue of antisemitism in promoting the film. This seems to be continued vindication of the late Fr. Edward Flannery's remark that Jews know best the pages of Christian history which Christians have frequently torn out of their textbooks. With good reason many Jews in the dialogue have expressed disappointment at the lack of Christian acknowledgment of the antisemitic aspects of *The Passion of the Christ*.

If Christian leaders are to restore a sense of moral credibility with regard to the film they must make it clear that the film cannot become a central educational tool within the churches as Gibson hopes it will. The film cannot replace the revised textbooks in terms of understanding the crucifixion of Jesus. This must be communicated in a clear and decisive manner by Christian leaders to the people in their churches responsible for educational programs if we are to return to the moral high ground after *The Passion of the Christ*.

Apart from the morally challenging issue of antisemitism in the Gibson film, there are other important ethical questions that arise from the theological perspective that undergirds the film. The first has to do with the theological significance of Jesus' death in terms of human salvation. For Gibson, the only dimension of Jesus' life that ultimately matters in terms of redemption is the intensity of his suffering and painful death. His public ministry and even his resurrection are relegated to second place at best. Orthodox Christian leaders have reacted quite negatively to what they regard as Gibson's downgrading of the resurrection in the film.

It is important to recognize the theological orientation of *The Passion of the Christ* in terms of atonement as well as the moral problems this orientation raises. Images of devils, ravens, and other satanic symbols are frequent in the film. These images are meant to highlight Satan's central role in the drama of salvation in Gibson's eyes. In this theological understanding Jesus' death brought about the reconciliation of humanity and God by overcoming its deep-seated sinfulness. The question of how Jesus' spilling of blood accomplished this resulted in various theological understandings up to the year 1200.

Gibson has set *The Passion of the Christ* in the framework of the oldest and grimmest of these theologies. He ignores the more recent and appealing approaches which first surfaced around 1100 and which continue as the prevailing theories in our time. The theological framework selected by Gibson is usually referred to as the "ransom theory." Developed by early church writers such as Origen, Irenaeus, and Augustine, it revolves around the belief that Adam's original sin delivered humanity into satanic hands. Humans could experience liberation from Satan's powerful grip only through the payment of a ransom by God to the Evil One. Augustine compared this atonement process to a mousetrap. Jesus' crucifixion involved substitution of a sinless Christ as trap to trick Satan into exceeding his power which extended only to sinners. When Satan overextended his reach by claiming a sinless Christ, he in fact relinquished any power over future humanity. In this theological vision, adapted by Gibson, the big loser is Satan. The intense suffering of the sinless Jesus has deluded him and appeased him, leaving him with no remaining influence over the salvation of the human community.

The atonement theology that serves as the substrate for *The Passion of the Christ* generally lost its appeal in Western theological thinking around 1100. It is virtually absent from the theologies of Eastern Christianity. The Benedictine Archbishop of Canterbury, Anselm of Bec (c. 1033–1109), replaced the ransom theory in his famous essay *Cur Deus Homo* which appeared in 1098. Satan has no role in the atonement process according to Anselm. Rather he argued that only a being who combined divinity with humanity could provide God the infinite compensation for the profound offence he had endured through human disobedience. In Anselm's perspective, God had no interest in a ransom being paid to Satan as the older theological viewpoint had maintained. Rather he required a repayment of an infinite value from humanity. Only a God-Man could in fact make such a repayment because it had to have infinite value while at the same being offered to God by someone fully human. What mattered for Anselm was not neutralization of Satan but the willingness of a God-Man to sacrifice all in the name of humanity. The manner of Jesus' death was inconsequential for Anselm.

A generation or so later Abelard advanced Anselm's perspective by interpreting the atonement not as a legal transaction consummated in Jesus' crucifixion but rather as flowing from God's infinite love for humanity demonstrated in Christ's public ministry. Jesus' sacrifice on Calvary is not divorced from his public ministry, as is largely the case in the Gibson film, but represents the pinnacle of his life of loving service of humanity. A life of love which may well involve ultimate sacrifice demonstrated by Jesus becomes the model for members of the Christian community. While Abelard's view drew opposition from the likes of a St. Bernard in his own time, by 1800 it had gained widespread acceptance in Western theological circles.

However, another approach to salvation also was becoming influential. According to the "substitutionary atonement" perspective, God's justice could be satisfied only if the punishment that all sinful human beings deserved was actually administered. It could not simply be rescinded. Jesus, in this view, substituted himself as the one upon whom this righteous divine punishment fell and thereby appeased God. In a distortion of Anselm, the punishment that Jesus was able to endure because of his divinity was thereby sufficient to satisfy God's honor. Lost in this perspective is the God of limitless mercy and forgiveness of whom Jesus preached in such parables as the Prodigal Son, the Lost Coin, and the Unforgiving Servant.

The Passion of the Christ returns us to the theology that prevailed prior to Anselm and Abelard in which Satan is depicted as roaming the world in search of whomever he might devour and blends it with the substitutionary atonement stress on the infinite amount of pain necessary to make things right with God. In largely striking Satan from the process of human salvation Anselm and later Abelard placed divine love at the center of the redemptive process. Satan's alleged need for a payoff was basically shelved until Gibson sought to revive it. Combined with the film's fixation on Jesus' pains, the movie obscures the infinite mercy and love of the One Jesus called Abba.

Gibson's theological perspectives are explained by his reliance on the visions of Anna Katharina Emmerich. For Clemens von Brentano, the priest who converted Emmerich's visions into a written text, was involved in trying to undermine the growing dominance of the theological understanding of atonement championed by Anselm and Abelard as way of overcoming what he saw as the deep-seated sinfulness of his contemporaries. Thus Gibson's inclusion of episodes from her visions serves the goal of restoring the pre-Anselmian version of atonement to a place of primacy in Christian belief as an antidote for contemporary sinfulness in his own society of today. Professor Will Johnston of the Yarra Theological Union in Melbourne, Australia, has rightly argued that the von Brentano-Gibson perspective is far more medieval than biblical.

This theological background of the Gibson film is particularly important for the issue of morality in light of the Holocaust. Ethicians such as Peter Haas and Didier Pollefeyt as well as a historian such as Peter Hayes have pointed to the destruction of any notion of personal commitment within the so-called "Nazi ethic." Haas first raised this problem in his 1988 volume *Morality After Auschwitz: The Radical Challenge Of The Nazi Ethic*.[8] As Haas sees it, the Nazis created an approach to human activity that froze out all sense of morality as a matter of personal commitment. What went awry in terms of morality during the Nazi era, according to Haas, was the pre-definition of what constituted morality. Nazism proclaimed only what was right and wrong from a scientific perspective and therefore was unquestionable. This resulted in people engaging in the most atrocious forms of action because they regarded such activities as morally mandated. People, even the highly educated, fell into line because they had lost any genuine sense of an intimate relationship between the human person as a moral agent and the moral act. To counter the "Nazi ethic" there is need in Haas' view to restore human relationship, cooperation, openness to the other, and compassion for the other.

Didier Pollefeyt takes issue with Haas' language about a "Nazi ethic." He prefers to speak of Nazism's perversion of authentic morality. But, despite this disagreement with Haas over terminology, Pollefeyt acknowledges the same negative characteristics as Haas in terms of the Nazis' approach to human behavior. In a manner similar to Haas, Pollefeyt speaks of a "moral sameness" in Nazi ideology. Such a mindset has the effect of removing any personal sense of responsibility from the framework of human response. In this setting there is a total absence of any fundamental moral notions such as mercy and compassion.[9]

In my judgment both Pollefeyt and Haas have brought to the fore a critical aspect of Nazism that remains a central dimension of any post-Holocaust discussion of ethics. In highlighting the crucial importance of the Nazi framework for human response, whether one decides in the end to term it an "ethic" or not, they have uncovered a destructive impulse in modern society (and in postmodernity as well)—the programming of human societal responses through political, cultural, and economic structures.

Historian Peter Hayes has further illuminated this dimension of Nazism in his continuing research on business leaders in the period of the Third Reich.[10] Hayes' work offers some of the most incisive insights into the consciousness and conscience of those shaping the dynamics of human response on the Nazi side during World War II. In the end, Hayes concludes, German big business was willing to "walk over corpses," as he puts it, despite an initial moral hesitation regarding the Nazi program. Hayes admits that there were numerous internal factors that aided the process of moral numbing within the German business community. But especially influential was Nazism's construction of a social framework in which the successful pursuit of corporate survival had to serve, at least outwardly, the established goals and ideological requirements set by the Nazi political authorities.

The indifference of German business leaders which became increasingly commonplace in the later days of the Third Reich exposes the penchant to hide behind professional responsibilities in the face of deep moral challenges, a reality that continues unabated in contemporary society. During the Nazi era an unquestioned belief within the German business community that its members were obliged to seek the best possible return for the firm and to secure its future, which in decent contexts can serve as a barrier against corruption and inept management, deteriorated into a mere excuse for participation in cruel and eventually murderous actions and even a sense that there existed a mandate to do such. For Hayes the most alarming aspect of this development was not merely complicity in mass murder, but a morally destructive conviction of innocence in the process among many of the business leaders. They found it increasingly easy to submerge any moral hesitations that might arise within them with the response, "What else can I do?" losing sight of the far more critical question, "What must I never do?" The divorce between personal moral responsibility and societal activity spoken of by Haas and Pollefeyt is clearly validated in Hayes' research on the German business community.

The so-called "Nazi ethic" has opened up what unquestionably is one of the most decisive moral questions today. How can the human community maintain a sense of human responsibility in a global system of human organization? The Holocaust has shown us how destructive a failure to address this question head-on can be for human and creational survival.

Now how does this connect with the Gibson film? As I see it, the basic theological perspective on atonement chosen by Gibson as the foundation for the film plays right into the destruction of personal commitment described by Hayes, Pollefeyt, and Haas. For the emphasis in the early patristic-based approach to atonement places the burden of human salvation entirely on God and his suffering Son. Neither Jesus' ministry in the world nor human activity matter much in terms of personal redemption. This stands in sharp contrast to the subsequent theological outlook developed by Anselm and Abelard and confirmed by Pope John Paul II in his writings on human co-creatorship.

Such a viewpoint also contradicts the basic moral thrust of the II Vatican Council, especially its declaration on the Church and the Modern World (*Gaudium et Spes*), and subsequent central documents such as the 1971 Roman Synod document on Justice in the World where the pursuit of justice is described as integral to the authentic proclamation of the gospel. Thus in my judgment the basic theology of *The Passion of the Christ*, whether directly intended by Gibson or not, opens the door to the marginalization of concrete human activity in terms of personal salvation. It is not what I do but what God has done for me and the rest of humanity that matters. No authentic theology would deny the primacy of divine action in the process. But the reduction of expressed moral commitment to an inconsequential status opens the door to the kind of moral deterioration in the Nazi era described by Haas, Pollefeyt, and Hayes.

Gibson himself has unfortunately demonstrated in his own actions in connection with the process of editing *The Passion of the Christ* some semblance of the moral numbing that became a trademark of the Shoah. This is particularly evident in how he has cynically manipulated the use of the blood curse from Matt 27:25 in the film. A scholars group of which I was a part initially identified the inclusion of this problematical text as one of the disturbing aspects of the original shooting script which we examined. After its inclusion became known and public criticism began to surface, Gibson announced its removal from the script. But he added that he was taking it out for fear that Jews would have his throat if he retained it. It stayed out for much of the time the early cuts of the film were being developed. But in the final pre-screenings a few weeks before the film's formal release it was suddenly restored. As criticism again arose Gibson announced he might remove it. In the end, at least in the version released in the United States, the curse is spoken by the High Priest in Aramaic, but it is not translated in the subtitles.

This verse from Matthew is arguably the most toxic New Testament text historically in terms of the suffering and death of Jews over the centuries in Christian societies. It served as the biblical basis for much of the social legislation that marginalized Jews and reduced them to a miserable, wandering status for much of Christian history. Yet in dealing with the text, Gibson shows not the slightest degree of sensitivity to the profoundly immoral amplification of it throughout history. He has a theological framework for this film with regard to atonement. Nothing else really matters. In so doing, he establishes through his personal stance a model for human activity in which the demonstrated history of Jewish suffering at the hands of Christians over the centuries matters little. And as the biblical scholar Elisabeth Schüssler Fiorenza has argued, the degradation of the Jews opened the door to the degradation of women and other groups. Gibson's moral failure in this regard extends to those Christian leaders who likewise have shown zero sensitivity to the moral cancer that antisemitism has seeded in the heart of Christianity virtually since its birth.

The final point I would raise concerns the violence in the film. It is destructively excessive in my judgment. There exists neither a historical or biblical basis for the bloody gore given to us by Gibson. Clearly Jesus' death was painful. But there is no basis for presenting it as a total ripping off of Jesus' flesh which Gibson's Jesus actually invites by forcing himself to stand again after the first round of beating (in line with substitutionary atonement theology). Nor is there any warrant for showing the Romans scourging Jesus frontally, an action which they knew would literally rip out their victim's internal organs. The New Testament certainly does not present salvation as resulting from the extremity of Jesus' sufferings.

But there is even a more profound point involved in Gibson's bloody depiction of Jesus, one that is especially pertinent to a discussion of the film's ethical implications. What we see in Jesus in this film is a hunk of humanity totally torn apart. We see little or nothing of the soul and spirit of Jesus. A number of perceptive film critics such as Michael Wilmington of the Chicago *Tribune* have pointed this out. Jesus is totally dehumanized by Gibson as are the Roman soldiers directly involved in beating him to a pulp. Chicago Theological Seminary President Susan Thistlethwaite has described this aspect of the film as sadomasochistic. I think she is basically correct in her assessment.

The fundamental dehumanization that marks the film becomes particularly disturbing when we consider that a number of prominent Holocaust scholars such as Henry Friedlander have pointed to dehumanization as a central feature of Nazi ideology.[11] In reporting on the daily activities in death camps Nazi administrators removed all human references to their victims. Religious leaders today such as Pope John Paul II have continually pointed to the need to reaffirm the dignity of all human persons. Biblical scholars such as Donald Senior have emphasized "love of enemy" as a distinguishing dimension of Jesus' basic proclamation in the gospels,[12] a dimension paid lip service to by the movie, but neutralized by the raven's pecking out the eye of the crucifixion victim who had dared to mock Jesus. The whole anti-human ethos of *The Passion of the Christ* significantly undercuts these vital themes in Christian faith. Religion's most important contribution today may in fact lie in an uncompromised defense of human dignity in the face of the growing depersonalization in our increasingly globalized world. If the extreme violence and human brutalization so central to *The Passion of the Christ* become a centerpiece of the contemporary understanding of Jesus' message, suffering and death, it can seriously undercut the challenge now facing religion to become a proactive force in the protection of human dignity worldwide that is so much a moral imperative in light of the experience of the Holocaust.

Overall, *The Passion of the Christ* remains a highly problematic film from the standpoint of contemporary morality, especially when we reflect on ethical commitment through the lens of the Holocaust. Although I am not arguing that Mel Gibson is a Nazi sympathizer or anything of that sort, his film nevertheless poses serious ethical questions. Christian leaders and educators have a basic decision before them. Will they allow the basic ethos of the Gibson film to dominate Christian faith understanding and expression in the coming years? If they do, I believe they are failing to honor the memory of the victims of the Holocaust.

Notes

1. Pontifical Council for Justice & Peace, *The Church and Racism: Towards a More Fraternal* Society (Washington, DC: United States Catholic Conference, 1988), 34 (#24).

2. Pontifical Council, *The Church and Racism*, 23 (#15).

3. Pope John Paul II, "The Sinfulness of Antisemitism," *Origins* 23, no. 13 (5 September 1991): 204.

4. Pope John Paul II, *Crossing the Threshold of Hope*, ed. Vittorio Messori (New York: Alfred A. Knopf, 1994), 96.

5. Leuenberg Church Fellowship, *Church and Israel* (Frankfurt am Main, Germany: Verlag Otto Lembeck, 2001), 102.

6. John T. Pawlikowski, "The Vatican and the Holocaust: Putting *We Remember* in Context," in *Ethics in the Shadow of the Holocaust: Christian and Jewish Perspectives*, ed. Judith H. Banki and John T. Pawlikowski (Franklin, Wisconsin and Chicago: Sheed & Ward, 2001).

7. Religious News Service, 2 April 2004.

8. Peter J. Haas, *Morality after Auschwitz: The Radical Challenge of the Nazi Ethic* (Philadelphia: 1988); also, "The Morality of Auschwitz: Moral Language and the Nazi Ethic," in *Remembering for the Future*, vol. 2, ed. Franklin Littell and others (Oxford: Pergamon, 1989), 1893–1902; and "Doing Ethics in an Age of Science," in *Good and Evil After Auschwitz: Ethical Implications for Today*, ed. Jack Bemporad, John T. Pawlikowski, and Joseph Sievers (Hoboken, New Jersey: KTAV, 2000), 109–17.

9. Didier Pollefeyt, "The Morality of Auschwitz? A Critical Confrontation with Peter Haas' Ethical Interpretation of the Holocaust," in *Good and Evil*, ed. Bemporad, Pawlikowski, and Sievers, 119–37.

10. Peter Hayes, "Conscience, Knowledge, and 'Secondary Ethics': German Corporate Executives from 'Aryanization' to the Holocaust," in *Ethics in the Shadow of the Holocaust*, ed. Banki and Pawlikowski, 313–35; also *Industry and Ideology: I. G. Farben in the Nazi Era* (Cambridge: Cambridge University Press, 1988); and "Profits and Persecution: German Big Business and the Holocaust" (Washington, DC: Center for Advanced Holocaust Studies, United States Holocaust Memorial Museum, 1998).

11. Henry Friedlander, "The Manipulation of Language," in *The Holocaust: Ideology, Bureaucracy, and Genocide,* ed. Henry Friedlander and Sybil Milton (Millwood, New York: Kraus International Publications, 1980), 103–13.

12. Donald Senior, "Jesus' Most Scandalous Teaching," in *Biblical and Theological Reflections on "The Challenge of Peace,"* ed. John T. Pawlikowski and Donald Senior (Wilmington, Delaware: Michael Glazier, 1984), 55–69.

CHAPTER FOURTEEN

~

Were You There When They Crucified My Lord? The Psychological Risks of "Witnessing" the Passion

Maddy Cunningham

The words of the African-American spiritual "Were you there when they crucified my Lord?" are meant to evoke the reality of the passion, death, and resurrection of Jesus, which are central events in the spiritual lives of Christians. The suffering and death of Jesus, for Christians, is the greatest act of love for humankind; his resurrection, the greatest hope.

On Ash Wednesday 2004, Mel Gibson's *The Passion of the Christ* opened in theaters throughout the United States. This film stirred great controversy regarding its historical accuracy, its use of the New Testament, and concerns about antisemitism. However, there has been little focus on the potential psychological impact of this film on the viewer.

The Passion of the Christ graphically portrays the last twelve hours of Jesus' life. The film depicts the suffering and torture of Jesus in stunningly gruesome detail. From the arrest in the Garden of Gethsemane to his death on the cross, Jesus is hit, beaten, whipped, spat upon, and jeered at. From the blood-thirsty crowd to the soldiers in charge of his arrest and death, startlingly few individuals display any compassion or sense of decency. Along with visual images of horror, the viewer is exposed to the sounds of suffering which accompany the violence. This graphic portrayal does not rely on the imagination of the viewer, but rather recreates scenes so realistically that viewers actually experience the events as witnesses. Could this film have adverse psychological impact on viewers? Why would this impact differ from other spiritual practices that encourage Christians to meditate on the events associated with the passion and death of Jesus? In this essay, I propose that *The*

169

Passion of the Christ may have a negative psychological impact on some viewers. I will support this using the research on media violence and the theoretical framework of secondary traumatization that considers those affected by indirect exposure to extreme events. I further propose several reasons viewers may have adverse reactions to the film.

Exposure to Media Violence

In the past several decades numerous research studies have documented a relationship between exposure to media violence and negative aftereffects. A major focus of these studies is the potential for viewers to re-enact aggressive acts after exposure. Although this potential is significant, James Potter, a scholar on media violence, criticizes limiting the focus of attention to behavioral consequences alone. These effects are easier to measure, are what people tend to notice, and in children, the most studied group, are a prevalent reaction. Potter argues, however, that we need to broaden our view to include psychological reactions as well as delayed and long-term effects of violent media content. He further argues that most viewers are not aware of the impact of exposure on themselves, partly because they do not know what to look for. Viewers often think others are vulnerable to negative effects of a particular exposure, without realizing the same potential for themselves. Focusing on behavioral reactions only, such as imitation, underestimates the potential harm of exposure to media violence. A common assumption is that if one does not imitate aggressive behaviors immediately after exposure, there are no negative effects. Pertinent to the discussion in this essay is the concern that research studies of media exposure rarely include emotional responses. To what extent does a film evoke fear, rage, or sadness? Exclusion of such effects can lead one to underestimate the importance of these responses after exposure.[1]

Secondary Traumatic Stress

Along with the research on exposure to media violence, the concept of secondary trauma provides a useful framework to understand the possible negative psychological impact on viewers of *The Passion of the Christ*. Trauma experts originally focused on the direct victims of disasters and other extreme events. However, over the last few decades there is an increasing awareness that those indirectly exposed to extreme events are also adversely affected. For example, loved ones of trauma victims or those that witness the suffering of others often demonstrate signs of traumatic stress. This phenomenon is referred to by traumatologists as secondary or indirect trauma.[2] Numerous scholars within this field have studied several groups to support this concept. Groups studied include disaster recovery personnel, families of rape victims, families of Vietnam veterans, playmates of kidnapped children, and trauma therapists working with survivors. Furthermore, research on the effects on viewers of media coverage of the Challenger disaster[3] and the Oklahoma City bombing[4] indicate that one does not have to be a witness to the actual event to have adverse reactions.

Secondary trauma theory, then, allows one to understand that "witnessing" the suffering of another, especially someone who is meaningful to us, poses risk for traumatic stress.[5] Because of the graphic depiction of the events in The Passion of the Christ viewers will feel like witnesses to the actual events, which may increase the likelihood of distress. Therefore, it is plausible that witnessing the intense suffering and torture of Jesus can be extremely upsetting for viewers, especially Christian viewers who have a significant relationship with the "victim."

Why *The Passion of the Christ* May Be Psychologically Harmful

I am not arguing that viewers of this film will develop post-traumatic stress disorder or any other psychological disorder from seeing it. However, using the research on exposure to media violence and secondary trauma theory as a context, I do propose that there are several reasons why this particular movie may be in a unique position to generate unusual distress among moviegoers, and that this distress may be psychologically harmful for some. These reasons include that The Passion of the Christ is not like other violent films, that the viewers of this film are different from other viewers of violent movies, and that the encouragement of clergypersons increases the risk for viewers.

Not Just Another Violent Film

The Passion of the Christ may have adverse psychological effects because it is not just another violent film released by Hollywood, such as Nightmare on Elm Street, Psycho, or Silence of the Lambs. The central "character" in this movie is Jesus Christ, a historical and spiritual leader with whom many viewers believe they have a personal relationship. Key to understanding secondary trauma is the capacity for empathy and identification.[6] Witnesses who feel a deep emotional attachment or have a high capacity for caring are at higher risk for distress. Furthermore, when one can identify with the victim, it is more likely that one will suffer vicariously along with him. Therefore, viewers who identify with Jesus or have a deep emotional attachment to him will theoretically feel distraught by witnessing the graphic portrayal of his suffering. And unlike other characters that one may become identified with or attached to in the course of a film, Christian viewers feel this connection and identification with Jesus before the movie begins. This makes it even more likely that they will be deeply affected by witnessing these events portrayed in such a realistic manner. For many Christian viewers this film is tantamount to watching a loved one tortured and executed. Although Christians are aware of the events of Holy Week long before the release of this movie, they have never before been exposed to these events in such an unrelenting realistic manner. Gibson, himself, refers to other films as "sterilized religious epics." One favorable review of the movie underlines the difference from others by stating that one does not "view" this film, but rather "experiences" it. He stated it "was an encounter, unlike anything I have ever experienced."[7] And it is the fact that one "experiences" these events that presents the potential for adverse reactions. Furthermore, this film is not only violent, but the violence is gratuitous. One is left confused about the extent of hatred and abuse perpetrated on Jesus. Since the ministry of Jesus is omitted from the film and the motivations of his opponents are not developed, the treatment of Jesus is without context.

There are many disturbing aspects to *The Passion of the Christ*. The graphic brutality of the scourging scene, which continues for over ten minutes, is quite disturbing in itself. However, the violence is not only unrelenting, it is sadistic. The perpetrators and some onlookers have looks of sheer delight and glee on their faces. Likewise, many individuals in the crowd scenes throughout the movie are portrayed as jeering and bloodthirsty. Rarely does one see a compassionate face. This debased view of humanity is very disturbing. A diminished view of humanity often accompanies exposure to cruelty which is intentionally perpetrated.[8]

A particularly disturbing scene occurs after Judas betrays Jesus and, regretting his deed, attempts to return the silver coins he had been paid. When denied, he leaves and, clearly filled with torment, is found sitting by a large rock. A group of young boys at play approach him. Initially, the boys appear concerned that Judas is so distraught, but, when dismissed by him, these children turn into demons and ultimately chase Judas into the hills where he commits suicide. Although the demons may exist in the mind of Judas, the portrayal of young children and the change from kind, considerate boys to demonic figures is quite distressing.

One scene, which in itself is not gruesome, highlights the emotional effect of the movie. Veronica, moved by compassion for Jesus, attempts to give him a drink of water. Out of nowhere a soldier viciously kicks the jug from her hand. The jug shatters on the pavement. So tense is the viewer at this point that one becomes startled by this comparatively mild display of violence. This type of reaction is an example of the hyper-alert or hyper-startle response associated with traumatic stress.[9] Because one's anxiety has been aroused to such a high level when one has endured or witnessed a horrific event, relatively mild stimuli may cause reactions one usually expects only with a stronger stimulus.

Signs of Secondary Trauma

Along with the hyper-startle response described above, there are two major categories of traumatic responses, those associated with flooding or intrusion and those associated with avoidance or numbness.[10] When individuals are overwhelmed by the events witnessed, they may have difficulty managing their emotions and intrusive images of violence come to mind unintentionally. Some viewers of *The Passion of the Christ* reported similar reactions such as "sobbing uncontrollably," feeling "nauseous," or difficulty getting "the images out of their mind." Other viewers report feeling overwhelming sadness or grief as they watched someone who was vitally important in their spiritual lives being brutalized. Nightmares or re-experiencing the horrific images from the film when exposed to the Passion narratives during Holy Week or other times when the events of the Passion are recalled are other indicators of flooding responses.

The other category of reactions, avoidance, or numbing refers to those reactions used by individuals to block out feelings and avoid reminders of the events. Many viewers, including a film critic,[11] said they needed to "look away" in order to avoid the images being depicted. Others stated they "wanted to walk out of the theater."[12] A sense of numbness is a common response to exposure to distressing material. The images, which at first are shocking, no longer evoked that response. Individuals feel a sense of being immune to the horror before them. And although this numbness may feel like relief, a great deal of emotional energy is used to protect them from the shock. Extreme attempts at avoidance are referred to as dissociation. In this phenomenon, the individual emotionally distances him- or herself from what is happening before their eyes. I found myself "wondering" if the special effects used to create the scarred body of Jesus were achieved with makeup or a costume. Having worked with trauma victims for several years, I was quite aware that I was dissociating from the horrible images playing out before me on the screen. Whether viewers experienced a hyper-startle response, or signs of flooding, or avoidance and numbing, these reactions support the premise of this essay that viewing the brutal torture of Jesus was highly distressing. Such reactions are not expected at clinically significant levels associated with psychological disorders, such as post-traumatic stress disorder, but there is still enough distress to cause concern about the emotional effect of this film.

Why This Exposure Differs from Other Practices

Contemplation and meditation on the events of the Passion and death of Jesus are common spiritual practices for Christians. Why is *The Passion of the Christ* different from the Stations of the Cross or meditating on scripture passages, all of which are intended for reflection on the reality of Jesus' suffering? The spiritual practice *lectio divina*[13] originated with the monastic tradition. Monks chose a particular passage from the daily scripture reading on which to reflect. Using this practice, contemporary devotees choose to meditate on a particular aspect of a scripture reading that appeals to them and to place themselves in the scene depicted. How would it feel to be among the crowd as Jesus was questioned by Pilate? What would you experience if you were in the Garden with Jesus and asked to pray? If you stood at the foot of the cross what would you feel, or what would you say to Jesus or he to you? The goal of the practice is to be present in the events that unfold in the scripture passages. Believers are asked to choose a passage that has particular appeal to them in the present moment and to observe in detail the setting of the passage. What is seen, heard, smelled, or felt? Next, one focuses on the weather, what is happening in the story, or the atmosphere evoked. Who is he or she in the crowd, how does he or she feel about what is happening? Is he or she drawn to anyone in the scene and if so, is he or she able to enter into a dialogue with this person? This exercise can be particularly powerful for believers, helping to evoke the reality of the events and the significance of them in their personal life.

A common devotion, especially during the liturgical season of Lent, is the Stations of the Cross. Fourteen scenes from the passion and death of Jesus are depicted and the devotee meditates and prays at each Station. I remember as a school child attending the Stations of the Cross each Friday afternoon during Lent. At the station "Jesus is nailed to the Cross" the accompanying prayer suggested we contemplate on the pain we feel when we prick our finger with a pin and to think about how much more painful it must be for Jesus to have nails hammered into his hands. One of the most gruesome scenes in *The Passion of the Christ* is the nailing of Jesus to the cross. The realism is nauseating. In fact, it is so realistic that one shuns away from meditation. In contrast, the approach mentioned above was effective. I remember it clearly almost forty years later. When the scene is as graphic as that depicted in the movie, one is likely to avoid reminders of it because it was too painful.

In the above-described devotions, one can use the practice similarly to a Rorschach inkblot. The practice is neutral enough that each individual can project whatever images he or she finds meaningful at the particular time of the practice and interpret the passage according to what the person needs spiritually at the time. For example, at one point in the spiritual journey, an individual may find it helpful to focus on Jesus' endurance of his suffering during the Passion. At another time, one may benefit from understanding his or her own capacity for meanness or cruelty. However the practice is used, the stimulus is not overly graphic and therefore, the mind is capable of protecting itself. Spiritual seekers will go to their own edge of endurance. When exposed to a graphic film such as *The Passion of the Christ* one has no control over the images and sounds that accompany the suffering of Jesus. And therefore, one can be overwhelmed by these events and suffer adverse psychological reactions. The shocking imagery portrayed in this film is intentional. Mel Gibson in his *Primetime* interview with Diane Sawyer said, "I wanted it to be shocking and I also wanted it to be extreme. I wanted it to push the viewer over the edge. And it does that." And it is because it "does that," pushes the viewer over the edge, that one can experience psychological harm from the graphic details depicted in this film. The events in life which overwhelm the person's usual capacity to cope are those which individuals find the most distressing.

The Passion of the Christ's Audience is Different

The second argument, that this film may be extremely distressing for viewers, is that many of the patrons are different from those who usually attend violent R-rated movies. Because the film is about the Passion of Jesus, many of the individuals who will attend are seeking a spiritually moving experience and may not be people who ordinarily expose themselves to violent media content. Therefore, the potential for them to be shocked and horrified by the violence is higher. They may not be prepared for what they will encounter, they may be highly sensitive to the graphic violence, and they may find the imagery presented especially distressing. As stated above, it is the individual's capacity for empathy and identification with the victim that poses the risk for extreme distress. This combined with the lack of exposure to media violence may make them doubly vulnerable to psychological harm.

Encouragement by Religious Leaders to Attend Film

And finally, many Christian religious leaders encouraged their congregants to see *The Passion of the Christ* because it is "so moving." One such minister portrayed on the news told his congregation, "Go see this R-rated film." This encouragement increases the likelihood that the movie will be seen by naïve viewers who are unprepared for the exposure to the graphic imagery. Expecting to be spiritually moved, they may in fact be overwhelmed and distraught. And since their reactions are not expected, the adverse effects of exposure may go unrecognized. Furthermore, the unexpected reaction may add another complexity of distress; that is, they think their reactions are not normal because they are different from what they were told they would feel and experience.

Potential for Hostile Acting Out

Although the focus of this essay is on the internal distress viewers may experience, one controversy raised by this film is the potential for increased antisemitism. There are two psychological theories to support this concern. The social learning theorists propose that we imitate the actions of those who model certain behaviors; thus we learn to be aggressive or violent by watching others partake in violent actions. From this perspective, violence, a learned response, becomes an acceptable option.

Alternatively, others explain the potential for violence by a defense mechanism called identification with the aggressor. This mechanism is often seen in children of abusive parents. As a defense against the helplessness that the child feels in a situation where he/she has no control, the child identifies with and takes on the characteristics of the one who does have power, the abuser. The child then reenacts the violence with others who are in the role of helpless victim. The aggressor feels power over the victim and thereby defends against feelings of helplessness. Understanding the potential for antisemitism or acting aggressively against any other group which may be perceived as "responsible" for the suffering and death of Jesus, the mechanism may work as follows. The Christian viewer may attend the movie with a strong identification with Jesus, even perceiving one's self to have a personal relationship with him. This viewer will feel not only anger at the abuse directed at Jesus, but also a sense of helplessness as he or she watches his suffering perpetrated by others. To avoid feeling powerless and to avenge the suffering, he or she may feel "justified" in vengeance against those who "did this to Jesus." While there is a great deal of well-founded concern about hostility to Jews, I believe that other groups may be potential targets as well. Feminists, homosexuals, or any other group perceived to not follow the "straight and narrow" as defined by a particular individual or group may be at risk.

DVD and Videotape Format

Eventually, *The Passion of the Christ* will be released in DVD and videotape formats. When individuals attend a newly released controversial movie, there is a great deal of conversation and viewers have the opportunity to compare their reactions to those of others. When individuals watch the video or DVD, perhaps alone, in their own home, with whom will they discuss their reactions? Furthermore, children and young adolescents who may be very disturbed by the content will have greater access to the film. In movie theaters, the R rating provides some protection for young viewers, but this diminishes when it is released in easily accessible formats.

Conclusion

The graphic portrayal of the suffering and death of Jesus in *The Passion of the Christ* leaves little to the imagination. For some viewers this film may be a powerful experience, but for others there will be a high emotional cost. Should people watch this film? Will they be moved spiritually or harmed psychologically? Individuals vary in their ability to tolerate the suffering of others, especially when it is someone who is significant to them. Individuals who have a personal history of trauma may be particularly at risk for psychological harm. They are more likely to be disturbed by the graphic portrayal of violence and suffering which may trigger painful images, feelings, and memories of their own suffering. Since prevalence rates of traumatic events in the general population are reportedly high,[14] the likelihood that many viewers will find this film distressing is also high. Individuals may underestimate the effect of these personal events, especially if they occurred in the past. Likewise, they may not realize that exposure to the violent content in this movie may trigger recall of their own traumas which may leave them frightened and confused.

Potential viewers will make their own decision to see the film or not, and reactions to it will vary. Although it is difficult to predict with certainty the psychological effect of the film prior to viewing it, pondering the following questions may help prospective viewers make a more informed choice. Can one tolerate the unrelenting gruesome portrayal of violence in this film? Is one prepared to view two hours of cruelty perpetrated on the person of Jesus? Is one well-informed about the negative consequences of media violence, especially delayed or psychological effects, so he or she may recognize them if they occur?

And finally, if viewers of this film experience a great deal of distress, it is important they find someone with whom they can discuss their thoughts and feelings. This is especially true if they have a previous history of trauma and thoughts or memories of those experiences are triggered by the violence portrayed in this movie. Regardless of personal history, distressing feelings and intrusive imagery of the graphic violence portrayed are not abnormal reactions. Processing one's experience afterwards will enable viewers to deal with these negative effects in a constructive manner.

Some might argue that the emotional distress generated by this film is a catalyst for spiritual growth. A realistic portrayal of the suffering and death of Jesus may compel viewers to re-examine their lives and change their priorities, leading to transformation. Indeed, emotional pain and adverse life circumstances at times provide the seeds of personal growth. I believe, however, that *The Passion of the Christ* will not transform, but will, in fact, overwhelm many viewers. And when overwhelmed, without help, individuals often do not move forward, but become stuck or regress. Abraham Maslow describes a *peak experience* as "an intense life-changing event that propels a person into a profound sense of communion with self, other people, the universe, or divinity." This is an apt description of a positive spiritual experience, where one grows as a result. Maslow contrasts this, however, with a *nadir experience*, which is "an intense life-changing event that plunges one into a pit of confusion, despair, or grief." Therefore, this type of experience is fraught with emotional danger.[15]

It is risky business to expect a Hollywood production to be the catalyst for spiritual growth. And if one gains spiritual insights from the film, these insights are only beneficial if they promote growth and movement toward wholeness. Otherwise, these insights "are merely fireworks displays at night that wink out and leave only the darkness."[16]

Notes

1. For more thorough discussion of media violence, the reader is referred to W. James Potter, *On Media Violence* (Thousand Oaks, CA: Sage Publications, 1999) and W. James Potter, *The 11 Myths of Media Violence* (Thousand Oaks, CA: Sage Publications, 2003).

2. For further information about secondary trauma, the reader is referred to Charles R. Figley, *Compassion Fatigue: Coping with Secondary Traumatic Stress Disorder in Those Who Treat the Traumatized* (NY: Brunner/Mazel, 1995).

3. Lenore Terr, *Too Scared to Cry: How Trauma Affects Children and Ultimately Us All* (NY: Basic Books, 1990), 324–29.

4. B. Pfefferbaum, S. Nixon, R. Tivis, D. Doughty, R. Pynoos, R. H. Gurwitch, and D. Foy, "Television Exposure in Children after a Terrorist Incident." *Psychiatry* 64 (2001): 202–11.

5. American Psychiatric Association, *Diagnostic and Statistical Manual of Mental Disorders, 4th Edition* (Washington, D.C.: American Psychiatric Association, 1994), pp. 424, 429.

6. C. R. Figley, *Compassion Fatigue*.

7. This comment was initially attributed to Paul Harvey, but was in fact made by Keith A. Fournier, founder of the *Catholic Way*, where it was originally published.

8. L. I. McCann and L. A. Pearlman, *Psychological Trauma and the Adult Survivor: Theory, Therapy, and Transformation*. (New York: Brunner/Mazel, 1990).

9. American Psychiatric Association, *Diagnostic and Statistical Manual*, pp. 424–425, 429.

10. American Psychiatric Association, *Diagnostic and Statistical Manual*, pp. 424–425, 429.

11. Joel Siegel, ABC Eyewitness News, New York City in his February 24, 2004 review.

12. These comments were made by moviegoers on local news channels and on websites after seeing the film.

13. For an excellent description of *lectio divina* see Margaret Silf, *Close to the Heart: A Guide to Personal Prayer* (Chicago: Loyola Press, 1999), 125–38.

14. In a study by S. Vrana and D. Lauterbach, 84 percent of the sample reported a traumatic event; see *Journal of Traumatic Stress* 7, no. 2 (1994): 289–302.

15. Cited in E. R. Canda and L. D. Furman, *Spiritual Diversity in Social Work Practice: The Heart of Helping* (New York: The Free Press).

16. Canda and Furman, *Spiritual Diversity*, 225.

~

CHAPTER FIFTEEN

Educating for a Faith that Feels *and* Thinks

Mary C. Boys

For a full year, I have been involved in the intense discussion and debate about the film *The Passion of the Christ* by Mel Gibson—and I anticipate that the controversy the film has spawned will continue to engage me for a considerable time to come. Truth be told, I would rather turn my attention elsewhere, as I have grown weary of the media frenzy and the inordinate attention devoted to a Hollywood movie. Yet my commitments as a religious and theological educator oblige me to pursue the important issues the film has evoked.

In a recent essay, I have tried to account for the inability of many Christians to see the ways in which Gibson magnified Jewish culpability for the death of Jesus.[1] I remain deeply concerned by the failure of so many within Christian communities, particularly authorities, to hear with understanding and empathy the concerns expressed by Jews (and some Christians) about the potential of the film to unleash (or exacerbate) antisemitism. Yet not only are Jews and Christians talking past each other, so too are Christians who hold divergent views about the interpretation, both biblical and theological, of the passion, death, and resurrection of Jesus.[2]

This deeply disturbing controversy reveals a crisis in the education of Christians. In this essay, I propose to identify the contours of what has become a crisis in Christian-Jewish relations and to muse about responses in the light of an educational theory.

The Crisis

The following incident reveals one dimension of the crisis. Several weeks ago a rabbi and I led an informal session on the film for a group of about twenty Jews in New York City. Those I met that evening were professionals also committed to Jewish learning and affiliated with a synagogue—in short, they were well-educated in both secular and religious contexts and to all appearances secure, successful persons. The next day I asked a friend, my house guest who had accompanied me to the session, what she had thought of the evening. She responded, "What I observed most of all was the fear in the room. I was so surprised because they seemed an unlikely group to have such a reaction. And then I began to realize how deeply the scars of history continue to affect Jews."

Of course, the experience of this particular group of Jews is not normative; they do not constitute a statistically reliable sample nor does my friend's reading of their response represent a replicable methodology. Nevertheless, it allows a glimpse into one element of the crisis: the way in which representations of Jews in the passion and death of Jesus evoke visceral feelings among Jews. Jews come to enactments of the passion with vivid memories of the ways in which that story has been used to disparage them as faithless, perfidious "Christ-killers." Jews have paid a tremendous price for Christian misrepresentation of the events of the Passion.

Yet, too few Christians are sensitive to this and many, unlike my friend, are tone-deaf when it comes to antisemitism. Insofar as they think about Jews at all, they view them as success stories, safely embedded in a religiously tolerant society. It seems many Christians simply cannot (or will not) stop to consider what it might mean for Jews one or two generations removed from the Shoah to once again be depicted as responsible for the death of Jesus. This failure of empathy not only complicates relationships between Jews and Christians, but contributes to a lack of interest in learning interpretations of the Bible that situate the Passion of Christ in a more complex context.

Thus, a second element in the crisis is the disregard for ways of reading Christianity's sacred texts in their historical and literary contexts. That fundamentalists reject contextual approaches is not surprising, but what is shocking is that the controversy over the film has revealed that many in the so-called "mainline" Protestant churches and the Roman Catholic Church pay no attention to biblical scholarship—including many who hold ecclesial office. At least in my own Catholic communion, one of the great accomplishments of the past sixty years or so has been the proliferation of significant resources for the study of Scripture at both academic and popular levels. Particularly in the wake of the Second Vatican Council, the riches of Scripture became more widely available, eliciting considerable interest and even excitement among many. Learned scholars with deep immersion in the life of the church, such as Gerard Sloyan, John Donahue, Donald Senior, and the late Roland Murphy and Raymond E. Brown (my beloved mentor), opened the Scriptures to millions of people through their prolific writings, public lectures, and teaching.

These biblical scholars made a signal contribution to the church by opening up the possibility of more profound understandings of the passion narratives of the Gospel. Not only did Raymond Brown write a massive two-volume work, *The Death of the Messiah*, but he authored a number of briefer, more popular works on the passion as well. Donald Senior's four commentaries on each Gospel's passion narrative provide access to the best of scholarship and pastoral acumen. Gerard Sloyan's *The Crucifixion: History, Myth, Faith* is more densely written and thus less widely accessible, but offers a learned compendium of biblical exegesis, theological reflection, and analysis of popular religiosity. John Donahue's one-page commentary on the Sunday lections that appeared each week in *America* offered ways of understanding and praying with the Scriptures that concisely and skillfully provided alternatives to anti-Jewish readings of the Gospels.[3]

Less well known, but just as significant, is the way in which scholars such as these contributed to the development of the church's traditions of interpretation. In particular, their exegetical insights and theological-philosophical knowledge made possible extensive development of the admonition of *Nostra Aetate* (1965) that "Even though the Jewish authorities and those who followed their lead pressed for the death of Christ (see Jn 19:6), neither all Jews indiscriminately at that time, nor Jews today, can be charged with the crimes committed during his passion." Biblical scholarship underlies the two explications of *Nostra Aetate* §4 published in 1975 and 1985, respectively, as "Guidelines and Suggestions for Implementing the Conciliar Declaration *Nostra Aetate* (n. 4)" and "Notes on the Correct Way to Present the Jews and Judaism in Preaching and Catechesis in the Roman Catholic Church."[4]

Their influence upon the Pontifical Biblical Commission was also profound. Two texts the PBC promulgated, "The Historical Truth of the Gospels" (1964) and "The Interpretation of the Bible in the Church"(1993), are crucial for intelligent reading of Scripture; they deserve to be widely read and taught. Its most recent document, "The Jewish People and their Sacred Scriptures in the Christian Bible" (2001), is lengthy and more difficult to read, but bears important insights.[5]

Given this wealth of resources, readers might rightly wonder what the crisis is here. To put it bluntly, the riches of this scholarship are being squandered. Many among the clergy and episcopacy evidently have little grasp of the

breadth and depth of this scholarship—and of its vital importance for relationships with the Jewish community. This is a serious problem, the depth of
which has been graphically revealed in the controversy over the film. So when
the homilist in my parish began his Easter Sunday sermon with reference to
"that great Catholic film of 2004, *The Passion of the Christ*," I could only wonder whether he has ever taken the time to immerse himself in a study of the
passion accounts with people better informed about official Catholic teaching
on biblical interpretation than Mel Gibson, who, according to criteria voiced
by Cardinal Roger Mahony, is a schismatic Catholic.[6]

Yes, this homilist has a right to his judgment on the film—but in his enthusiasm for it (he mentioned it in glowing terms at least five times in his sermons for Holy Thursday and Easter Sunday), he has at least implicitly given
the impression that Gibson's interpretation of the passion is, if not definitive,
at least pretty close. Yet, as other essays in this volume develop in detail, the
film goes counter to some extremely important principles of Catholic biblical interpretation—but apparently this did not trouble our homilist, nor, it
seems, many others in the church.[7]

When those with pastoral and educational responsibilities in the church
give little credence to important streams of Catholic interpretation in their
enthusiasm for the film, they compound a cultural problem. Persons today
are more shaped by the visual (and its aural accompaniments) than by texts.
The staying power of images gives them authority. Will Gibson's depiction of
the passion become definitive? When subsequent generations read the
Gospels or hear them proclaimed, will Gibson's representation of the malev-
olent, sadistic Caiaphas and his cronies immediately come to mind when
they hear references to the high priest and the Sanhedrin? When they read
or hear John 8:44 ("You are children of your father, the devil"), will they picture the devil moving among the Jewish crowds or the young Jewish boys
who turn into demons when they meet up with Judas? When they read or
hear "the Jews" cry, "Crucify him, crucify him," will they conjure up the
huge, bloodthirsty mob that Gibson has pictured? And when they read of an
earthquake at Jesus' death in Matthew 27:51–54, will they understand that
Jesus' resurrection is the first fruits of the resurrection of all the dead as
Matthew intended, or will they picture instead the dramatic destruction in
the Jewish Temple of Gibson's imagining?

A Vociferous Reaction

Another aspect the controversy over the film has revealed deserves mention:
the vitriolic rejection of new knowledge, whether regarding the Bible or the
"teaching of contempt," by certain Christian fans of Gibson.

In nearly all of many speaking engagements related at least in part to the film, I have found that at least one member of the audience reacts with enormous anger to *any* criticism of the film, as well as to the claim that the gospels are not primarily historical records or that the church's treatment of Jews has been other than just. In every case, I have experienced that nothing I or other speakers say mollifies their rage. Moreover, this rhetorically violent response differs dramatically from my previous experience; in the hundreds of presentations, lectures, and workshops I've done over the years, the sort of response the Gibson film has elicited is rare.

My Gibson-related e-mail reflects a similar degree of hostility, although none has been quite as cryptic as the writer who said to another critic of the film: "I will pray for you, but I hope you go to hell." Insofar as I can detect a pattern among e-mail correspondents, four principal areas of reaction have arisen.

The first is the most numerous: Facts are facts, and history is history. Thus, I am told, "The film presents just what the New Testament says, so if you condemn the film, you are condemning the New Testament." Another correspondent claims: "It's clear from history: the Jews condemned Jesus. We cannot change history, the Jews were much more culpable for killing Jesus than the Romans . . . I certainly do not want anti-Semitism to occur, but you cannot change the facts of what occurred at that time in history." Still another writes,

> We as Catholics have been meditating on the Passion of Christ for 2003 years. While we appreciate the desire to get along with all faiths we can not dismiss that the reason Jesus was killed by the Jews was that he claimed to be God. There is no FIXING that truth. Perhaps you should pray and ask Our Lord what He wants your response to be. The world needs to meditate on His PASSION. We all killed Him with our sins. . . . That is what you need to tell the Jewish people who dont [sic] even recognize Him for who He is.

A second pattern, less frequent but more toxic, suggested an analogy between those who killed Jesus and the Nazis. One correspondent, certain that the film "is true to the Bible," equated first-century Jews with Germans and Nazis: "Last time I checked, the Jews at that time, and at that place, WERE the antagonists. They are the ones who WANTED Christ to die. It's amazing how you never see Germans complain of their constant negative portrayal in the media concerning the Nazis, yet you can't even make ONE movie that is true to the Bible?" Similarly, another asks: "Do all the programs and efforts exposing the diabolical nature and practices of the Nazis and their allies encourage hostility toward the Germans of today?"

A third set of e-mails claimed, "This film could change many hearts and minds, and bring people back to Christ and to the church." Several messages of this variety, however, were accompanied by offensive comments, such as: "The godless, secular media (and Jewish Hollywood moguls) make films that trash Christianity/Catholicism, and now, finally we have a film about all Jesus Christ suffered and you have the audacity to criticize? Where were you when *The Last Temptation of Christ* was released, etc.?"

A fourth set of e-mails revealed antipathy to scholars of religion. As one e-mail said, "Forget all this nonsense we call scholarly. Why have you turned on Jesus in derision and denigration?" Another told me to turn away from my "prideful" scholarship and work with lepers. A number told me I had lost my faith, as did one person face-to-face after a lecture in Miami. Apparently, Christian charity is not applicable to scholars.

An Analysis

It is difficult to gain sufficient distance from this disillusioning experience to understand all the factors that are involved. Yet the invitation to write this essay has sent me back to a work I had read a decade ago in search of insight, namely, to British religious educator John Hull, whose 1985 work *What Prevents Christian Adults from Learning?* offers a trenchant examination of education in the church.

Hull notes that many people lack curiosity about their faith and thus hold their beliefs largely at the unconscious level. In a chapter titled "The Need to be Right and the Pain of Learning," he asserts that adults are typically less able than children to bear cognitive dissonance, perhaps because the school system socialized them to the view that "to be right is not only to be sane but to be good and to be entitled to reward. . . . Thinking that you are right may be necessary to sanity but it may also be an obstacle to learning."[8] Hull suggests that attention to the work of developmental psychology, and especially to the use of dilemmas similar to those used by Lawrence Kohlberg and other psychologists, will help adults deal with cognitive dissonance.

Personal construct theory is of even greater value, Hull argues. Thus, a word of explanation about this theory is in order. All of us order our worlds by construing experience a certain way; a construct is an "anticipation, based upon our experience and continually modified in the light of more experience, which is intended to offer predictions about the way things will be."[9] We must distinguish a construct from a *percept* (a cognition based upon immediate sense experience), an *image* (the memory of a perception, usually in visual form), and a *concept* (an intellectual, mental, or logical structure assigned to a percept and its image). Concepts differ from constructs in being open to public discussion and philosophical analysis; constructs emphasize the individual and subjective element of knowing.

One of the most important insights Hull gleans from personal construct theory is that a term—e.g., God—carries associations that are often individual and highly personal. Each term is a personal construct that has a particular "halo of significance and reverberation" and is situated in a constellation with other constructs particular to the individual's religious beliefs. As a consequence, no two Christians possess the same faith.

Personal construct theory bears importance for theological education. Education involves more than informing persons of various Christian doctrines and aiding people to make connections to their own lives. Receiving other people's constructs—that is, church teaching—will not be meaningful unless those being educated let it affect their own construct system. This means dialogue with the constructs others have formed, as well as situating them in history. Moreover, as Hull points out, it is vital to remember that the process is one of "concept-education," not of mere "concept-transmission."[10]

Other implications may be derived. Because both cognition and emotion constitute constructs, attentiveness to the affective component of what people believe is essential. Because constructs exclude as well as include, understanding the polar opposite of one's construct enhances the possibility of understanding. Because a person's construct system is the entirety of what she or he has learned thus far, further learning can develop that system. Yet, if learning is to happen, educators must pay attention to other characteristics of constructs. Are they *permeable*—or *impermeable*, and thus resistant to new experience? Are they *preemptive*, restricting possibilities of future elaboration—or *propositional* constructs that make affirmations without restricting the entire field? How are constructs arranged in a system? Are they so *tightly construed* as to allow no room for ambiguity— or so *loosely construed* as to be virtually meaningless? It follows that the more impermeable, preemptive, and rigidly construed, the less possibility for learning. Personal construct theory also makes possible a new perspective about "being wrong": "There may well be times when a person simply cannot afford to be wrong, for the damage to the system as a whole would be unacceptable. People prefer to be meaningfully wrong than nonsensically right."[11] Particularly insightful is Hull's admonition:

When the danger of being wrong is great, the system will close up. The authority for the alternative point of view will be contested, the information presented will be filtered out so as to disregard the potentially threatening material, and other tactics of denial, avoidance and distortion will be employed in order to protect the system.[12]

Hull's explanation of cognitive dissonance and personal construct theory elicits new perspectives on the controversy over *The Passion of the Christ*. Those of us who raised questions about the film and criticized elements of it apparently evoked cognitive dissonance among many who were deeply moved by the film. Our critical observations threatened some of those captivated by the Christ Gibson had depicted. Moved by the visual representation of the extent of his suffering, they took umbrage at scholars who took issue with other aspects of the film. It is as if our criticisms meant they were wrong for their high regard for the film. We were perceived as denying their experience. And because they regarded themselves as persons of faith, Gibson's critics, therefore, must lack faith.

In retrospect, I now realize that some of the harshest e-mails I received came after interviews for television. In every case, those interviews, which sometimes required an hour or ninety minutes of filming, were heavily edited, juxtaposed with other interviewees in order to highlight conflicting views, and stripped of nuance. So this was education by sound bite: a most unsatisfactory medium. Moreover, the television coverage of the film was, in Hull's language, "concept transmission," not "concept education": There was no opportunity to dialogue with viewers, to clarify how one was heard, or to expand upon complex points.

Yet even the various public forums in which I participated permitted little "concept education." In contrast to television, they were much more satisfactory in terms of having opportunity to develop several points, albeit with a certain brevity. Still, the size and diversity of the audiences meant it was impossible to reach each person; we lacked knowledge of their needs and the limits of time restricted that extended interaction that is so crucial in education. It was impossible to dialogue adequately with the varied personal constructs of our audiences.

In a number of instances, furthermore, we encountered rigid constructs. Some refused to entertain the possibility that the Bible could be true other than in a factually historical way. Some held tenaciously to the theological view that salvation could only happen through the crucifixion of Jesus, that he had to die in this brutal fashion in order to atone for our sins and satisfy God: no other explanation could be countenanced. Some believed there was nothing antisemitic in the film, and rejected out of hand any analysis of the film that examined problematic aspects of Gibson's depiction of the

Jews. Some, hearing that many Christians over the course of nearly two thousand years had drawn upon representations of the passion to fuel hostility against and violence toward Jews, responded that Jews had persecuted Christians, too. This sort of intolerance for ambiguity and complexity makes teaching very difficult, and requires time and considerable pedagogical skill to overcome.

Rigid constructs, however, may not have been the major factor in the controversy. I suspect that the single most important aspect is the "halo of significance and reverberation" that the suffering and death of Jesus have for Christians. People cherish this doctrine; for many it is deeply embedded in their identity as religious persons. By offering biblical and theological perspectives that were in many cases new, we unintentionally jeopardized their self-understanding as Christians. In addition, our scholarly approaches may have exacerbated the perceived threat, as we were not as sensitive as we should have been to the affective component of personal constructs. Perhaps our educational efforts would have been more welcome had we given greater attention to the way in which the passion of Jesus Christ has significance for us. Had we revealed more of how it "reverberates" in our own lives as Christians, we might have been better able to be heard by those who so vociferously resisted our analysis of the film.

Allowing the affective layer of personal constructs to surface is always important in the educational process, but all the more so in the case of this film. Gibson himself stressed in a television interview with Diane Sawyer that he was committed to making a film in which people would *feel* the enormity of Jesus' suffering and death. The media reports told about viewers sobbing in the aisles of theaters, so it is evident that Gibson's desire to make his audience *feel* succeeded in many cases. The challenge for us was to help those who held such feelings to step back and explore their feelings in such a way that they might allow for a more complex response. That is, viewers might still treasure the film's portrayal of Jesus *and* see problems of the depiction of the Jews.

Helping viewers to form more complex reactions requires reaching the affective dimension of their personal constructs. One effective way in which this happens is by speaking "affect to affect." I witnessed an example of this quite recently. William Cardinal Keeler, the archbishop of Baltimore and the United States Conference of Catholic Bishops' moderator for Catholic-Jewish relations, had generally been approving of the film, despite several sessions with the Catholic scholars concerned about the film's potential for unleashing antisemitism on the basis of reading the shooting script. Yet, after an extended candid exchange with Jews at a meeting of delegates of the

Bishops' Committee on Ecumenical and Interreligious Affairs and the National Council of Synagogues in New York City on April 20, 2004, Cardinal Keeler apparently began to reconsider. Later that week he went again to the film, this time in the company of Jews. Seeing the film through their eyes awakened him to elements he had missed. In a column, "The *Passion* Revisited," written for the archdiocesan paper on April 28, 2004, he wrote:

> And then, at a meeting in New York, I was told by Jewish leaders of their heightened concerns and even fears. And thus, last week, I took my own advice and saw the movie with a rabbi and a well-informed Jewish layman, both of them articulate and sensitive. While I had heard and read criticisms before, this second viewing opened my eyes to aspects of the film I had not caught previously, and I saw why some of our Jewish neighbors view it with understandable concern and even a measure of fear.
>
> Afterwards, we talked about the picture and its context in our increasingly secular society. For this conversation, the rabbi's wife joined us. She too had seen the film. . . .
>
> I can see the worry, even the fear, of our Jewish partners in dialogue, of evil as a possible result from Christians viewing this film unprepared. They spoke of some individual cases in the United States where Jewish children were spoken to abusively by some Christian youth. We agreed in hoping that through discussion and joint Catholic-Jewish statements genuine good can be accomplished, as we look together for the reconciliation and peace so much sought after by Pope John Paul II.

While I do not know the precise content of the cardinal's conversation with his Jewish companions, I believe that their perspective on the film largely matches what we Catholic scholars had told him.

In sum, a great deal was at stake for those who heard us as saying they were wrong for championing the film. For them it was tantamount to saying that their faith was invalid—and for a number the best defense was to attack us in return as lacking faith. Without an affective exchange with Jews such as Cardinal Keeler described, or in the absence of other ways of engaging the affective faith dimension, the sense of an assault on one's personal faith was hard to overcome.

The controversy over the film invites religious and theological educators to reflect critically on our own practice. As we redouble our efforts to educate for more discerning interpretations of the Bible, we must pay careful attention to those factors that impede adult learning as well as those that enhance it. Mel Gibson has produced a film that evoked feeling. Our task as educators is to join thinking with feeling.

Notes

1. Mary C. Boys, "'I Didn't See Any Anti-Semitism.' Why Many Christians Don't See Any Problems with Gibson's 'The Passion of the Christ,'" *Cross Currents*, Spring, 2004 at http://www.crosscurrents.org/BoysSpring2004.htm.

2. See Mary C. Boys, "Seeing Different Movies: Talking Past Each Other," in Jonathan Burnham, ed. *Perspectives on* The Passion of the Christ: *Religious Thinkers and Writers Explore the Issues Raised by the Controversial Movie.* (New York: Miramax Books, 2004), 147–164.

3. The titles of Donald Senior's four books are *The Passion of Jesus in the Gospel of Mark, The Passion of Jesus in the Gospel of Matthew, The Passion of Jesus in the Gospel of Luke* and *The Passion of Jesus in the Gospel of John* (Wilmington, Del.: Michael Glazier, 1984). John Donahue's columns are collected in three volumes, *Hearing the Word of God: Reflections on the Sunday Readings, Year A, Year B, Year C.* (Collegeville: The Liturgical Press, 2001–2003).

4. These statements and other relevant texts may be accessed at www.jcrelations.net or www.bc.edu/cjlearning

5. See www.bc.edu/cjlearning or http://www.vatican.va

6. See the Cardinal's comments in a Feb. 20, 2004 online discussion hosted by *Beliefnet.com* at www.beliefnet.com/story/140/story_14062_1.html. Mel Gibson has underwritten the costs of building a church in Malibu, within the Archdiocese of Los Angeles, but says Mahony, "It is certainly not in communion with the Universal Catholic Church nor the Archdiocese of Los Angeles." Cardinal Mahony also noted that, "If one chooses to set aside any of [the sixteen documents of the Second Vatican Council], then they choose to separate themselves from the unity of the Church." For public comments by Gibson on Vatican II see www.adl.org/Interfaith/gibson_ii.asp, including his 1990 statement on CNN that "the Roman Church is wrong, but I believe it is at the moment, since Vatican II."

7. Another example of this dismissal of Catholic biblical scholarship and authoritative ecclesial teaching is a small book by Tom Allen et al. titled, *A Guide to the Passion: 100 Questions about "The Passion of the Christ"* (Ascension Press and the Catholic Exchange, 2004). The book touts itself as "a comprehensive Catholic resource book for this momentous film." It is claimed to have sold nearly one million copies and has also been widely distributed in some parishes and described in articles in Catholic diocesan newspapers. Like the movie, it presents an ahistorical reading of the Bible. Readers who interpret the book's prominent use of the word "Catholic" to mean that it conveys normative Catholic teaching on biblical interpretation are mistaken.

8. John M. Hull, *What Prevents Christian Adults from Learning?* (Philadelphia: Trinity Press International, 1991), 100–101.

9. Hull, *What Prevents Christian Adults,* 102.

10. Hull, *What Prevents Christian Adults,* 106.

11. Hull, *What Prevents Christian Adults,* 108.

12. Hull, *What Prevents Christian Adults,* 110.

~

Glossary

Antisemitism is hatred of Jews. It originated in the nineteenth century at a
time when the classification of humanity into various "races," including
the "Semitic" race, was popular. The more common hyphenated form
"anti-Semitism" is not used in this book, both to reject the racist categories that lie behind the term's beginnings and because the term refers
particularly to Jews and not to the non-Jewish peoples who might be included under the term "Semites."

B.C.E./C.E. are alternatives to the Western practice of naming the historical epochs that do not presuppose faith in Christ and hence are more appropriate in interfaith contexts than the conventional B.C./A.D. They
stand for *Before the Common Era* and the *Common Era.*

Christ is the Greek form of the Hebrew word *mashiach* or messiah, which literally means an "anointed one," someone appointed to a particular task or
role by God. For Christians, Jesus Christ is the one whom God anointed
as the inaugurator of God's Kingdom or Reign, but whose messianic work
will not be completed until his return in glory when God's Kingdom will
be established in all its fullness (cf. Acts 3: 19–21).

Covenant, from the Hebrew word *b'rit*, is an agreement between parties, especially that between God and Israel, or later, between God and the
church through Jesus Christ. In these religious senses, covenant is more
than just a contractual agreement. It is a sharing in life together for all
time with mutual duties and obligations.

Deicide, literally meaning the murder of God, refers to the long-lived Christian charge that the Jews collectively were under a divine curse for their crucifixion of Jesus, the Son of God.

Incarnation is the Christian doctrine that the Word or Son of God became flesh as a fully human Jewish individual by being born of Mary through the power of the Holy Spirit. The Council of Chalcedon (451) defined this doctrine in Greek metaphysical terms as the union of a human and a divine nature in which the two natures are not melded or blurred but retain their distinctive characteristics.

Kingdom of God or **Reign of God** is the Jewish metaphor used by Jesus to speak of the Age or World to Come or the New Creation. Conceptually rooted in the Hebrew Torah and prophetic traditions, it refers to the inevitable destiny of everything that exists to conform to God's will. Biblical metaphors speak of the lion laying down with the lamb and swords being beaten into plowshares. In the fullness of the Kingdom, universal shalom and justice will prevail and all people will acknowledge and glorify God.

Messiah, from the Hebrew word *mashiach*, literally means an "anointed one," someone appointed to a particular task or role by God. The term no longer has the same meaning for today's Jews and Christians. For Jews, the "messiah" will usher in the Age to Come or the Kingdom of God at the end of time, when universal shalom and justice will finally be established. For Christians, Jesus Christ (the Greek form of *mashiach*) is the one whom God anointed as the inaugurator of God's Kingdom or Reign, but whose messianic work will not be completed until his return in glory when God's Kingdom will be established in all its fullness. For Christians, Jesus' life, death, and resurrection were necessary preconditions for the Kingdom of God to be established.

Passion is the term used by Christians in reference to the suffering and crucifixion of Jesus.

Passion Narratives are the sections of the four Gospels in the New Testament that narrate Jesus' final hours. They are widely understood to encompass five scenes: (a) the nighttime arrest of Jesus in the garden; (b) the encounter between Jesus and the Temple priests; (c) the encounter between Jesus and the Roman governor Pontius Pilate; (d) the crucifixion of Jesus; (e) the burial of Jesus.

Passion Plays are dramatizations of the Passion that began in the late Middle Ages and were popular for many centuries. In many places, they became a major endeavor of the local village.

Redemption refers to God's activities that restore people back into relationship with God.

Resurrection (1) is a Jewish concept referring to the restoration to earthly life of all who have died (or perhaps only of the deceased righteous) in the messianic age. (2) is the Christian term that refers to the exaltation or lifting up of the crucified and deceased Jesus to transcendent, glorified life with God. It is also understood as a divine pledge and a foretaste of the eternal life with God that awaits all the righteous in God's Kingdom.

Salvation, while certainly a concept known to Judaism, is a much more prominent concern in Christianity, where it has developed a multiplicity of meanings (see the essay by Clark Williamson, "What Does it Mean to be Saved?"). At the most fundamental level, salvation might be understood as being enabled to participate willingly in God's unfolding plans for creation. For Christians, the life, death, and resurrection of Jesus have made universal salvation possible. The theological study of various understandings of salvation is known as soteriology.

Shalom is a Hebrew word that refers to the peace and wholeness that is the result of right relationship.

Shoah, from the Hebrew word for a "devastating whirlwind," refers to the Nazi genocide of Jews during the Second World War that is commonly referred to as the "Holocaust." Since the latter biblically means a burnt sin offering, it is problematic for some when applied to the six million Jews murdered by the Nazis and their collaborators.

Supersessionism is the Christian theological claim that Christians have superseded or replaced Jews as God's Chosen People as a result of the alleged Jewish murder of God's Son ("deicide"). This premise has consequences for other aspects of Christian theology, including how the first part of the Christian Bible is interpreted, how Jesus and salvation are understood, and how the mission and nature of the Church are comprehended.

Trinity refers to the Christian understanding and experience that God is intrinsically relational, even in God's own being. God is Source, Creator, Sustainer, or Father of all that exists, who eternally generates the Revealing Word, Wisdom, or Son through which all things are made and made comprehensible, and whose creative and irrepressible Spirit animates, inspires, and draws all things to God. Christians also believe that God's Word, God's revealing and inviting Self, was incarnated in Jesus, a first-century Jew.

Index

Contributors

Pamela Berger, Ph.D., is a Professor of Art History and Film at Boston College. Her books deal with Late Antiquity and the Middle Ages, and she is particularly interested in religious syncretism. She has written, produced, and/or directed three feature films: *Sorceress*, about a medieval woman healer accused of being a heretic; *The Magic Stone*, about an Irish slave who escapes from a Viking ship and is rescued by Native Americans, and *Imported Bridegroom*, adapted from the classic story by the Jewish writer, Abraham Cahan.

Mary C. Boys, S.N.J.M., Ed.D., is the author or editor of seven books, including two on Jewish-Christian relations: *Jewish-Christian Dialogue: One Woman's Experience* and *Has God Only One Blessing? Judaism as a Source of Christian Self-Understanding*, both published by Paulist Press. After many years of teaching at Boston College, for the past decade she has served as the Skinner and McAlpin Professor of Practical Theology at Union Theological Seminary in New York City.

John Clabeaux, Ph.D., is Associate Professor of Theology (Biblical Studies) at Creighton University. His nineteen years of teaching Latin and Greek at St. John's Seminary College in Boston focused his attention on the pastoral actualization of the scriptures and Roman Catholic teaching on biblical interpretation. His research and lectures have consistently involved the relationship between Judaism and Christianity, including published and forthcoming articles on Marcion and the *Didache*.

Rabbi Michael J. Cook, Ph.D., is Bronstein Professor of Judeo-Christian Studies, Hebrew Union College-JIR (Cincinnati). He focuses on the New Testament's impact upon Christian-Jewish relations; rabbinic literature in Pauline and Gospel study; and the meaning of Jewish symbols in Christian iconography. He recently published "Evolving Jewish Views of Jesus," in *Jesus Through Jewish Eyes*, B. Bruteau, ed. (Orbis), and his book in progress is titled *Modern Jews and the New Testament: Removing the Veil*.

Maddy Cunningham, D.S.W., is Assistant Professor at Fordham University Graduate School of Social Service. Her research interests include the treatment of survivors of childhood sexual abuse, vicarious trauma, and the role of spirituality in mental health and healing from traumatic experiences.

Philip A. Cunningham, Ph.D., is Executive Director of the Center for Christian-Jewish Learning and Adjunct Professor of Theology at Boston College. Interested in biblical studies, religious education, and theologies of Christian-Jewish relations, his two most recent books are *A Story of Shalom: The Calling of Christians and Jews by a Covenanting God* and *Sharing the Scriptures*, both published by Paulist Press.

Rev. Walter Harrelson, Th.D., is Professor Emeritus of Hebrew Bible at Vanderbilt University Divinity School and Adjunct University Professor at Wake Forest University. He is the author or co-author of books on Jewish-Christian relations, the Hebrew Bible, biblical languages, and biblical translation. He chaired the committee that completed the New Revised Standard Version of the Bible and is general editor of The New Interpreter's Study Bible. His ordination is recognized by the American Baptist Churches and the Christian Church (Disciples of Christ).

Raymond G. Helmick, S.J., S.T.L., teaches Conflict Resolution in the Boston College Theology Department. He has acted as mediator in the Northern Ireland conflict, the Israeli-Palestinian and Lebanese conflicts, for the Kurds of Iraq and Turkey, and in the Balkans. Music is his constant avocation. Recent publications are *Forgiveness and Reconciliation: Religion, Public Policy and Conflict Transformation*, edited with Rodney L. Petersen (Templeton Foundation Press), and the forthcoming *Negotiating Outside the Law: Why Camp David Failed* (Pluto Press).

John J. Michalczyk, Ph.D., is currently Chair of the Fine Arts Department and Co-Director of Film Studies at Boston College. He is the author of several books dealing with the Holocaust and World War II. His twelve documentary film productions, primarily for PBS television, include *The Cross and the Star* and *Of Stars & Shamrocks: Boston's Jews & Irish*. He also co-produced the educational film series, *Walking God's Paths: Christians and Jews in Candid Conversation*.

John T. Pawlikowski, O.S.M., Ph.D., is Professor of Social Ethics at the Catholic Theological Union in Chicago where he also directs the Catholic-Jewish Studies Program in the CTU's Cardinal Bernardin Center. He is the author or editor of many books on Christian-Jewish relations including the forthcoming *Covenantal Identity in the Presence of the Other*. He currently serves as President of the International Council of Christians and Jews.

Louis Roy, O.P., Ph.D., is Associate Professor of Theology at Boston College. He is interested in mystical and intellectual approaches to God, in religious experience and revelation, and in interreligious dialogue. His most recent book is *Mystical Consciousness: Western Perspectives and Dialogue with Japanese Thinkers* (SUNY Press).

Rabbi A. James Rudin, D.D., is the American Jewish Committee's Senior Interreligious Adviser and Distinguished Visiting Professor at Saint Leo University. He is the author or editor of seven books including *Israel for Christians: Understanding Modern Israel*. He writes a weekly commentary for Religion News Service/Newhouse Syndicate. For many years he worked with Oberammergau Passion Play officials to effect positive changes and he attended a 1984 performance of the Play.

Claudia Setzer, Ph.D., is Professor of Religious Studies at Manhattan College, Riverdale, NY. Her interests are Judaism and Christian Origins, and women in early Judaism and Christianity. She is the author of *Jewish Responses to Early Christians* (Fortress) and *Resurrection of the Body in Early Judaism and Early Christianity* (Brill). She is active in Jewish-Christian Relations at the academic and popular level, and a former chair of the Early Jewish/Christian Relations Group at the Society of Biblical Literature.

Rev. George M. Smiga, S.T.D., serves on the scripture and homil⸍ ⸍ facul-
ties of St. Mary Seminary and Graduate School of Theology in
Ohio, and as pastor of St. Noel Catholic Church in Willoughby J
He is a regular author for *The Faith Connection*, a weekly adult
tool (Resources for Christian Living) and *God's Word Today*, a n

study resource. He has also written the books *Pain and Polemic: Anti-Judaism in the Gospels* and a commentary on the Gospel of John for *The Word Set Free* series (both by Paulist Press).

Rev. Clark Williamson, Ph.D., is Indiana Professor of Christian Thought, Emeritus, at Christian Theological Seminary, an Indianapolis seminary related to the Christian Church (Disciples of Christ). Long involved as a theologian in Christian-Jewish Dialogue and post-Shoah theology, his two most recent books are *Way of Blessing, Way of Life: A Christian Theology* (Chalice Press) and *Preaching the Gospels without Blaming the Jews: A Lectionary Commentary*, co-authored with Ronald J. Allen (Westminster/John Knox Press).